MW00655763

Sonic Mobilities

Chicago Studies in Ethnomusicology

A series edited by Philip V. Bohlman and Timothy Rommen

Sonic Mobilities

Producing Worlds in Southern China

ADAM KIELMAN

The University of Chicago Press
Chicago and London

The University of Chicago Press, Chicago 60637
The University of Chicago Press, Ltd., London

Published 2022
Printed in the United States of America

31 30 29 28 27 26 25 24 23 22   1 2 3 4 5

ISBN-13: 978-0-226-81774-3 (cloth)
ISBN-13: 978-0-226-81780-4 (paper)
ISBN-13: 978-0-226-81779-8 (e-book)
DOI: https://doi.org/10.7208/chicago/9780226817798.001.0001

An earlier version of chapter 4 appeared as "'We Sing in Dialects Even as We Wander Far from Home': Performing the Local in Polyglot Southern China," *Popular Music and Society* 42, no. 5 (2019): 513–37. An earlier version of chapter 7 appeared as "Sonic Infrastructures, Musical Circulation, and Listening Practices in a Changing People's Republic of China," *Sound Studies* 4, no. 1 (2018): 19–34.

Library of Congress Cataloging-in-Publication Data

Names: Kielman, Adam, author.
Title: Sonic mobilities : producing worlds in southern China / Adam Kielman.
Other titles: Chicago studies in ethnomusicology.
Description: Chicago ; London : The University of Chicago Press, 2022. | Series: Chicago studies in ethnomusicology | Includes bibliographical references and index.
Identifiers: LCCN 2021032856 | ISBN 9780226817743 (cloth) | ISBN 9780226817804 (paperback) | ISBN 9780226817798 (ebook)
Subjects: LCSH: Popular music—China—Guangzhou—History and criticism. | World music—China—Guangzhou—History and criticism. | Mabang (Musical group) | Wanju Chuanzhang (Musical group) | Music and globalization—China. | Music—Social aspects—China.
Classification: LCC ML3502.C58 G835 2022 | DDC 781.6309512/75—dc23
LC record available at https://lccn.loc.gov/2021032856

♾ This paper meets the requirements of ANSI/NISO Z39.48-1992 (Permanence of Paper).

Contents

Note on Romanization

Throughout this book, I use the Hanyu Pinyin system of romanization for all Chinese words and phrases when I am referring to their written form or to their Standard Mandarin (Putonghua) pronunciation. I use Jyutping (The Linguistic Society of Hong Kong Cantonese Romanisation Scheme) for Cantonese and Peng'im (Chaozhouhua Pinyin Fang'an) for Chaozhou (Teochew) dialects. Except in cases where I am drawing special attention to proper oral pronunciation of words and phrases in Standard Mandarin, I omit tone markers for typographical ease and readability. In cases where I am drawing specific attention to linguistic sounds in dialects other than Standard Mandarin in comparison to their Standard Mandarin pronunciation, I use a modified Hanyu Pinyin system. I discuss this practice at greater length in chapter 4, as such practices and questions surrounding them relate directly to the broader issues discussed in that chapter. I follow the preferred spelling of personal names in cases where they depart from Hanyu Pinyin (e.g., names of musicians from Hong Kong and Taiwan).

1

Musical Cosmopolitanism and New Mobilities

The band Mabang is on stage in a large warehouse venue in a former industrial area in Guangzhou, China's third largest city. Beyond the converted warehouse, several eighty-foot-high concrete distilling vats connected by huge aluminum pipes are illuminated by shifting colored lights. No longer producing beer, the towers provide a stark backdrop to the many bars and restaurants clustered on this bank of the Pearl River. On stage inside the warehouse venue, the members of the band Mabang are wearing elaborate costumes that were designed and stitched for this event celebrating the launch of a new record label, Liuzhen Yinyue, a sublabel under Xingwaixing Records, one of China's largest record companies. Over two thousand audience members fill the warehouse, many holding the sampler CD of six bands signed to the label that was distributed at the door.

Ye Honggang, Mabang's lead singer, takes a deep breath, and, with one hand raised, exclaims "Zou qilai!" into the microphone, his southwestern pronunciation communicating as much as the sentiment itself, "Let's go!" The drummer, wearing a loose saffron-colored tunic, launches into a song called "Carp Crag in Liuzhou" with a common reggae drum intro that moves from a rim shot on the snare drum to a series of three sixteenth notes played in its center. Another band member, wearing flowing brown linen, joins in, playing a simple melody on the gourd-like *hulusi*, a free-reed aerophone associated with southwest China. After two measures, Ye Honggang, wearing an elaborate feather headdress and mesh shirt that resembles chain mail, begins to sing:

> Liuzhou is filled with mountain songs.
> Open your mouth, and they flow like a river.

Lang-a-lei-a jia-gu-gun-na, lang-a-lei!
Singing makes the sun rise in the East,
Singing makes the moon unwilling to set.
Lang-a-lei-a jia-gu-gun-na, lang-a-lei!
The water of the Liu River is clear and pure,
It brings up generation after generation of people who love to sing.

He sings of Liuzhou, his hometown, a major industrial hub in southwest China. But he also references broader associations of China's southwest with *shan'ge* (mountain songs), a classifier for folk songs that encompasses a wide variety of music from China's rural regions, including various musical traditions in the southwest that Mabang's music draws on. Another drum fill sets up the chorus:

Mountains joining mountains, water joining water.
Mountains and water joining the hearts of those living far from home.
. . . .
People come and go through all the years and all the seasons,
and the singing voice floats through the myriad mountains.[1]

"Liuzhou you ge Liyu Yan" ("Carp Crag in Liuzhou"),
lyrics and music by Ye Honggang, performed by Mabang,
copyright 2015 Guangdong Xingwaixing Wenhua Chuanbo Youxian Gongsi

Far from home himself, Ye Honggang sings of the distinctive landscapes that surround Liuzhou, his voice rising and falling, rhythmically floating over and through the one-drop reggae bass far beneath him. The lyrics, sung in a southwest dialect of Mandarin, evoke stylistic elements and images from a long history of classical Chinese poetry. Behind the band, large projection screens intercut live close-ups of the performers' faces with black and white images of lush scenery, karst peaks, and winding rivers of Guangxi Province. Highly stylized calligraphy of the band's name, Mabang, is occasionally superimposed. Mabang (literally "horse gang") is often translated as "caravan," though it refers specifically to the horse or mule caravans that transported goods along the Ancient Tea Horse Road (*Chama Gudao*), more commonly known in English as the Southern Silk Road. The route, which stretched from southwest China into the Himalayas, may have brought tea and other products as far as Guangzhou, where they might have been loaded onto the ships that docked on the banks of the river where Ye Honggang now sings. *Mabang*—the name evokes a particular Chinese cosmopolitan formation that stretches back two thousand years and that is being restitched into contemporary cosmopolitanisms. "Mountains joining mountains, water joining water. / Mountains and water joining the hearts of those living far from home . . ."

This book explores the relationships between musical circulations, emergent forms of musical creativity, and an evolving geography of contemporary China. It is an ethnographic account of musical cosmopolitanism in Guangzhou as a process of knowledge making, connected both to much older forms of cosmopolitanism and routes of exchange and to contemporary experiences of mobility, migration, and urbanization. Bridging ethnomusicology, popular music studies, cultural geography, media studies, and the anthropology of infrastructure, it examines the cultural dimensions of shifts in conceptualizations of self, space, publics, and state in a rapidly transforming PRC.

The ethnographic focus of this book is two bands based in Guangzhou and their relationships with one of China's largest record companies. The first band, Wanju Chuanzhang (Toy Captain, fig. 1.1), performs a self-described "island mix" of poppy, Latin-infused music sung in the Min subdialect spoken on Nan'ao Dao, a small island off the southeast coast of China. Drawing on genres ranging from reggae to flamenco to salsa, the band's front man Li Yihan crafts songs that describe and express themes most often related to his hometown on Nan'ao Dao (Nan'ao Island) with lyrics about parties on the beach, the sea, watching Chaozhou opera, and returning to one's hometown from the big city. The second band, Mabang (fig. 1.2), performs a blend of folk, rock, and reggae peppered with elements from folk musics of southern China and *caidiao* opera from Guangxi Province. Front man Ye Honggang sings in Guiliuhua, the subdialect of Mandarin spoken in his hometown on the outskirts of Liuzhou. Many of Mabang's original songs are about local life in Guangxi, depicting country fairs, rural life, and song and dance. The locations of Guangzhou, Nan'ao Dao, and Liuzhou are shown in figure 1.3.

Wanju Chuanzhang and Mabang are part of a broader cohort of musicians who have coalesced in China's third largest city over the past decade and who participate in a flourishing scene of independent music in southern China that has galvanized in recent years as an important counterpart to both the mainstream Chinese popular music industry and to well-received independent rock and folk scenes centered in Beijing. These musicians, many of whom have moved to Guangzhou from small towns and rural areas throughout southern China, selectively draw on transnational genres of popular music and Chinese folk musics. They sing in local dialects of Chinese about themes related to their hometowns, urban/rural difference, migration, and broader changes in Chinese society. Increasingly successful commercially, these bands have become central to a new business model adopted by one of China's largest record companies that seeks to integrate traditional industry approaches with new strategies and new media that cater to an increasingly mobile citizenry. Focusing on these musicians and the music industry in which they

FIGURE 1.1. Wanju Chuanzhang performing at the 2014 Beijing MIDI Music Festival. Photograph by Jonah M. Kessel.

FIGURE 1.2. Mabang performing at the Liuzhen Yinyue label launch in 2014 described at the outset of this chapter. Photograph by the author.

FIGURE 1.3. Map showing the locations of Guangzhou, Liuzhou, and Nan'ao Dao. Map by Jonathan Levy, JL Cartography.

participate, this book explores the changing economics, politics, and aesthetics of popular music in China through an ethnography of the social worlds of cultural production in Guangzhou.

Thinking Musical Cosmopolitanism through *Tianxia*

An important gathering place for these musicians and their fans is Tutu Kongjian (Tutu Space), an independent music venue with a capacity of about two hundred in downtown Guangzhou. Prominently displayed next to the stage is a hand-painted horizontal scroll that reads "pengyou tianxia" (friends all under heaven).[2] I asked one of the owners of the venue, Dao Jianghua, about the calligraphy, the phrase, and the prominent position it was given next to a stage that hosts musicians from throughout China and the world and styles from rock and folk to jazz and experimental music. "'Pengyou tianxia,' this means 'one love,'" he explained, using the English words "one love," then continuing in Chinese: "One family under heaven. This is an ideal, a Utopia, it's the idea that your friends are everywhere under heaven, without borders. In every corner of the world we can become friends, can achieve peace and love, and can come together through music."

In this statement, Dao articulates an orientation toward the world and a perspective on music that are intertwined through tianxia, a Chinese concept for the world as "all under heaven." Dao offers "one love" as an English equivalent of pengyou tianxia, self-consciously making reference to the Bob Marley song and the Rastafarian ethical stance, identifying pengyou tianxia as a universal sentiment with multiple vernacular interpretations. He also uses the Chinese transliteration of Utopia, *wutuobang*, identifying pengyou tianxia not only as a form of friendship and interpersonal connection but also as embodying a political ideal. For Dao, and for the musicians and audiences who frequent this venue, music is a resource for fashioning knowledge about the world in its complexity.

Artists in contemporary China create music reflective of their own lives and mobilities and grapple with shifting ways of understanding space, place, where they are from, where they are going, China's place in the world, and the world's place in China. Both Wanju Chuanzhang and Mabang create music expressive of the landscapes, sounds, and ways of life where their lead singers grew up. Both bands are based in Guangzhou, China's third largest city, and include members from throughout southern China. And both bands draw more on globally circulating popular musics than on the folk or traditional musics of the regions they seek to express through music. Rather than any sort of contradiction however, I bring attention to these details because they are quite typical of musical practices—practices often termed *cosmopolitan*—in diverse locales throughout the world. Since the 1990s such practices have received extensive attention from ethnomusicologists, who have looked to music as a metaphor for broader cultural processes of globalization.[3]

A key insight of this literature on musical cosmopolitanism is that music is not merely reflective of broader global systems in a passive sense; rather, musical creativity is a process of "worlding" in which human agency and creativity play active roles in constructing new understandings of global connection from geographically and historically situated perspectives (Stokes 2008). As China has emerged as a global superpower in a span of mere decades, Chinese perspectives on globality have gained influence. Understanding musical cosmopolitanism as an "active process in the making of 'worlds'" (Stokes 2008, 6) is thus especially relevant in the context of contemporary China, where an official ideology of Xi Jinping Thought on Socialism with Chinese Characteristics for a New Era promotes a particular articulation of power, knowledge, and subjectivity as well as a new role for China in a neoliberal world order. Anthropologist Lisa Rofel (2007, 112) discusses what she describes (playfully) as "cosmopolitanism with Chinese characteristics" as "a site for the production of knowledge about what it means to be human in this reconfigured world, knowledge that is being embraced, digested, reworked, contested, and resisted in China." Music, sound, and listening are important dimensions of these processes of producing, embracing, digesting, reworking, contesting, and resisting knowledge (Ochoa Gautier 2014).

By suggesting that musical cosmopolitanism in southern China is part of these knowledge processes, my goal is to build on understandings of cosmopolitanisms (musical and otherwise) as multiple, discrepant, and vernacular (Clifford 1997; Werbner 2006). Returning to Stokes (2008, 8), my aim is thus to think through cosmopolitan formations, that is, the "various ways of imagining musical belonging, as various musical spheres of exchange and circulation . . . [and] mediations of broader ideological tensions and contradictions." Or as Steven Feld (2012, 7) puts it more simply, "how cosmopolitanism, mine, others', is embodied, lived, uneven, complicated, and not just some heady abstraction."

Pengyou tianxia, the calligraphy that decorates the stage at Tutu Kongjian, and Dao's parallel invocation of "One Love," the famous Bob Marley song, envision a mode of musical belonging and a broader cosmopolitan formation as embodied and lived in contemporary urban China. While the English term *cosmopolitanism* is often translated into Chinese as *shijie zhuyi*, which most directly translates as "worldism," recent scholarship in China and abroad have increasingly turned to *tianxia* as a useful analytic in understanding the global order from a Chinese perspective. Tianxia consists of two characters: *tian* (heaven or sky) and *xia* (under) and is most often translated as "all under heaven." It is a concept derived from Confucian political thought that describes a broad moral and civilizational complex unifying the world. While the concept is popularly attributed to the Duke of Zhou, a ruler who helped unify China under the Zhou Dynasty three thousand years ago, tianxia has gone through diverse incarnations as a way of thinking the world. During the Republican Era (1912–1949), the term appeared in Sun Yat-sen's slogan *tianxia weigong* (tianxia is for all), articulating a new engagement with and role in a global community. In the last decade the term has once again experienced a renaissance in the popular imagination (Wang 2017).

This is in large part due to the work of Zhao Tingyang, a philosopher at the Chinese Academy of Social Sciences. In 2005 he published *The Tianxia System: An Introduction to the Philosophy of a World Institution*, a best-selling book whose influence extended well beyond philosophy and academia. Through an archaeology of the concept of tianxia and a discussion of the political orientation adopted by the Duke of Zhou (ca. 1000 BCE) toward the disparate tribes and substates that had previously been ruled by force by the Shang Dynasty (ca. 1600 BCE–1046 BCE), the book articulates a contemporary political philosophy where "internationality," as the relationships between nation-states, is subsumed under "worldness," the global interest.[4] In Zhao's (2009, 9) formulation, tianxia is "a dense concept meaning 'world.' It has three meanings: (1) the Earth or all lands under the sky; (2) a common choice made by all peoples in the world, or a universal agreement in the 'hearts' of all peoples; (3) a political system for the world with a global institution to ensure universal order." Explicitly contrasting tianxia with Wallerstein's (1974) notion of "The Modern World-System," Zhao proposes tianxia as a utopian alternative to a neoliberal world order wherein the core continuously extracts value from the periphery, consolidates its power, and exerts economic, political, and cultural domination.

Zhao's formulation of tianxia has been extensively critiqued inside and outside of China,[5] just as it has deeply influenced discussions around and implementations of a reorientation of China's role in the world. My goal, however, is not to debate the merits of this philosophy or its influence on recent Chinese foreign policy but rather to draw attention to its influence as a way of thinking the world. I want to reflect on what its popularity reveals about transforming modes of engagement with the broader world and how the notion of tianxia might be helpful in thinking musical cosmopolitanism in China. In the context of broader efforts to "rethink China" as it emerges as a world power,[6] tianxia may be understood as what Raymond Williams (1977, 132) calls a "structure of feeling"—that is, as a "cultural hypothesis" and as a processual social experience that permeates not only political but also cultural formations and is reworked through diverse creative domains, including popular music.

In "pengyou tianxia," as in the calligraphy adorning the stage at Tutu Kongjian, tianxia is invoked as a way of framing musical production and cultural exchange. As a pillar of a developing independent music scene in Guangzhou and as a destination for touring musicians, this venue connects Guangzhou to places near and far through music and functions as a node on a cosmopolitan infrastructure that reorients Guangzhou as an important global city. In 2015 Dao and his partners opened another larger music venue in the gilded Zhujiang New Town area of Guangzhou. The name of this second music venue, Yuefu, is borrowed from the name of the imperial music bureau that came to prominence in the Han Dynasty, around the second century BCE, and was in various formations under various dynasties charged with collecting folk song and verse from diverse regions under central rule and reformulating these musics into performances for the imperial court. The venue's name thus self-consciously makes reference to this history of music collecting and curation as a territorial project and recasts contemporary musical circulations within the context of much older ones.

Tianxia, as a cosmopolitanism formation, interprets contemporary spatial formations and movements of people, objects, and ideas within frameworks, concepts, and terminologies drawn from China's long history and imperial past. The term *tianxia* itself is of course the most obvious example, but it is worth mentioning China's Belt and Road Initiative, which frames President Xi Jinping's development strategy in terms of earlier trade routes, as its full name indicates: "The Silk Road Economic Belt and the 21st-century Maritime Silk Road."[7] The name of the band Mabang, which references a particular mode of transportation used along the Southern Silk Road, operates similarly, as does Yuefu, the name of the Guangzhou music venue. With four decades passed since the beginning of China's reform era and a new political climate since Xi Jinping's ascendency in 2013, China is reasserting its role in the world in new ways. Tianxia encapsulates a form of global connection that is at once very new and very old.

Tianxia as political philosophy applies an ancient moral and civilizational complex to an emerging world order with China at the center. Tianxia as structure of feeling is an affective geography of global connection. Tianxia as a form of musical cosmopolitanism is a way of imagining global connection through music, of reclaiming creative authority, and of absorbing and reinterpreting transnationally circulating popular musics to rethink and reinvent China. A key element of tianxia as a way of thinking the world is the ways configurations of difference are reworked and incorporated through relational processes, and the boundaries between inside and outside are murky.[8] As the subsequent chapters demonstrate, musicians adapt and redeploy diverse musical materials, forging connections that reframe their own experiences of globality. Thus, a key element of musical cosmopolitanism in China, as elsewhere, is mobility.

Actual and Vicarious Mobilities: Spatializing China's Transformations and Rethinking Music and Place

As recounted in the ethnographic vignette that frames this introduction, Mabang's lead singer, Ye Honggang, begins nearly every performance with an exclamation: "Zou qilai!" (Let's go!). The phrase as Ye recites it is significant in part because it sounds to listeners notably southwestern.[9] But the meaning of *zou qilai* is significant as well—in the context of Mabang's musical cosmopolitanism, it may be understood as an invocation of mobility through music, pointing to "the workings of the imagination in a deterritorialized world" (Appadurai 1996, 63). For Ye and the other musicians discussed in this book, actual corporeal mobilities—leaving their hometowns, working in factories in the Pearl River Delta or attending college there, performing throughout China—are tied to vicarious musical mobilities and inform the ways they consciously connect their movements and personal histories to ways of listening to, drawing on, and reformulating musics, narratives, and languages from disparate places.[10]

With people, objects, ideas, and sounds always on the move but still bearing traces of where they come from and where they are headed, mobilities are central dimensions of musical worlds. Inspired by Urry's (2007) articulation of a "new mobilities paradigm" in the social sciences, this book examines music as part of a " 'social world' [consisting of] a wide array of economic, social and political practices, infrastructures, and ideologies that all involve, entail, or curtail various kinds of movement of people, or ideas, or information or objects" (Urry 2007, 18).[11] Two kinds of mobility—*actual* and *vicarious*—are connected and mutually constituted, in part, through emergent forms of musical creativity and modes of circulation.[12]

By *actual mobilities* I mean to refer to people and things physically moving through space, including but not limited to labor migration, tourism, educational migration, privatized cultural institutions that bring musicians and performers on tour, and circulations of ideas, images, and sounds. By *vicarious mobilities* I mean to refer to people imagining being elsewhere through sensory practices, economic participation, or affective political connection,[13] including, for example, listening to music while associating it with a faraway place, watching a depiction of New York in a television series streamed online, feeling a connection to Beijing while watching the annual Spring Festival Gala on television, or being on either end of a wired remittance between a factory worker in the Pearl River Delta and their family in rural Guangdong.[14] Attention to the intertwinedness and disjuncture of these two kinds of mobilities—actual and vicarious—is productive in understanding music and culture industries as domains where new spatial practices and relationships are articulated.[15]

Understanding mobility as a contingent potential for movement complicates idealizations of music and sound as boundlessly mobile agents of globalization by acknowledging the generative possibilities of "immobilities" and "obduracies" (Steingo 2016) alongside actual movements. Paying attention to the ways that musics on the move intersect unevenly with lives on the move reveals the roles of subjective experiences of listening to and creating music as imaginative processes of worlding. This is especially important in the context of China, where in recent decades both movements of people and circulations of music and other media have been inconsistent and intertwined with evolving state policies.

An extended discussion of the evolving mobilities and immobilities of ideas, sounds, and cultural products in the PRC must wait until chapter 7, where I discuss the infrastructures through which musics have circulated within, to, and beyond China in the past century. It is more important at this point to note that one of the most remarkable effects of China's reforms since the early 1980s has been the emergence of new kinds of actual mobilities that are restructuring economic, political, and cultural realms. Shifting state interventions in citizens' mobilities over the course of the past century as well as the deep historical roots of contemporary ways of thinking spatially make it important to contextualize some of the ways that China's reform era—in part through its imbrication in broader processes of neoliberal globalization—has built on, altered, or supplanted ways of thinking about mobility, space, place, and scale.[16]

Since the establishment of the PRC, the most important policy initiative that has shaped mobilities as well as political and economic spaces and scales has been the *hukou* system of household registration (Chan 2009; Chen and Fan 2016). Established in 1958 through the *hukou dengji tiaoli* (Household Registration Regulation), this institution categorizes Chinese citizens as either agricultural (*nongye*) or nonagricultural (*fei nongye*) and affords them different rights and access to state services according to the type (*leibie*) of their hukou. A major overhaul of the system in 2014 lessened this distinction and promised other reforms accompanied by new regulations aimed at increasing the urban population but funneling it to smaller provincial cities. Still today though, a person's hukou ties them to the specific locale—village or urban district—of their hukou registration, which has been, and in most cases remains, extremely difficult to change. Through the 1980s the percentage of people who lived outside of their place of hukou registration was miniscule—estimated at only 0.6 percent of the population. Alongside China's economic reforms, establishment of special economic zones, a push for industrialization, and now a new technology and creativity-driven economy, more and more people have moved from rural areas to the cities for work. However, they maintain strong ties to their hometowns, and in a sense they live *between* places. Thus, subtle and slow reforms to the hukou system have encouraged mass mobility in China over recent decades but have also dictated the terms of these mobilities. According to official estimates, now one in six Chinese citizens lives outside the place of their hukou registration.

These people are often referred to as China's *liudong renkou*, a phrase that is most often translated as "floating population" but that more importantly, especially in the context of the theoretical project of this book, implies a sense of flow, movement, and mobility. While a large portion of these migrants are low-skilled laborers, many work in new industries and are part of an emerging middle class in China. Among the musicians at the center of this book—all of whom work, perform, and rehearse in Guangzhou—few actually hold Guangzhou hukou. Some have worked in factories and construction in smaller Pearl River Delta cities before ending up in Guangzhou, where after many years struggling, they are now able to subsist on performing and teaching. Others are university graduates from middle-class backgrounds. While differing class backgrounds certainly shape people's opportunities and particular experiences of mobility and immobility, lacking the hukou of the place one lives inevitably leads to a precarious existence. For example, non-hukou-holders in China's major cities have difficulties sending their children to public schools or seeking subsidized treatment in public hospitals. Some musicians leave their children with their parents in their hometowns or other cities for extended periods and frequently travel back and forth. Still others live in smaller Pearl River Delta cities where they have established hukou status through marriage or buying property and commute to Guangzhou for rehearsals, gigs, and meetings.

As the music at the center of this book demonstrates, local place-based identities continue to be salient anchors in contemporary subjectivities while serving as grounds for diverse forms of cultural production. However, the forms that these localities take on are undergoing transformation as they are inflected by economic and political formations and intersect with regional imaginaries and transnational contact zones (Dirlik 2008).[17] Increasingly, the production of the local is imbricated in translocal imaginaries that destabilize isomorphic linkages between places, cultures, and people.[18] My analysis draws on Oakes and Schein's (2006) particular use of the term *translocal* in describing contemporary China's spatial reorganization brought about by both new kinds of mobility and new conceptions of the local. While acknowledging that the reform era, related economic reorganization, and the relaxation of the hukou system of residence permits has led to new forms of mobility on a massive scale, the authors also examine the linkages between mobilities (in a literal and physical sense) and "other forms and functions of connectedness" (1), that is, the connections between what I am calling (drawing on their work) actual and vicarious mobilities.[19] New modes of belonging to multiple physical places intersect with new ways of imagining connection to even more places. The consequences of industrialization and mass internal migration in the reform era, as Sun and Chio (2012, 20) argue, "is neither a flattening of hierarchy nor an erasure of locality and place as an important point of identification . . . [but rather] the emergence of a new 'geography of inequality,' on the one hand and an unprecedented level of translocal linkages and connections on the other." Mobilities, actual and vicarious, are intertwined with hierarchies and inequalities and with the economic and political transformations of China in recent decades.

New kinds of translocal linkages in China demonstrate a fundamental tenet of cultural geography, that is, that spatial formations undergird economic and political ones. Spatial reorientations necessarily both reflect and shape changes in economic and political structures as well. As Zhang Li (2001, 203) summarizes in her ethnography of China's floating population, "in a period of increased spatial mobility and marketization . . . the production of new social spaces and spatial relations brings about a higher-level social transformation." As anthropologists and cultural geographers of contemporary China observe, new mobilities and spatial transformations are at the heart of broader shifts in contemporary China, social transformations that resonate through the music of this cohort of musicians who float between Guangzhou and their hometowns.

In ethnomusicological theory, focus on the "musical construction of place" (Stokes 1994) has evolved toward attention to the ways that "circulation itself *constitutes* cultures" (Novak 2013, emphasis in the original).[20] Scholars have explored the ways in which musical circulations under globalization reflect an unmooring of music from place, nation, identity, and emplaced subjectivities.[21] This book builds on such work, exploring music's relationship to dynamic mobilities rather than its role in producing static notions of place or identity, while attending to the generative possibilities of the feedbacks and frictions of circulation.

However, two distinctive characteristics of China's cultural, political, and historical contexts necessitate nuancing such approaches. First, mobilities—musical and otherwise—are nothing new. While theories of globalization and cosmopolitanism, to varying degrees, imply an originary situation in which places, people, cultures, and musics were static, this implied stasis conflicts with reality—which, in his call for a field of "mobility studies," literary theorist Stephen Greenblatt (2010, 6) notes, "for most of the past as once again for the present, is more about nomads than natives." The widely circulating notion of China as a "closed" culture until the 1980s is an Orientalist fantasy; as Lisa Rofel (2017, 229) observes, China "has long been an active creator of various worlding projects, from dynastic tianxia to anticolonial nationalism, to socialist internationalism, to the contemporary worlding project of global capitalism." While movements of people and ideas have rapidly accelerated over the twentieth and twenty-first centuries, musics, musicians, and discourses about music have moved throughout and beyond China for millennia, and Guangzhou has been an important cosmopolitan port city and hub in these sonic exchanges for hundreds of years. Contemporary mobilities—of people, sounds, and ideas—must be considered in relation to historical ones rather than as evidence of a uniquely modern condition enabled by contemporary technologies.

Second, people's deep and enduring identifications with national, provincial, and local imaginaries mean that historical ideas about place (particularly in relation to music) still inform the production and consumption of all kinds of music, including popular music. As I discuss further in the epilogue, the intellectual history of thinking about the relationships between person, place, and sound in China threads together two-millennium-old Confucian treatises on music with Maoist cultural policy in the mid-twentieth century. Neoliberalization and globalization have not brought with them the annihilation of older cultural, social, and geographic formations in China nor have they brought about wholesale replacement of older ways of thinking about music in relation to these formations. Studying music through the lens of mobility means acknowledging this tension between ubiquitous mobility and illusory but nonetheless durable emplacements.

Given the strong affective connections people draw between musics and places as well as the long-standing pervasiveness of mobility as an element of all musical worlds, this book theorizes musics on the move by examining the actual and vicarious mobilities inherent in cosmopolitan musical worlds. While emphasizing the generative possibilities of musical circulation (Novak 2013), my approach recognizes enduring attachments to ideas of place, considers stasis and immobility alongside movement and mobility, and understands contemporary movements of people, ideas, and music in the context of much older ones. Against the dual backdrops of historically constituted understandings of the relationships between music, space, and scale in China as well as a contemporary era where people and sounds are mobile in remarkably new ways, this book aims to theorize music and space in China in terms of music's unequal and unpredictable movements, detachments, attachments, and cleavages, thereby also nuancing concepts often invoked by ethnomusicologists, from the simple dyad of "local" and "global" (Guilbault 1993; Slobin 1993; Stokes 2004 ; Taylor 1997) to ideas of "cosmopolitanism" (Feld 2012; Regev 2013; Turino 2000) and "circulation" (Novak 2013) that theorize musical flows in a globalized world. Thus, the book attends to the ways that contemporary musicians' different modes of mobility—both actual and vicarious—enact new spatial-creative imaginaries, jump scales, make places, and reveal spatial and scalar transformations brought about by China's reforms and their connections to broader processes of neoliberal globalization.

Tianxia Cosmopolitanism, Mobilities, and Music in Guangzhou

Beijing Lu is a wide and bustling pedestrian street in central Guangzhou lined with outlets of Chinese and international clothing retailers, crowded snack stalls, a cinema, book shops, and other stores. Running down the center of the street for several hundred meters is an excavated stretch of ancient road covered in glass. About four to eight feet below the current ground level, cobblestones of various shapes and sizes are unearthed at different depths with labels pointing to origins from ten different dynastic periods stretching from the Nanyue Kingdom (second century BCE) through the Qing Dynasty (1644–1912 CE). Geographies, like the thoroughfares that reticulate them, layer in diachronic accretions with the spatial imaginaries and practices of the past existing in dynamic relation with those of the present. A plaque introducing the "Beijing Road Cultural Tourism Zone" reads as follows:

> Beijing Road Cultural Tourism Zone is located at the site where Guangzhou was first established. It has undergone more than 2200 years of vicissitudes, yet its role as business center remained unchanged. . . . Now it has grown into a dynamic zone featuring the integration of culture, commerce, and tourism.[22]

Historical sites, museums, and institutions in Guangzhou materialize and perpetuate an official narrative of the city as a cosmopolitan hub with a history stretching back two millennia. This narrative positions Guangzhou as a central actor in a Chinese imperial and national history that is nonetheless on the geographic and political periphery. It bills the city as a center of commerce above all else and foregrounds the role of linkages with places far away—most significantly but not exclusively the Middle East, South Asia, and Africa. As an anchor of the Maritime Silk Road, the long-standing presence of a large foreign population in Guangzhou is often highlighted, as is the movement of Guangzhou people to places far afield. A brief overview of some of these sites offers a glimpse into the ways Guangzhou positions itself with reference to various geographic scales, historical narratives, and vernacular cosmopolitanisms.

A few minutes' walk from the north end of Beijing Lu lies the Nanyue Kingdom Palace Museum. Established in 204 BCE after the fall of the Qin Dynasty—the short-lived first-unified imperial dynasty in China—Nanyue was a kingdom that ruled over much of the present-day provinces of Guangdong, Guangxi, Hainan, and some of Yunnan as well as northern Vietnam. The kingdom's capital was here, in what was then called Panyu, a name that now refers to a southern suburb of Guangzhou. The museum sits atop a large open archaeological site displaying artefacts in the ground as well as in curated expositions narrating the history of the Nanyue Kingdom. As the museum introduction to the palace summarizes, "Being the witness to the city's development over 2000 years, it testifies to the fact that Guangzhou has all along been the political, economic, and cultural center in the *Lingnan* region." Another common term, *Lingnan*, refers here to the broader cultural area south of the Nanling Mountains over which the Nanyue Kingdom ruled.[23] It is noteworthy that Guangzhou is defined here on regional scales instead of national ones—looking beyond the nation as the "ultimate ground of history" (Duara 2009, 2; 1995), the projection of the footprint of an ancient kingdom onto contemporary geographies articulates a subnational and transborder entity of southern China and Southeast Asia for which Guangzhou is now, as in the past, a political, economic, and cultural center.

About a kilometer west of this museum is a white and unadorned thirty-six-meter-high minaret. First built in the seventh century, the minaret is part of the Huaisheng Mosque, which was the center of a community of Muslim traders and businessmen who lived in the surrounding neighborhood beginning in the Tang Dynasty (618–907 CE). The area is often portrayed as a historical precursor to present-day Xiaobei Lu, where a large population of African and Middle Eastern foreigners live. Most are traders and businessmen who participate in what anthropologist Gordon Mathews (2017) calls "low-end globalization." The mosque is described in official literature as a "much cherished historical site that has witnessed Guangzhou's history as the starting point of the Maritime Silk Road as well as a witness of the early Sino-Arabian cultural exchange." During the Tang Dynasty (618–907 CE), the Middle East and Africa were connected to Guangzhou by way of the Silk Road, an overland route that stretched through Central Asia, as well as by the Maritime Silk Road, a sea route connecting Chinese ports to South Asia, the Middle East, and Africa. Discourse about the Huaisheng Mosque is thus part of a broader positioning of Guangzhou as a key node on both these historical trade routes and their reimagining through Xi Jinping's Belt and Road development initiative.

Jumping several centuries into the future and several kilometers to the east, Huangpu Ancient Port sits on what is now a muddy bank of the Pearl River. A reconstructed customs house on the site of the historic port recounts Guangzhou's role as China's exclusive maritime port for foreign trade from 1757 through 1842 and highlights "the imprints of its past glory and prosperity" as a "testimony to the history of China's exchanges with the world." Exhibits trace Guangzhou's role as an important seaport stretching back to the Qin Dynasty (221–206 BCE), highlighting the transforming role of the city in broader cosmopolitan formations as well as the historical (and contemporary) centrality of Guangzhou as a gateway from China to the rest of the world.

Leaving the Huangpu Ancient Port, one is bound to pass the nearby Canton Fair Complex, a huge futuristic building that appears as a large suspended oblong cylinder on a nearby bank of the Pearl River. With an interior area of over one square kilometer, the complex comes to life twice a year during the China Import and Export Fair, a massive three-week-long trade fair that dominates the city while it is in session. Held since 1957, it is the most important international trade fair in China, with twenty-five thousand exhibitors and two hundred thousand attendees. Especially since Reform and Opening Up, this complex has been central to Guangzhou's integration with global economies through the Pearl River Delta region's industrial development, and it is a magnet for foreign traders who travel to and reside in Guangzhou.

Beginning in 1978 and spearheaded by reformist leader Deng Xiaoping, the Chinese state embarked on a project of drastic economic reforms that dramatically pushed the pendulum of China's political rationality away from the disastrous agricultural collectivization of the Great Leap Forward (1958–1961) and the violent anticapitalist purges of the Cultural Revolution (1966–1976) toward a system of partial privatization and limited market economy packaged as "socialism with Chinese characteristics" (*zhongguo tese shehui zhuyi*). As part of Deng's policy of "Reform and Opening Up" (*gaige kaifang*), five Special Economic Zones (*jingji tequ*; hereafter SEZ) were established in the southern provinces of Guangdong and Fujian that allowed for international trade and foreign investment. Throughout the 1980s, more SEZs were established, economic reforms were expanded, and China's economy rapidly grew and became more and more imbricated in global capitalist systems.[24] Shortly after the crackdown in 1989 on protesters calling for democratic political reforms to match the pseudocapitalist economic ones, Deng's Southern Tour (*nanxun*) of Guangzhou, Shenzhen, and Zhuhai in 1992 reinforced both the particular ways that capitalist reforms could coexist with socialist ideology and the central roles of southern China and the Pearl River Delta in this transition.

Also key to this transition was the reintegration of the former colonies of Hong Kong and Macau into the PRC state; the intertwined cosmopolitan and colonial histories of Guangzhou, Hong Kong, and Macau permeate Shamian Island, several kilometers west of the Huangpu Port and Canton Fair Complex. The island was part of the Thirteen Hongs, a trading system and commercial district administered by the Qing government that delegated all international business activities to a series of Guangzhou-based business entities called *hongs*.[25] Broad tree-lined streets are flanked by elegant buildings in European style that now house cafes, restaurants, art galleries, and souvenir shops. The area became an island only in 1859 when a canal was dug around the area of concession to England and France after the Opium Wars. In addition to connecting Guangzhou to European colonial powers, Shamian linked Guangzhou to the new British colony of Hong Kong and the Portuguese colony of Macau, where European and other traders had previously retreated outside of the short trading season in Guangzhou.[26] Over the next century, Hong Kong and Macau grew into major cosmopolitan hubs with distinctive blends of Chinese and European cultures. Since their return to Chinese rule in 1997 and 1999, respectively, Hong Kong and Macau join Guangzhou, Shenzhen, and seven smaller mainland Chinese cities as part of the Greater Bay Area (Yuegang'ao Dawanqu), a recent coinage of the Xi Jinping era (since 2013) that is replacing the term Pearl River Delta (Zhujiang Sanjiaozhou) in official and unofficial discourse. As the borders of these urban areas once separated by countryside expand into one another and contentious policies reintegrate Hong Kong and Macau with the mainland, a single massive megalopolis is emerging with a population of over one hundred million.

These various sites illustrate some of the ways the long history of Guangzhou as a cosmopolitan hub, transborder region, and cultural center of southern China is intertwined with reclaiming and rethinking its role in the world today. As the largest urban metropolis in southern China and a magnet for migrants from throughout the region, Guangzhou's music and arts scenes are important counterparts to those in Beijing and Shanghai, which receive far more attention in the academic and popular presses both in China and abroad.

Parallel and related to the central role that Guangzhou played in China's economic development since reform, it was also key to the cultural redevelopment of mainland China's popular music industry in the 1980s and 1990s. While Hong Kong and Taiwan had been the centers of Chinese-language popular music production in the broader Sinophone world for decades, record labels based in Guangzhou were central to jump-starting a homegrown music industry beginning in the early 1980s. Just as regulations on music and the monopoly held by the China Record Corporation (Zhongguo Changpian Gongsi) were being loosened through processes of partial privatization, China Record Corporation Guangzhou (Zhongguo Changpian Guangzhou Gongsi) and Guangzhou New Era Audiovisual Company (Guangzhou Xinshidai Yingyin Gongsi) were among several Guangzhou-based record labels responsible for a first generation of mainland Chinese pop stars who came to prominence in the early 1990s. Guangzhou's central role in developing a new mainland Chinese popular music industry was intertwined with broader perceptions of the region as a center of economic as well as cultural innovation.

By the 1990s Beijing and Shanghai eclipsed Guangzhou as centers of China's mainstream popular music industries. At the same time, both cities—though especially Beijing—became homes to diverse rock and independent music scenes that have been well chronicled elsewhere (Baranovitch 2003; De Kloet 2010). Beijing-based record labels such as Modern Sky (Modeng Tiankong), and major music festivals such as Strawberry Festival (organized by Modern Sky) and Midi Music Festival (organized by the Beijing Midi School of Music) were key actors in the development of an infrastructure of interconnected independent music scenes throughout China. At the same time, such a Beijing-centric understanding obscures the influence of other cities in this process—Wuhan, Chengdu, Lanzhou, Kunming, Shenzhen, and of course Guangzhou, just to name a few—as well as the roles of venues, music festivals, record labels, artists, and fans outside of Beijing. Guangzhou produced several early pioneers of Chinese independent music, from rocker-turned-reggae dub artist Wang Lei to folk singer Zhu Fangqiong, and is now home to many music venues and a lively music scene featuring a diversity of genres, styles, and musical approaches.

Music in Guangzhou draws on the diversity of languages, musics, and ways of living in southern China and is inflected by an orientation toward the world that has been shaped by the unique role that the city has played in China's global interactions. From a worldly metropolis in the Tang Dynasty (618–907 CE) to the exclusive international port in the Qing Dynasty (1644–1912 CE) to a relatively liberal and open city at the heart of China's reforms beginning in the 1980s, Guangzhou has been defined by mobilities and cosmopolitan formations, movements and connections that reverberate through a vibrant music scene that has emerged in the city in the past two decades.

Performance and Production as Ethnography

I first moved to Guangzhou in March 2005 to work at Guangzhou Ruixin Technology Ltd., an outsourcing company that offers North American, European, and Hong Kong companies "employee leasing" services for their software and IT needs. I had recently graduated from college with a BA in East Asian Studies and was a jazz saxophonist by training. As a hobby throughout high school and college, I had also spent many years developing practical skills as a recording engineer and home studio producer. I was hired to work in a small music production studio for Asia Entertainment and Communications, a subsidiary of the outsourcing company. The studio worked on various projects for both the parent company and its subsidiary, from producing incidental music for video projects and an online magazine to recording and editing voice-overs for clients—I am reminded of the time I spent working there every time I board any of Air China's domestic fleet of Boeing 737s and hear the familiar sounds of their safety video, the voiceover for which was produced by the company and voiced by a good friend and colleague.

During this time I began to collaborate with a wide variety of musicians in Guangzhou. At first I played weekly gigs at a small jazz club called Blue Note (no affiliation with the famous New York club with branches in Japan and now Beijing) and the occasional daytime gig for real estate sales parties and similar commercial events. After about a year, and several months spent back in New York, I stopped working for the IT outsourcing company and started pursuing more opportunities as a musician in Guangzhou.

As I discuss in more detail in chapter 5, I began to meet more and more musicians in Guangzhou's *minyao quan* (folk circle) by spending most of my nights at a venue called Loft345. Located on the middle floor of a compound of artist's studios in Haizhu District, the venue attracted many musicians, students at the nearby Zhongshan University, and young creative professionals. Along with the owner of the venue, a drummer named Dao Jianghua, and several other regulars who were also from southwest China, I formed San Duojiao, a band that blended musical traditions of the Bulang, Wa, Hani, Dai, and Lahu minorities with reggae, dub, jazz, and electronic music. Together we played widely in Guangzhou and elsewhere in China and were involved with the operation of music venues in Guangzhou and Shenzhen.

Over the subsequent five years (from 2005 through 2010), I worked closely with these people and others as a fellow musician, recording engineer, and business partner. I returned to Guangzhou for a month every summer after moving back to New York and beginning a PhD in 2010 and for a sustained year of fieldwork in 2014, during which time I started playing regularly with the two bands at the center of this book. Since beginning an academic position in Hong Kong (which is now connected to Guangzhou by a forty-five-minute high-speed train), I have continued to work with these and other musicians based in Guangzhou. This book emerges from these experiences and is grounded in participant observation in many overlapping dimensions of music making and the music industry in southern China.

Paraphrasing Steven Feld (2012, 6), this book recounts a critical entanglement "in other searching musical lives," where research and writing form one part—albeit an important one—of a broader collaboration and exchange with people through music. It is anchored in participant observation as a collaborator with both bands, playing saxophone in Wanju Chuanzhang and various wind instruments in Mabang; as a recording engineer, arranger, and sometimes translator; and as a longtime participant in Guangzhou's music business. I rehearsed and performed with Wanju Chuanzhang and occasionally with Mabang, creating horn arrangements and backup chorus arrangements for Wanju Chuanzhang and assisting with the process of recording and producing Mabang's debut album in Xingwaixing Records' studio. I participated in approximately twenty performances on tour and at music festivals outside of Guangzhou with the bands and performed regularly with the bands and other musicians in more casual shows and jam sessions at Tutu Kongjian and other venues in Guangzhou. I attended musical performances by other Guangzhou-based bands and touring bands from elsewhere in China and abroad on a nearly nightly basis whenever I was not performing, and I socialized extensively with both the musicians at the center of this book and other musicians that I do not focus on. I also attended business meetings between band members, their managers, and representatives and executives from the company. My ethnographic research was supplemented by historical and archival research on media systems, the music industry, and state-sponsored music and performance in China.

While theoretical approaches and methodologies borrowed from cultural studies dominated the study of popular music through the 1990s, ethnography has emerged since the 2000s as an increasingly influential mode of analyzing the social, cultural, and political worlds of popular music.[27] During the same period, popular music in North American ethnomusicology has gone from serving as a foil for the folk and traditional musics worthy of study (think Mantle Hood's [1971] Adornian diatribe on the "social nightmare" of "beatle music"[28]) toward occupying a central place in the discipline.

This book is one of countless other ethnographies of global popular musics that push ethnomusicology to take popular music seriously and popular music studies to enlarge its scope beyond North America and Europe. While many of these works focus on audiences and the socialities of popular musics in circulation, this book is inclined toward performance and production as ethnographic methods. Taking such an approach, it reinvigorates a research methodology intertwined with the earliest days of ethnomusicology of folk and traditional musics; Mantle Hood's (1960) concept of bimusicality stressed the importance of musical competency in musical ethnography, and even though Hood's focus was on gagaku, gamelan, and other high-art traditional musics, his outlook nonetheless offers insights for the role of participation in an ethnographic approach to the study of popular music in its social and cultural contexts. Bimusicality may be extended to other forms of musical competency, including production, recording, and mixing that are as central to popular music as bodily techniques are to other performance traditions. As Chris Washburne (2008, 6) observes in his bandstand ethnography of salseros in New York City, a musician-ethnographer's "dual roles as scholar and performer create an ongoing dynamic of alternating perspectives." Intertwining my own cosmopolitanism and mobility with those of my interlocutors, I emphasize the *participation* in participant observation in order to explore cosmopolitan creative processes and musical worlds marked by mobility.

As a participatory and multisited ethnography of musics and people on the move, this book focuses on Guangzhou and several other cities and towns in southern China, on interconnections between these locations, and on the "circulation of cultural meanings, objects, and identities" (Marcus 1995, 96) that emanate from them sonically. Following the book's focus on musical cosmopolitanism and new mobilities, I am inspired by anthropologists of the media, who offer a model for a "mobile ethnography" (Abu-Lughod 1997, 121) that explores the social worlds of media and the lived particularities they help bring about (Ginsberg, Abu-Lughod, and Larkin, 2002); these scholars inspire me to examine musical scenes, media worlds, and sonic infrastructures as the connective tissues in which subjectivities are embedded and as important conduits through which mobilities are expressed and explored.

While I touch on events that happened before and since, this book is based on primary fieldwork that took place in 2014. In the years since, the bands have continued to develop, and the musical scenes of which they are a part have continued to evolve. One member of Mabang moved on and was replaced, and the band started to work with a new label, Pollux Music (Beihesan Yinyue), which is a collaboration between Xingwaixing and Modern Sky. Pollux Music is developing in new and exciting directions the work started by Liuzhen Music that I focus on in this book. Wanju Chuanzhang continues to play widely as an independent band, and its lead singer has also performed increasingly often in a solo project wherein he plays *zhongruan* and electronics. Both bands have been featured in prominent national and international music festivals, television programs, and other venues. However, this book takes as its focus the period in and around 2014, when both bands were beginning to meet more wide acclaim and the music field in southern China was in the midst of transition.

Producing Worlds

Understanding musical cosmopolitanism as a process of knowledge making, this book examines music's role in producing worlds—in forging understandings of global connection, senses of self, and emplaced ways of being in the world. It does so through close ethnographic analysis of the worlds of musical production. By "production," I mean to encompass the variety of processes and negotiations that are involved in the creation of popular music, including rehearsal, performance, recording, mixing, marketing, and others. Exploring how personal histories intersect with creative processes, my focus skews toward musical producers over consumers. "Producing worlds" thus also gestures toward the dispersed networks of people, activities, and things that go into the creation and circulation of popular music; musical corollaries to what Becker (1982) calls "art worlds."

Chapter 2 offers ethnographic and musical analyses of the collaborative creative processes behind Mabang's debut album and the band's promotion by Xingwaixing Records. The chapter recounts the transformation of the band from Mifen Yuedui (Noodle Band) into Mabang (Caravan), and the shift from describing their music as *minyao* (folk) to the record label's genre category and marketing label *nanpai shijie yinyue* (southern branch world music). Understanding recording and mixing as negotiations that mediate sonic and social worlds (Meintjes 2003), I analyze an assemblage of practices inflected by interconnected concerns about musical genre, the market, and ideas of the local, national, and global.

Chapter 3 explores Wanju Chuanzhang's "island sound" as a form of cosmopolitan engagement with global island cultures. Attending to affective dimensions of practices of musical signification, I examine how musical elements, timbres, and stylistic conventions from diverse genres are redeployed as sonic representations of Nan'ao Island, a small island off the southeast coast of China. Offering analyses of several songs and their lyrics, I discuss the ways the band's leader and songwriter Li Yihan conceptualizes his connection to his hometown on the island through his and others' movements to and from it; I argue that a creative disjuncture between lyrical content and musical style is generative of new ways of thinking about the local and situating it in the world.

Chapter 4 investigates the intersecting aesthetic and political dimensions of the use of *fangyan*—alternatively translated as dialects, local languages, or topolects—by both Wanju Chuanzhang and Mabang as well as an expanding cohort of musicians in southern China. Attending to processes of composition, rehearsal, performance, and listening in a polyglot cosmopolitan setting marked by uneven linguistic competencies, I suggest a framework for understanding how the sounds of language in popular music—even when minimally understood—communicate notions of place and articulate social formations. I apply this framework to an analysis of the ways the production, circulation, and consumption of this music relates to shifting conceptions of the local in contemporary China. I argue that the resulting disruption of isomorphic ways of linking dialect and place inspire creative reflection on the movements of people and spatial reconfigurations at the heart of China's broader transformations.

Chapters 5 and 6 introduce the people at the center of this ethnography and look to the intersections of personal histories, national histories, cosmopolitan formations, and creativity as a means of exploring the role of individual agency and expressive culture in broader cultural shifts. Anchored around detailed biographies of the members of Mabang (chapter 5) and Wanju Chuanzhang (chapter 6), and building on scholarship that links China's economic privatization and its particular form of late socialist neoliberalism to a fundamental transformation of subjectivities, these chapters explore the process of becoming a musical cosmopolitan in contemporary China as one that is structured by political, economic, and cultural factors but that is nonetheless profoundly personal and unique to thinking, feeling, reflecting, and listening individuals.

Putting sound studies in dialogue with the anthropology of infrastructure, chapter 7 explores the ways that evolving modes of musical circulation and the listening practices associated with them reveal and contribute to broader transformations of state, society, and space. By focusing on the infrastructural foundations of mediated circulations of sound as well as on the sonic aspects of broader infrastructures, I bring attention to the materialities and spatialities of the technical and cultural systems through which sounds have circulated in the PRC, from wired radio to Mabang and Wanju Chuanzhang's record label, Xingwaixing Records. With this approach, I highlight how practices of listening are connected to broader political and economic rationalities and how the production of space occurs in part by means of infrastructural circulations of sound.

In the epilogue, I step back to consider musical cosmopolitanism and mobilities against a much broader intellectual history of thinking music, place, and governance in China. Returning to the concept of tianxia once again, I reflect on what the producing worlds at the center of this book offer for rethinking the relationships between music, China, and the political.

2

Worlding Genres

Everyone is gathered in the studio control room. Members of Mabang lounge on the sofa, a manager from the record company stands in the corner looking at his cell phone, and the engineer sits at the studio desk. He clicks the "S" for "solo" in the tracks that show the waveforms of the bass drum and floor tom that have just been recorded and then hits the space bar. As each sharp attack of the bass drum gives way to a resonating thud, the floor tom plays a staccato rhythm that turns to mud. The drummer shakes his head. "This isn't going to work," he says, and goes on: "This sounds like *minyao* (folk), not like Mabang." His contrast of *minyao*, a genre name, with Mabang, the band's newly minted name, in reference to the timbre of the floor tom and the rhythm it plays, intertwines several threads whose connections this chapter explores.

Creativity in popular music production is a collaborative process that occurs at various intersections between musicians, producers, corporate executives, recording engineers, audiences, and many other players. Focusing on the production of Mabang's debut album on Xingwaixing Records and the band's transformation from an independent unsigned *minyao* (folk) band called Mifen Yuedui (Noodle Band) into a *shijie yinyue* (world music) band called Mabang (Caravan), this chapter traces that collaborative creative process and explores the ways it is inflected by interconnected concerns about musical genre and ideas of the local, national, and global. Drawing inspiration from ethnographies of the recording studio (Bates 2016; Meintjes 2003; Porcello 2004; Thompson and Lashua 2014), my goal is to listen through the recording studio's control room to the interplay between structure and agency that permeates discussions around and enactments of musical genre in the popular music field in contemporary southern China and attend to the ways that such negotiations mediate broader constellations of cosmopolitanism, mobilities, space, and place.

From Simon Frith's (1996) "genre worlds" to Keith Negus's (1999) "genre cultures," many popular music scholars have described the ways genres function as both corporate categories and broader practices that link musical sounds to social worlds.[1] While I am drawing on these frameworks in order to understand the ways in which fields of cultural production articulate with economic fields, I mean to look more deeply at the ways ideas about musical genre articulate with the spatial dimensions of cosmopolitan social worlds marked by mobility. As Novak (2008, 16) observes, "the emergence of new musical genres takes place in an ongoing cycle of multi-sited, multi-temporal interpretations, which must be situated within a global history of exchange." Genres not only intersect with social worlds—they are resources for imagining and refashioning ideas about cultures and geographies in their gendered, emplaced, and historicized complexities.

Such an approach is aided by scholarship that expands from an understanding of genre as based in intertextuality (Briggs and Bauman 1992) toward an understanding of genre as assemblage (Born and Haworth 2017; Ochoa and Botero 2009). Drawing on DeLanda's (2006) development of Deleuze and Guattari's (1987) notion of assemblage, a key insight of this scholarship is that genres exist as emergent and heterogeneous networks of relation, wherein the components of a genre—social, cultural, sonic, aural, visual, affective, technological, and so on—participate in and connect to other genre assemblages.[2] By examining these connections and forms of participation, my goal is to contribute to an understanding of genre that looks to listening as a "distinctly virtuosic and creative practice of circulation" (Novak 2008, 15) and that pays attention to local particularities and to reception.

The remainder of this chapter ethnographically explores musical creativity as an assemblage of practices (Ochoa and Botero 2009, 160), including listening, interpretation, performance, recording, mixing, and selection of instruments as they intersect with one another, with emergent genre categorizations, and with cosmopolitan circulations of knowledge. Exploring how these relations and intersections inflect creative processes in the recording studio offers insight into the ways cosmopolitan subjectivities reformulate globally circulating knowledge through sonic and aural practices.[3]

What's in a Name?

Ye Honggang,[4] Fan Feng, and A Fei coalesced as a band under the name Mifen Yuedui (Noodle Band) in 2010.[5] From the start, Ye Honggang was the major creative force behind the project—the band played exclusively Ye's original songs, which were acoustic-guitar-driven compositions with poetic lyrics, accompanied by Fan Feng on djembe (referred to in Chinese as *feizhougu* [African drum]) and A Fei on various Chinese woodwinds including *dizi*, *hulusi*, and *suona*. Stylistically, the songs resembled the music of other groups in China's *minyao* (folk) circles, drawing on the singer-songwriter aesthetic popularized by 1960s North American folk revivalists like Bob Dylan while also incorporating elements of folk musics and traditional operatic forms from China's southwest, where Ye himself is from. From 2010 through 2014, Mifen Yuedui played regularly at prominent bars in Guangzhou that featured nightly live music—including Xiwo, 191Space, and Tutu Kongjian—and were invited to play at several major music festivals in the Pearl River Delta region and in other provinces. During this time, the only recordings of the band's songs were on Ye's self-produced 2009 album. These recordings were available streaming and for free download on several social media sites, including Douban.com.[6]

In 2014, Mifen Yuedui signed a five-year contract with the newly launched Liuzhen Yinyue sublabel. As a subsidiary of Xingwaixing Records, the label had already existed for several years, rereleasing popular independent bands' self-produced albums for wider circulation. The critically acclaimed debut album of now-famous Beijing-based Mongolian folk-rock group Hanggai was rereleased on Liuzhen, for example. During the course of 2014, the Liuzhen sublabel was reorganized with the goal of launching several of the label's own bands.[7] Mifen Yuedui was one of the first of these bands; in the process of preparing to record and promote their debut album on Liuzhen, the band underwent a transformation and reorientation from independent *minyao* (folk) band with strong ties to Guangzhou's music scenes to a *shijie yinyue* (world music) band signed to a major record label seeking performances in nationally and internationally prominent music festivals.

On the surface, this transformation was marked by a change in the band's name. Before 2010, Ye Honggang had played with several bands and various sidemen but performed often under his own name, "Ye Honggang and his Band." "Mifen Yuedui" was proposed as a band name only in 2010, when the band, in its infancy, was invited to play at the Beishan World Music Festival in Zhuhai. The name, meaning "Noodle Band" in English, was a playful one. Many who heard the name assumed it was a reference to a kind of noodle shop that is ubiquitous throughout China that sells a particular kind of noodle from Ye's native Guangxi Province, *Guilin mifen*. Thus, for many, the name evoked the southwest in a lighthearted way. Ye himself denies the explicit reference, however. He describes it simply as a good name for a "folk" band: "Everywhere has its own noodles. And everywhere has its own music. We didn't think about it too much. We just thought it was catchy," he said.[8]

Band members had already grown somewhat tired of the name by 2014—even before signing to Liuzhen, drummer Dao Jianghua had urged the other band members to consider changing the name. After signing to Liuzhen, several advisers at Xingwaixing reinforced these calls. The band saw their relationship with the record label and the prospects it brought with it as an opportunity to reinvent themselves. For both record company and the band members themselves, the name Noodle Band was no longer in line with the increasingly ambitious goals of the group.

After much discussion, the band settled on a new name: Mabang, which literally means "horse gang" and is often translated as "caravan." More specifically, the term references a type of caravan using horses as pack animals that is associated with a trade route in southwest China. The trade route is referred to in Chinese as the *Chama Gudao* (Ancient Tea Horse Road) but is often referred to in English as the "Southern Silk Road," drawing a parallel with the more well-known trade route that passes through northwest China and Central Asia. The *Chama Gudao* stretched from southern Yunnan Province through the Himalayas into Tibet and beyond. As early as the Song Dynasty (960–1279 CE), it was an important infrastructure through which tea, salt, and livestock were transported. In recent years, the trade route has played a reinvigorated role in popular discourse in China about the southwest and its connections both to urban and political centers of China and to broader trade routes and cultural affinities that connect China to South Asia and Southeast Asia (Ma and Ma 2016; Sigley 2013). It has also been central to the formation of a particular form of cosmopolitan masculinity marked by mobility. While the route was historically a "multi-layered social and physical mechanism for political, social and economic exchanges and mobility" (Ma and Ma 2016, 237), scholars have observed that it functions in contemporary cultural and political imaginations as "a narrative of national and ethnic unity that attempts to reimagine the importance of the periphery vis-à-vis the center" (Sigley 2013). That is, its historical significance has been mobilized as a way of reimagining space and center-periphery relationships in the present, much like China's Belt and Road Initiative, as well as the concept of tianxia, as discussed in the introduction. Using *mabang* as a band name, then, evokes China's southwest, borderlands, cosmopolitanisms, movement, masculinity, and depictions of ancient China. The band's choice to reference these histories of mobility through their name may be understood as expression of a form of tianxia cosmopolitanism that connects contemporary mobilities to much older forms of Chinese cosmopolitanism.

FIGURE 2.1. Mifen Yuedui's publicity photo in 2012. Photograph by Jiu Hao.

Along with the name change from Mifen Yuedui to Mabang came an image makeover and changes in their onstage presentation and performance. As Mifen Yuedui, band members had worn casual clothes in performances—jeans, T-shirts, and sometimes collared shirts. The outfits worn by members in an early publicity photo (fig. 2.1) were also typical for performances: all members are wearing black jeans with patterned T-shirts or informal collared shirts in various shades of blue. The only element of apparel that approached a consistent band uniform was Ye's own black leather baseball cap; he wore this in all performances, and he continues to wear it at all times off stage. As Mifen Yuedui, there was a unity in image and fashion between on stage and off consistent with tropes of authenticity and approachability in *minyao* circles.

After signing to Liuzhen Yinyue, a designer, stylist, and fashion consultant hired by Xingwaixing created costumes for the band that they began to wear in all performances, and a photographer and designer produced promotional photos and materials featuring these costumes (fig. 2.2). Ye wears an elaborate headdress with long peacock feathers sticking vertically out of its top.

He wears typical Thai-style loose brown linen fisherman's pants, and on top, a long mesh shirt that looks and fits like chain mail. Over this garment, he wears a leather vest. Fan Feng wears an orange and red tunic over a black shirt and a long beaded necklace, together evoking Buddhist robes. A Fei wears flowing black pants and a translucent black top. Dao Jianghua wears an intricate sari-like woven drape that hangs diagonally over one shoulder. These costumes evoke a romanticized and fantastical ancient China, from

FIGURE 2.2. Mabang's publicity photo in 2014. Photograph by Alex So.

the monk-like outfit of the percussionist through the armor-like outfit of Ye Honggang himself, while also mixing a grab-bag of other cultural signifiers, such as the feather headdress and henna tattoos on every band member's forearm.

Producing Genres

The change of the band's name and makeover of its image were related to a shift in the way the band described and promoted its music. As Mifen Yuedui, they listed the genre (*fengge* or *liupai*) of their music on Douban and other social media sites as *minyao* (folk).[9] This label situated the band within a particular genre world (Negus 1996) prominent in Chinese independent music with a significant ready-made audience of young creative types. As Mabang, the band was rebranded under the self-coined genre label *Nan Zhongguo ronghe shijie yinyue* (Southern Chinese fusion world music), or *Nanpai shijie yinyue* (Southern branch world music). These phrases were used in marketing materials and press releases about the band and were part of the video projection at the Liuzhen label release party described in the introduction to this book. In streaming services and social media, the band began to self-identify as simply *shijie yinyue* (world music). As descriptions of an individualized musical style, these extended phrases—*Nan Zhongguo ronghe shijie yinyue* (Southern Chinese fusion world music) and *Nanpai shijie yinyue* (Southern branch world music)—are dense with signification.

It is first important to note that *shijie yinyue* (literally, "world music") as it is often used in the contemporary Chinese context means something quite different from the "world music" of the 1990s North American and European recording industries that has been discussed at great length by ethnomusicologists.[10] As part of a broader expansion in major music festivals, several prominent and well-attended annual "world music festivals" (*shijie yinyuejie*) have been held in recent years in China, including the MIDI Taihu World Music Festival outside of Suzhou, the Ditan Park Folk and World Music Festival in Beijing, and the Beishan World Music Festival in Zhuhai. Each of these festivals has booked prominent Chinese bands that self-identify as *minyao* ("folk," the original term used by Mifen Yuedui) as well as international touring acts that have included jazz and rock from North America and Europe. Mabang and Wanju Chuanzhang have also been regularly booked at these festivals in recent years. Music festival organizers often also mine the significant ranks of foreign musicians working in China to bring "world music" to their festivals without having to buy international plane tickets; Ghanaian and Nigerian singer Sunny Dada's Afrobeat band Afrokoko Roots, and

Brazilian guitarist Fabão Funker's Brazilian funk band Vida Dura, both based in Beijing, are two acts that I have personally worked with as a horn player performing at "world music" festivals in China. Thus, the term *world music* as used in China has somewhat less of the fetishization of the local and third world than its western counterpart. As a corollary, it is interesting to recall that the Chinese term for cosmopolitanism, *shijie zhuyi*, is also formed as a compound of "world" and–ism. Whereas the "world" in the English "world music" nearly always implies *third* world (Feld 2000), the *shijie* in *shijie yinyue* does not, and *shijie yinyue* prominently includes music from North America and Europe including rock (*yaogun*), jazz (*jueshi*) and experimental (*shiyan*), as well as popular musics of Africa, Latin America, and the Caribbean. It also includes cosmopolitan musics from China and broader East Asia that might draw on any of these aforementioned traditions as well as on musical traditions from East Asia.[11]

Thus, three interrelated points about the meanings of *shijie yinyue* (world music) in relation to *shijie zhuyi* (cosmopolitanism) in China are worth reiterating. First, the corporate workings of a fledgling music infrastructure devoted to *shijie yinyue* in China are distinct from the well-chronicled ones of the North American and European contexts and are connected to other parts of the Chinese media and entertainment industries. Second, there are still important institutional gatekeepers who regulate the circulation of musics to, from, and within China, so notions of an unmoored "World Music 2.0" (Novak 2011) are not adequate in describing the Chinese context. Third, the "global order" (Stokes 2004) against which music is heard and performed is perceived differently from a Chinese perspective.

Returning to the larger discussion at hand, it is important to keep all of this in mind when considering Mabang's genre self-categorizations, *Nan Zhongguo ronghe shijie yinyue* (Southern Chinese fusion world music) and *Nanpai shijie yinyue* (Southern branch world music). While the *shijie yinyue* (world music) in these compound phrases carry all (and more) of the abovementioned connotations and implications, *shijie yinyue* is also modified by several other terms. *Nan Zhongguo* (Southern China) or *nanpai* (Southern branch), identify the region of origin of this "world music" in China's south and articulate with a common way of imagining China's cultural geography as split into a "northern branch" (*beipai*) and a "southern branch" (*nanpai*). The final word, *ronghe*, is a common word used to refer to mixtures or fusions of multiple elements, musical or otherwise, and is often used in very similar contexts as the English word "fusion." In the context of Mabang's genre self-categorization, it is meant to evoke the multiple musical influences the band draws on.

The band's official bio explicitly enumerates these influences, and the inclusion of both Chinese and English text necessitates including the original:

> Chinese: 融合了南方原生态山歌、彩调、桂柳腔、摇滚、雷鬼、Ska等元素形成独特的南派世界音乐。
>
> Pinyin: Ronghe le nanfang yuanshengtai shan'ge, caidiao, guiliu qiang, yaogun, leigui, Ska, deng yuansu xingcheng dute de nanpai shijie yinyue.
>
> English translation: Fuses Southern *yuanshengtai* mountain songs, *Caidiao* [opera of Guangxi Province], the accent of Liuzhou and Guilin cities, rock, reggae, ska, and other elements to form a unique Southern branch world music.[12]

Once again, each of these elements listed as part of the "fusion" of Mabang's music is dense with signification.

The first phrase, "Nanfang yuanshengtai shan'ge" invokes a recent coinage that has become a buzzword and common descriptor for music since the early 2000s. *Yuanshengtai* is a portmanteau of *yuansheng* (original) and *shengtai* (ecology) and is often translated as "original ecology." *Shan'ge* (mountain songs) is a genre classification used in popular and academic discourse in China to refer to a variety of rural folk musics. Rees (2016) offers an in-depth discussion of the term *yuanshengtai* and its relationship to music and discourse about music in contemporary China. For the present purposes, it is most important to note the term's association with a broader nostalgia for minority and rural folk musics untouched by musical modernization and cultural assimilation. The term, then, signals a discourse of purity surrounding folk musics, amplifying and modifying the term *shan'ge* (mountain songs) that follows. Both of these terms are preceded by *nanfang* (southern), locating the geographic origin of these "original ecology mountain songs" within a traditional geographic imaginary dividing China into northern and southern regions with distinct cultural, dietary, bodily, musical, and other properties.

The second term in this list is *caidiao*, which refers to a regional dramatic genre originating in northern Guangxi Province. Ye Honggang's parents are from Guilin, and he grew up outside of Liuzhou; these are the historical centers of *caidiao* opera, traditionally an amateur dramatic genre popular in villages. Regional opera traditions abound in China; *caidiao* is most well known nationally as the source of the opera *Liu sanjie* (*Third Sister Liu*), which tells the story of a female folksinger of the Zhuang minority who defies her landlord. The opera was transformed into a well-known 1960 song and dance film of the same name. Thus, while certainly not as prominent in the national imagination as other forms of regional opera such as *jingju* (Beijing opera) and *yueju* (Cantonese opera), *caidiao* would be recognized as a traditional dramatic genre and associated with the region by many readers of this biography.

The third term, *guiliu qiang* (Guiliu accent) further identifies the region of China that this "fusion" expresses without referring to any specific folk or traditional musical style. *Guiliu* combines the first syllables of two city names, Guilin and Liuzhou, and describes a broad region of Guangxi Province. *Guiliuhua* describes the southwestern dialect of Mandarin of the region that Ye sings in. By using *qiang*—which can also mean tune or pitch in the musical sense, in addition to "accent" in the sense of a regionally marked form of speech—instead of *hua* (language, the term most often used in combination with place names to describe the local dialect spoken there, as in *Guiliuhua*), the phrase hints at the ways that the sounds of the dialect express place, as I discuss extensively in chapter 4.

The final three words—yaogun, leigui, ska—refer to globally circulating genres of popular music, but the particular ways that they linguistically signify these genres is worth noting.

Yaogun is a direct literal translation of the English "rock and roll" and has been used to refer broadly to rock music produced both outside and inside China since the 1980s (Jones 1992; Baranovitch 2003; De Kloet 2010; Campbell 2011). Most music festivals in China are dominated by *yaogun* bands, and many cities in China have extensive amateur rock scenes that support local bands; it is by far the most ubiquitous and well-supported music scene outside of mainstream pop and has been the near-exclusive focus of Anglophone academic attention to popular music in China.

Leigui is a transliteration of "reggae," rendered in the standardized fashion with characters meaning "thunder" and "ghost." As I discuss in the detailed biographies in chapters 5 and 6, several band members have come to appreciate reggae through various routes. While several reggae or reggae-influenced bands, including Long Shen Dao and San Duojiao, have reached somewhat wider audiences in China in recent years, reggae has a comparatively small audience—the broad audiences and subcultures that reggae has spawned in other parts of Asia (Sterling 2010) have never taken hold in China. However, as early as the mid-1980s, widely popular rock musicians including Dou Wei and Cui Jian have occasionally drawn on reggae rhythms and sensibilities in their music.

Ska, the final word in this list, is written in English because no standardized Chinese translation or transliteration of the term exists—this also points to the scarcity of the style in China and to its more recent importation. For these musicians, ska refers broadly to both 1950s Jamaican artists and to

North American and European punk-influenced groups of the later decades of the twentieth century.

Taken as a whole, this list of terms and phrases about genre and style paints a picture of the diverse musical sources that Mabang sees itself as drawing on in creating the band's own original music. This specificity lies in stark contrast to Mifen Yuedui's 2011 bio, which discussed only *Guangxi yinyue fengge* (Guangxi music styles) and *duli minyao* (independent folk). The way that this list juxtaposes Chinese terms for transnationally circulating popular music genres, English terms for related genres little-known in China, names of particular local musical traditions in China, and terms that reference a contemporary discourse of purity surrounding folk musics in China is significant because it represents a cosmopolitan-minded world musicalization that is related to but notably distinct from similar world musicalizations described by ethnomusicologists in other contexts (e.g., Guilbault 1993; Meintjes 2003; Waterman 1990). It is distinct because of the particular meaning that the Chinese term *shijie yinyue* (world music) has taken on in recent years; because of *shijie yinyue*'s relationship to notions of Chinese cosmopolitanisms new and old; and perhaps most significantly, because of the ways in which these genres, styles, and musical elements come together to form a particular musical *ronghe* (fusion) representative of *nan Zhongguo* (southern China).

These ideas about genre have significant influence on the creative processes and negotiations surrounding the creation of the music itself and may be further understood through ethnographic attention to the production of Mabang's debut album released on Liuzhen Yinyue in 2015.

Producing Mabang in the Studio

Xingwaixing's corporate offices—the entire eighteenth floor of a gleamingly new office building with well-appointed conference rooms surrounding a maze of cubicles—are located in Guangzhou's central business district. Walking ten minutes from the corporate offices and entering the lobby of a nondescript mixed-use high-rise, one would hardly expect that the fifteenth floor houses a recording studio operated by the same record company, one of China's largest. Ascending to the fifteenth floor, the studio itself has a metal grate that covers a glass double door leading to a small hallway with the corporate logo embossed on the wall. A separate ordinary apartment door (used exclusively, except when entertaining guests) leads into the lounge, which is decorated with CDs published by Xingwaixing, hung above two leather couches and a tea table.

Beyond the lounge is the control room, about fifteen feet square, seen in figure 2.3. At the back is another leather sofa. It faces a large control desk that sits about five feet back from a fifty-inch flat screen mounted on the wall. On either side of the screen are stereo monitor speakers; below it is the subwoofer. On the desk itself is another smaller flat screen, a keyboard, and a mousepad; below the desk is a desktop PC. The computer runs both Protools 10 and Cubase 7.5, widely used software packages for music recording and producing known as "digital audio workstations." There is no hardware mixer; the smaller screen shows the mixer view of the DAW (digital audio workstation), which resembles a flattened hardware mixer, while the larger monitor shows the project view, which shows the waveforms of each track. Next to the desk is a studio rack. In the top slot is a Lynx Aurora 8 8-channel 24-bit/192kHz A/D D/A converter. The unit serves to convert analog audio inputs to digital signals and vice versa. It is a relatively high-end professional unit, though only having a single unit means that recording in this studio is limited to eight tracks, which is an extremely small number for a professional studio. Below the converter are various hardware preamps and compressors. The stars of the rack, and the most often used units, are two Avalon VT-737SP signal processors, much-lauded high-end analog units that function as tube preamps with compressors for getting the ideal sound out of high-end condenser microphones. Next to the sofa is a cabinet with padded drawers filled with about twenty microphones of various kinds. Beyond the control room and separated by two thick soundproof doors is a single recording booth of about fifteen by twenty feet. A video monitor and PA enable communication between the two spaces.

As this studio setup suggests, the space was designed for smaller recording projects. In the past it was mostly used for MIDI production and for recording vocals or the occasional acoustic guitar as well as for voice-overs and other incidental recording for online media. Guangzhou is also home to one of the most advanced recording studios in Asia, Village Studios, funded and built by Cantopop star Hins Cheung, which features a spacious control room with massive hardware mixer facing a large live room surrounded by smaller isolation rooms separated by thick soundproof glass. Compared to such a studio that might be rented by Xingwaixing or other major labels to record albums of established acts, this smaller studio operated directly by Xingwaixing is more similar to a very well-appointed home studio. This is in large part due to the fact that Xingwaixing does little of its own recording; it is largely a music licensing company. In addition, a significant portion of contemporary pop music in China, as in the rest of the world, is realized entirely through MIDI production and virtual instruments with only vocals and selected parts

FIGURE 2.3. Ye Honggang and the recording engineer reviewing a recently recorded track in the studio's control room. Photograph by the author.

recorded live. For these purposes, Xingwaixing's studio is well equipped—with a variety of high-end vocal mics and the Avalon preamps, it is best suited for recording vocals, voice-overs, or single instrument overdubs.

Beginning in April 2014, Mabang had access to the studio and the assistance of Xingwaixing's experienced full-time recording engineer Xiao Sun whenever a more pressing project from Xingwaixing did not require them. The process of recording Mabang's album was typical for recording a full band in a small studio such as this one. Ye Honggang began by laying down guide tracks for each song on guitar and vocals according to arrangements that were agreed on in rehearsals and performances. All other tracks were overdubbed independently. Short ethnographic vignettes from this overdubbing process illustrate some of the ways a recording comes into being as the creative result of multiple actors comingling, collaborating, and, occasionally, colliding.

In analyzing these examples, I follow Albin Zak (2001, 1) in understanding record making—that is, as opposed to simply recording—as a "poetic collaboration" between individuals and technology, and as an "inclusive process" (xii) in which many actors play collaborative roles. Understanding the process of music production as a form of social mediation, I am inspired by

Louise Meintjes's ethnographies of a recording studio in South Africa (2003; 2012), in particular her understanding of "recording and mixing [as] a dramatized struggle over signs embodying values, identities, and aspirations" (2003, 9). Following Meintjes, the following examples illustrate how the studio functions as a site for the (re)production "of sound's physiological, social, and sensual dimensions" (2012, 272) and how the sounds it (re)produces thereby reflect and reformulate not only ideas about music genres and styles but also and interrelatedly ideas about space, place, nation, and gender, among others.

RECORDING THE DRUMS

How could a small studio with only eight channels and no drum set record live drums? From the start, this was the largest logistical challenge and one that the studio had never had to face before. The band and label considered renting a larger studio space, but the free availability of underutilized company resources made the decision to record everything at Xingwaixing's studio easy. Implementing the decision was less so. Dao Jianghua arranged to bring his own kit, a Yamaha Maple Custom with 18″ bass drum, 14″ floor tom, and a single 12″ rack tom.

We spent a full day experimenting with the placement of the drums in the room and with different microphones and microphone placements, recording countless test tracks with the eight channels at our disposal. The best setup was to use two overhead mics, a single large diaphragm mic on the bass drum, top and bottom mics on the snare, close mics on each tom, and an additional room mic about ten feet in front of the drum set, as seen in figure 2.4. Auditioning test tracks at the end of the day, there was lengthy discussion about the sound that the studio was capturing versus the ideal sound that was desired. Everyone came to a consensus that, regardless of the setup used, the sound of the drums, particularly the bass drum and floor tom, lacked power. Though the sound might be appropriate for *minyao* (folk) or jazz, it lacked the *liliang* (power) required for *Nan Zhongguo ronghe shijie yinyue* (Southern Chinese fusion world music). Returning to the moment that began this chapter, we listened to the tracks of the bass drum and floor tom in isolation, and Dao Jianghua summarized: "This isn't going to work. This sounds like *minyao* (folk), not like Mabang." From the start, discussions about the timbre of the recorded drums intersected with ideas about the self-categorized genre label that Mabang was now using. Thomas Porcello's work on studio technologies brings attention to the importance of discourse about timbre in the studio (Porcello 2004; Feld et al. 2005). In this case, the timbre of the drums was not

FIGURE 2.4. Dao Jianghua recording the drums. Photograph by the author.

only evaluated objectively for quality but was also connected to several other factors: the new name of the band, the related visual aesthetic, from costumes to stagecraft, and finally, genre worlds.

After once again discussing moving to a larger studio, the recording engineer suggested using a different drum set. He pointed out that Dao's drum set was great for live performance, and especially versatile for playing in multiple styles, but it might not be ideal for the sound that the band had in mind. We began looking for an alternative. A friend of the band's—Liao Peng, the percussionist who plays with Wanju Chuanzhang—had a Sonor Force 3005 Maple kit with 22″ bass drum and 16″ floor tom, a kit with a reputation for a powerful, deep sound. Dao called him that very moment, and the next day, we picked the drum set up at Liao Peng's apartment and moved it into the studio. Dao also swapped his sensitive and versatile Taye snare drum for a

Mapex Solid Bronze 14″ by 6.5″, an extremely heavy snare drum with a loud but balanced sound.

After recording several test tracks, we listened back, and band members were immediately pleased. One remarkable element of the discussions that ensued was that descriptions of the drum sounds were filled with language not only about musical genre but also about gender, overlapping in sometimes surprising ways. In conversations about the timbre, especially of the floor tom, low frequency and deep resonance were gendered male, whereas higher frequency and shorter decay time were gendered female. Drawing on these associations, the Yamaha Custom kit was judged as too feminine and too suited for the sounds of the genres of *minyao* and jazz, contrasted with the Sonor Force kit, which was seen as sounding masculine, martial, warlike, and even "heavy metal."

These discussions also intersected with ideas of masculinity encoded in Mabang's new image. In some versions of Mabang's newly minted publicity photo discussed previously (fig. 2.2), one notices that not only the costumes but also a background of traditional Chinese architecture that the band members are superimposed against draw on the visual language of recent Chinese *wuxia* films. Films of this genre often depict heroic fighters in fantastical historical settings; Zhang Yimou's 2002 film *Hero*, starring Jet Li as a nameless assassin in the Qin Dynasty (221–206 BCE) who ends up sparing the emperor's life for the sake of Chinese unity, is perhaps the most well-known example outside of China. Many film studies scholars, notably Sabrina Qiong Yu (2012), have traced the reimagination of Chinese masculinity through films that portray an ideal man who balances *wen*, scholarly refinement, and *wu*, characteristics of a warrior, while also infusing traditional Chinese conceptions of masculinity with contemporary transnational ideals. Mabang's new name and image also is connected to this *wenwu* masculinity; the sound of the drums, then, were imagined sounding masculine in a similar way.

At the same time, the particular rhythms and grooves of Mabang's songs influenced the desire for a deeply resonant bass drum and floor tom sound. This sound was better achieved with the Sonor Force kit than the Yamaha Maple Custom kit. Figure 2.5 shows a transcription of a representative excerpt of the drum set, auxiliary percussion, and bass for "Mountain Song" ("Shan'ge"), a song whose title references the Chinese genre of rural folk musics discussed previously. In the bass drum and low-tuned floor tom that were the focus of discussions about timbre, the deep four-on-the-floor beat of bars one and two gives way to a rhythm that cites Chinese *luogu* drum and gong music; this four bar phrase is a loop under the song's chorus. In this case, the bass drum and floor tom are meant to mimic the sound of *tanggu*, large

FIGURE 2.5. Transcription of drum set, auxiliary percussion, and bass in "Shan'ge" ("Mountain Song"). Lyrics and music by Ye Honggang, performed by Mabang, copyright 2015 Guangdong Xingwaixing Wenhua Chuanbo Youxian Gongsi.

wooden drums used in a variety of Chinese percussion music, and to interact and balance the *bo*, the Chinese cymbal that enters in bar three. *Tanggu* are commonly up to three feet in diameter (or more), and have leather skins played with wooden beaters. The sounds of these drums have a deep resonant sound that the Sonor Force drum kit came much closer to approximating than the Yamaha Maple Custom kit.

The process of achieving an agreeable sound in the drums involved mediating multiple sonic and social ideals and concerns—particularities of Mabang's *ronghe* (fusion), conceptions of masculinity, the band's image, marketing strategies, and genre worlds all intertwined and affected equipment choices, recording strategies, and playing styles. The final timbre of the drums in this recording thus refracts and articulates social, geographic, and gendered dimensions and components of genre assemblages.

Once the drums had been recorded on top of Ye's simple guide track, the remaining instruments were filled in one by one. Recording the bass proved to be another instance where the process of recording ended up significantly changing the musical product that the musicians entered the studio expecting to create, and once again, where negotiations of this process circulated around cosmopolitan ideas about genre intersecting with various extramusical factors.

RECORDING THE BASS

The original configuration of Mifen Yuedui was a trio: Ye Honggang on guitar and vocals, A Fei on woodwinds and backup vocals, and Fan Feng on djembe and miscellaneous percussion. When Dao Jianghua joined the band in 2010 as drummer, Fan Feng, the percussionist, began playing bass on several songs to fill in what all band members perceived was rhythmic redundancy and a newly apparent gap in the sound. Fan Feng was best known in music circles as an accomplished percussionist; he was a self-taught guitar player, but it was not his main instrument, and he did not start playing bass until 2010. Most of the bass parts that Fan Feng played were derived from Ye Honggang's own guitar parts and were relatively simple bass lines in a rock style.

Mabang originally planned to record all songs as they performed them live; that is, with Fan Feng, the percussionist, playing bass on about half the songs and djembe and miscellaneous percussion on the other half. After recording the drums, however, they decided that songs that previously had no bass part would sound better with one, and that the overdubbing process allowed for the flexibility to have Fan Feng play both bass and percussion and sing backup vocals, which was impossible in live performances. Fan Feng, however, is not a bass player by training, and after spending several days in the studio experimenting with new bass lines for every single song, no one was pleased with the results. Band members and the producer started to consider bringing in an outside bass player to record new bass parts.

They called Yu Dian, a bass player in his late twenties who is a graduate of Xinghai Conservatory's jazz studies program.[13] Yu Dian played regular weekly gigs in both jazz and funk groups at the bar and music venue Xiwo, and he is a voracious listener; in addition to jazz, he has a particular interest in reggae and dub music. Yu Dian had also played with members of Mabang several times in the late-night informal jam sessions that Xiwo was known for—these often veered toward long psychedelic dub grooves, particularly when Dao Jianghua was behind the drums.

Yu Dian came to the studio at noon one day, and by 3:00 am, fifteen hours later, he had composed and recorded new bass lines for all eleven songs. The next day, we sat in the control room and listened to the results. Upon hearing the first few songs, Ye Honggang exclaimed, "Wow, so reggae!" He was surprised but pleased at the transformation of songs he had been playing for years; while not every song had a reggae-style one-drop bass line, several songs did, and Ye's reaction to the bass playing in general was summarized in this comment about genre. Everyone agreed that the new bass lines were far more complex and interesting than the original ones, and grooved with Dao Jianghua's drumming in a way that Fan Feng's bass playing never had.

Listening to the songs recorded on Ye's self-produced 2009 album alongside the same songs rearranged and rerecorded in 2014 is remarkable, and one of the most notable differences is the presence of a bass. The song "Not Changing the Direction the River Flows" is a particularly good example. In the original, the strummed acoustic guitar is the most prominent instrument beneath Ye's voice; below it is a simple sixteenth pattern on the djembe. In the 2014 recording, an intricate bass line forms the foundation for a much richer sound. The drum set plays a standard eighth-note rock groove with congas playing a tumbao rhythm that interlocks with it. The acoustic guitar is still strummed in a folk style, above which more complex vocal harmonies float alongside a simple melody on the *dizi* (Chinese bamboo flute). The contrast between the two versions can be seen in figures 2.6 and 2.7, which offer transcriptions of a short excerpt from each version, focusing on the rhythm section.

The overall complexity of the second version compared to the first illustrates a cosmopolitan assemblage of rhythms, timbres, and melodies from diverse sources: a standard rock beat on drum set layered against a bossa nova feel on the conga with Chinese *dizi* forming a counterpoint to the vocals. The process by which the bass on this recording came to sound as it did gestures toward the complex ways each of these elements came to be part of Mabang's musical *ronghe* (fusion). In the case of Yu Dian's bass playing, several songs took on a much stronger reggae feel as a result of his personal tastes and musical proclivities. One example that exhibits this particularly strong reggae groove that came to several songs is Mabang's cover of the popular folk song "Yellow Poplar Shoulder Pole." A "one-drop" reggae style is used in several songs on the album including this one; a deep bass drum heard on the third beat of every measure grooves with Yu Dian's reggae bass line, which rarely plays on the first beat of the measure, as seen in the transcription of the bass and drums in figure 2.8.

After the recording was completed, band members were so pleased with the hired bass player's effect on Mabang's sound that they invited him to join the group full time. Yu Dian became a member of Mabang the same month that he first collaborated on their recording, and he began to play with them in all live performances. This allowed the percussionist to focus on a wider range of auxiliary percussion that was also added during the process of overdubbing as well as on more complex vocal harmonies. Coming to the studio to record revealed a shortcoming of the song arrangements and of the band's

FIGURE 2.6. Transcription of excerpt of 2009 recording of "Bu gaibian heliu de fangxiang" ("Not Changing the Direction the River Flows"). Lyrics and music by Ye Honggang, performed by Ye Honggang, copyright 2015 Guangdong Xingwaixing Wenhua Chuanbo Youxian Gongsi.

configuration. Addressing these shortcomings altered not only the final recorded product but also the band's live performances from then on, and the sound of Mabang received a reinfusion of reggae style linked to one musician's own cosmopolitan listening habits.

The process of recording the bass I have outlined here illustrates how one particular element of Mabang's musical *ronghe* (fusion)—reggae—came to have a weightier influence. It also highlights the role of the agencies of multiple individuals—and musical subjectivities—in forming a band's overall sound. As in the previous example, analyzing this process necessitates "a nonessentialist approach to genre as an assemblage of heterogeneous actors and

FIGURE 2.7. Transcription of the same section on the 2014 recording of "Bu gaibian heliu de fangxiang" ("Not Changing the Direction the River Flows"). Lyrics and music by Ye Honggang, performed by Mabang, copyright 2015 Guangdong Xingwaixing Wenhua Chuanbo Youxian Gongsi.

FIGURE 2.8. Transcription of an excerpt of "Huangyang biandan" ("Yellow Poplar Shoulder Pole"). Arrangement by Ye Honggang, performed by Mabang, copyright 2015 Guangdong Xingwaixing Wenhua Chuanbo Youxian Gongsi.

mediations" (Born and Haworth 2017, 609). It furthermore illustrates how, in the context of cosmopolitan music making in contemporary China, elements of musical styles contribute to an overall band's sound without definite isomorphic links to the cultural or geographic contexts of their sources, a theme I expand on in the next chapter. At the same time, my ethnographic focus here is meant to demonstrate that this is not a dissonant unhinging of sound from source, a form of "schizophonic mimesis" as Feld (1994) reformulates Schafer's (1977) concept of "schizophonia." Nor is it "remediation" in the sense that Novak (2011) discusses, connected to "an emergent open source culture of global media" (606), wherein new media (or, in this case, styles) repurpose and repackage older ones (Bolter and Grusin 2000). Rather, elements of diverse musical styles are consciously but casually conjoined and resignified by musicians who are deeply cosmopolitan listeners. This conjoining and resignifying is a process of knowledge making central to musical cosmopolitanism in contemporary China.

RECORDING THE VOCALS

One day about halfway through the recording process, two representatives from Xingwaixing came into the studio. One was a manager of Xingwaixing's expanding concert, festival, and event planning department. After listening to preliminary mixes of several songs, he complained that, put quite simply, audiences would not be able to sing along with this music. His critique was in large part accurate. Mabang's songs are difficult to sing along with for the average listener in part because of the southwest dialect of Mandarin in which the songs are sung. This is also because of Ye Honggang's complex and poetic lyrics and his expressive singing style. The visitor pointed out the importance of connecting to audiences through lyrics as well as the importance of audiences being able to sing along in popularizing music, and he suggested having at least one song on the album that was, in his words, "comparatively poppy." In sharing his opinions, he mentioned a few songs including one about Ye's hometown, "Carp Crag in Liuzhou," and suggested involving a female singer, simplifying the lyrics, and making them standard Mandarin.

Ye nodded in silent agreement throughout the visitor's suggestions, but the next day when the topic came up again, he subtly expressed his distaste for the idea. Nonetheless, he had already been considering adding additional vocal textures, and he sought a path of compromise. Ye called a friend who was an accomplished singer of southwestern folk songs to the studio. He proposed modeling the exchange between male and female voice after *duichang*, male-female antiphonal singing popularly understood through its mediated circulations as a courting ritual most associated with southwestern minorities. Such male-female antiphonal singing is also a prominent feature of *caidiao*, the operatic form from Guangxi Province that Ye Honggang counts as one element of Mabang's musical *ronghe*. In addition, he proposed adding an extended female vocal solo.

The female singer recorded the parts, and the flowing contours of her high nasal voice respond to each line that Ye sings. The vocal elements of the song are reminiscent of highly produced *shan'ge* folk songs, folk songs sung in a conservatory-trained pan-traditional style. However, the singing takes on a much different feel than conservatory-style *shan'ge*, layered as it is above a reggae feel. In the end, the song still is not very singable by the average singer, as the visiting manager had suggested, but it did involve the male-female back-and-forth that he suggested. While the manager proposed a change to make the music appeal more widely to a domestic market, band members deflected the suggestions and instead addressed the CEO Zhou Xiaochuan's separate pursuit of strengthening the "Chinese DNA" in the label's music; cognizant of a desired international market for their music, they foregrounded a star of Chinese singing styles on a reggae song that fits the genre label of "Southern Chinese fusion world music."

While much attention has been paid to the role of corporate actors in the formation of "world music" and its markets, this example reveals that corporate influence over the recording process is complex and far from monolithic, and it demonstrates how aesthetic disagreements are sometimes generative of new configurations of musical cosmopolitanism.

Creative Assemblages

In the context of the transformation of the band from Mifen Yuedui to Mabang discussed in the first half of this chapter, these three examples demonstrate how creative processes in the recording studio draw on but reformulate transnationally circulating knowledge about genre in popular music. Subjective understandings of genre intersect with ideas about the spatial, political, and gendered dimensions of social worlds. These creative processes in turn are embedded in personal relationships, corporate relationships, and mediated circulations and are guided by an evolving market and listening public in contemporary China. Attention to creative processes and the agencies of individuals over the structuring potential of genres reveals the fragility of concepts of genres as coherent wholes and points to some of the ways in which cosmopolitan circulations of musical knowledge articulate with local understandings, aural histories, and musical subjectivities.

3

Places and Styles Converging

Navigating the crowded sidewalk abutting the six lanes of Jiangnan Xi Road, my attention is split between the smartphone in my hand and the similarly distracted people walking toward me. Checking the image of a hand-drawn map on my phone, I walk past several malls and office buildings until reaching a small alley that a post on the ubiquitous social-networking app Weixin directs me to. I am searching for "LA Moni Co.," a small French-themed café that is holding an event called "Dreaming of Hawaii: Beach Culture Music Party" ("Mengqi Xiaweiyi haitan wenhua paidui").

The post on Weixin features a square, vintage-filtered photo of a woman in midjump on a beach with her hands raised in the air. The text below promises an "Island and Beach Culture Summit" (Haidao, shatan wenhua fenxianghui) in the afternoon followed by a "Music Party" in the evening. It advertises Hula dancing lessons, free coconut milk and various snacks, and appearances by "Ukulele Beach Princess Yi Xi" and "Wanju Chuanzhang's Island Prince Xiao Li." It advises a dress code—for men, shorts, Aloha shirts, straw hats, and sunglasses; for women, muumuus, shorts, floral patterns, and sunglasses. My sandals and cargo shorts are well suited for the sweltering late summer heat of this Saturday afternoon in September 2015.

I follow the alley behind the newly built ten-story buildings that line Jiangnan Xi Road into a small neighborhood of typical six-story walk-up apartment buildings built in the early 1980s with concrete facades and balconies filled with drying laundry. The small street has covered bike parking and a few spots for cars that an older neighborhood security guard watches over. On the ground floor of the apartments are a series of neighborhood shops: a hardware store; a kiosk selling cigarettes, beverages, and lottery tickets; and a casual noodle house with a few tables and plastic stools.

I soon spot a sandwich board with "LA Moni Co." written in chalk and notice a recently renovated storefront that stands out from its neighbors for its sleek concrete facade and large antique-looking window panes with black grills. I enter through a thick natural wood door and am greeted by Li Yihan (today the "Island Prince" Xiao Li) and a few other friends as well as ten or so people I don't know. One of the owners of the café, a well-traveled businessman who operates the space as a side project, greets me and places a lei made of brightly colored artificial flowers around my neck. As promised on Weixin, I am soon drinking a cool iced coconut milk. On the wall is a hand-drawn chalk illustration of palm trees, coconuts with straws, two bikini-clad women, and a guitar beneath an arched banner: "Dream of Hawaii."

As I chat with a few friends and sip my drink, my attention wanders to the music playing quietly in the background:

> They're anglin' in Laguna in Cerro Azul
> They're kicking out in Dohini too
> I tell you surfing's mighty wild
> It's getting bigger every day
> From Hawaii to the shores of Peru.

It's the Beach Boys' 1962 album *Surfin' Safari*, playing from start to finish, with songs about surfing, beaches, and American cars. After a while, the event commences and we take our seats in the café.

First, Yi Xi, an emerging singer-songwriter in Guangzhou's *chengshi minyao* (urban folk) scene, makes a presentation about the history of the ukulele and performs a few of her original songs in the Hakka dialect of Chinese from a bar stool in the corner of the café. She hands out grass skirts to all attendees and gives a short lesson in Hula dancing. "Move your hips!" she laughs.

After some time spent practicing our hula dancing, Li Yihan takes the stage (fig. 3.1). He first shows a ten-minute film that he and the members of Wanju Chuanzhang made on a trip to his hometown on Nan'ao Island, an island seven kilometers off of the coast of southeastern China. The film features scenes of fishermen coming into port and offloading their catches juxtaposed with images of tourists frolicking in the waves.

Li then performs a few solo renditions of Wanju Chuanzhang's most popular songs. They tell stories of eating barbecue and singing karaoke on the beach, of attending a Chaozhou opera performance in a seaside village, and other glimpses of life on Nan'ao Island, all set to poppy interpretations of Afro-Caribbean rhythms.

After playing a few songs, Li goes back to his PowerPoint presentation and shows images of a letter written by a great uncle accompanying a remittance

FIGURE 3.1. Li Yihan addressing the audience at La Moni Co. Photograph by the author.

of fifty Hong Kong dollars sent from Thailand back to his family in Nan'ao. "Island life isn't just about parties on the beach," he says, making reference to one of his popular songs he has just played, "Beach Party," but also to the theme of this event. He goes on to speak about the migration of people away from Nan'ao Island to Southeast Asian countries including Singapore and Thailand in the early and mid-twentieth century. This forms an introduction to another original song, a slow ballad which incorporates the text of the letter:

Heading to Siam with no money, no food, and no prospects,
just the rucksack on his back.
Tears streaming from his eyes,
as his parents, wife, and child look on tearfully.
His fate is in Heaven's hands—
he doesn't know when he will be able to return.

A letter home tells his family not to worry:

My Dearest Parents,
It is respectfully submitted, fifty Hong Kong dollars are hereby remitted.
I will send more as soon as I can. Please don't worry about me.
To my dearest wife: What is our son's name?

Please do everything you can to free our elder daughter from servitude.
With you tilling the fields, raising the pigs, and waiting for me to earn money,
I will return to reunite our family as soon as possible!
I wish my family luck, happiness, and good health.

Yours truly,
A Homesick Traveler

"Yi feng qiaopi" ("A Letter Home"), lyrics and music by Li Yihan, performed by Wanju Chuanzhang, copyright 2016 Guangdong Xingwaixing Wenhua Chuanbo Youxian Gongsi

By performing this song about an uncle who moved from Nan'ao Island to Southeast Asia in order to support his family, Li complicates a romanticized notion of "island culture" by bringing attention to economic and cultural links between coastal cities in China and Southeast Asia as an alternative way of imagining island life that reflects longer maritime histories, vernacular cosmopolitanisms, and the experiences and outlooks of migrant workers. The contrast with the "island culture" imagined by elite cosmopolitans holding a themed event in a French café in Guangzhou is palpable. Audience members listen, rapt, and occasionally sip their iced coconut milks.

Celebrating "island and beach culture," this event enacts a collapsing of geographic scale accomplished through a cosmopolitan musical aesthetics of place where cultural and aesthetic affinity connects distant places that share a proximity to water. For organizers and attendees, "Hawaii" is imagined as more than a place; it is a trope that links together the Beach Boys' songs about the American West Coast, Yi Xi's reflections about beaches in southern Guangdong Province, and Li Yihan's musical homages to his hometown on Nan'ao Island.

Extending the conversations about musical genre in the previous chapter, this chapter explores Wanju Chuanzhang's *haiyang minyao* (ocean folk) music as a form of cosmopolitan engagement with global island cultures wherein musical elements, timbres, rhythms, and stylistic conventions from reggae, salsa, flamenco, and other musics are resignified in creative ways that consciously attend to issues of mobility, space, and place.

Places and Styles Converging

"Life on Nan'ao Island and the life of the music converge. You've been to Nan'ao," Li Yihan, the lead singer of Wanju Chuanzhang says to me, and we spend a bit of time reminiscing about a trip we took there together in 2013. He continues: "People there, this kind of life, this kind of spirit . . . It's very warm and welcoming, very summery. So, when we are writing these stories, these elements of Nan'ao and the music style (*leixing*) that we want to express actually coincide" (personal communication, December 14, 2014).

Li's reflections on his music hint at a way of understanding the resignification of globally circulating musical genres in relation to culturally particular and historically constituted understandings of music, space, place, and mobility. Ideas of the local articulate with cosmopolitan cultural imaginaries, and globally circulating cultural forms may stand in as iconic signifiers for localities far removed from the places where these forms originated. Li continues: "When you leave your home, you think about the ways your home is different from other places. You think about the ways the state of mind in your hometown is different. It is only when you are already on the road that you come to think about these questions. So, I use these songs to solve these problems, as a record."

While Li has not physically traveled to the Caribbean, the south of Spain, or North America, where the styles of music he incorporates into his songs hail from, he has traveled widely in China and has broad cosmopolitan experiences, vicariously traveling through listening to music, watching television, reading, and meeting people from all over the world in Guangzhou and other international cities in southern China. Musical expressions of place are often formulated through such disjunctures between actual and vicarious mobilities and are arrived at through cosmopolitan listening practices and reflection that happens once one leaves home.

In their official biography used until 2014, Wanju Chuanzhang portrayed their music as expressive of Nan'ao Island through three elements of local culture incorporated into their songs: the exclusive use of the local Nan'ao Island dialect,[1] the use of "elements of the island's local traditional music culture," and narratives about local islanders and "the ocean around them":

> Toy Captain was established in 2008 and is a band that performs songs in the local dialect of Nan'ao Island in Chaoshan. Their creative output employs elements of the island's local traditional folk musical culture. The majority of their songs recount stories of the people of Nan'ao Island and the ocean that surrounds them. Their musical style is traditional but not stilted, fashionable but not merely trendy. Lyrics are full of poetic ruminations, and their live performances resonate with audiences. Their musical method provides another possibility for the roots of Chinese culture to merge with world music.[2]

The bio concludes with reference to an alternative "musical method" of expressing the local through a merging of "the roots of Chinese culture" with "world music." As discussed in the previous chapter, the term *world music* (*shijie yinyue*) in a Chinese context has related but notably distinct connotations from in North America and Europe. Since the band started playing together, they have drawn on salsa, rumba flamenca, bossa nova, reggae, and other Afro-Caribbean and Black Atlantic musics. It is notable that these influences are not mentioned in this bio; glossed as "world music," they are situated as representative of Nan'ao rather than as specific genres or styles linked to their geographical roots, and it is their merging with things distinctly Chinese rather than their foreignness that is emphasized.[3]

The album art of their 2012 CD (fig. 3.2) reflects this sensibility as well. The band, in Bermuda hats, plays in front of a backdrop of a sunset over mountainous islands. Above them, lamps in red, yellow, and green are a nod to the

FIGURE 3.2. Cover art of Wanju Chuanzhang's 2012 album, *Dadao xiaodao, xianxian jiu hao*. Artwork by Popil (Zhuoyin He).

FIGURE 3.3. Map of Nan'ao Island included in the liner notes of Wanju Chuanzhang's 2012 album *Dadao xiaodao, xianxian jiu hao*. Artwork by Popil (Zhuoyin He).

actual stage at Xiwo, their home bar, as well as to pan-African and Caribbean colors. The drummer is pictured playing an Afro-Peruvian cajón, one of which he owns but rarely plays in band performances. The album title, *Dadao xiaodao, xianxian jiu hao*, means roughly, "Island big or small, life's good for all."[4] On the cover of the booklet inside is a hand-drawn map of Nan'ao Island and a handwritten note that begins, "My home, Nan'ao Island" (fig. 3.3).

This album cover distills some of the ways that Wanju Chuanzhang situates their music as expressive of both Nan'ao Island in particular and of a deterritorialized "island and beach culture" in general. In the album, lyrics about life on Nan'ao are set to fusions of musical styles from diverse places, and lyrical content and musical style articulate to express a sonic portrait of Nan'ao Island.

Wanju Chuanzhang's Island Sound

Wanju Chuanzhang originally consisted of Li Yihan on acoustic guitar, button accordion, and vocals; Gao Fei on acoustic and electric guitars; and Zhou Yi on electric bass. Dao Jianghua joined the band as drummer in 2010. Shortly thereafter, two prominent members of Guangzhou's jazz scene joined the band: Yu Zhenhai on tenor saxophone and Liao Peng on congas, bongos, and other percussion.

It is in this configuration that the band recorded their well-received 2012 album mentioned in the previous section, *Dadao xiaodao, xianxian jiu hao*. The album was produced in Hong Kong by Peter Scherr in a well-appointed home studio.[5] Scherr, a retired double bassist in the Hong Kong Philharmonic Orchestra, overdubbed several of the bass parts himself; the congas and other percussion were recorded by Chris Polanco, a Hong Kong–based musician and bandleader from the Dominican Republic. Though released independently, the album garnered the band a wide following on social media. In these early years, Wanju Chuanzhang played frequently in bars in Guangzhou and several times a year in festivals or invited performances in other cities.

I began to play with the band regularly in January 2014 just as it was being invited to perform at more and more major music festivals. This same year, the band signed to Liuzhen Yinyue, and the original independently released 2012 album was rereleased on Xingwaixing Records under the Liuzhen sublabel with new cover art and wider promotion. The band expanded as well; in addition to myself on saxophone, a trombonist joined to fill out the horn section, and three backup singers completed a large eleven-person stage presence. During this time, the band rehearsed several new songs composed by Li Yihan, which were later released on the 2016 album *Ching Chun Photo Studio*. In what follows, I offer translations of lyrics and detailed musical descriptions of one song from the 2012 album and two songs from the 2016 album while contextualizing these songs within the social and historical worlds they comment on as well as the musical worlds with which they intersect.[6]

"BEACH PARTY"

Built on a poppy interpretation of bossa nova and cha-cha-cha rhythms with an ensemble of singers that interjects invocations to drink or dance in response to the lyrics of the verses sung by Li Yihan, "Beach Party" is a nostalgic and carefree portrait of a gathering on the shore of Nan'ao Island. Released on Wanju Chuanzhang's 2012 album, the song is one of the band's more popular songs; in live performance, fans regularly *tui xiao huoche* (push the small train) to this song—form a line that snakes through the audience in a style derived from the "conga line" originating in Cuba and popularized internationally in the 1950s.

The recording begins with sounds of waves gently rolling in and several voices chatting and laughing in the distance. A Spanish guitar plays a solo figure that brings in the band at 135 beats per minute. On the drum set, the hi-hat imitates a guiro rhythm, resembling a jazz hi-hat figure but with even eighth notes. Bongos are layered low in the mix, with the two open hits on the fourth beat punctuating the groove on the drum set. A second acoustic guitar plays a downward and upward strum on two eighth notes on beats one and three of each measure. The bass plays a dotted quarter-, eighth-, half-note rhythm. The chord progression for both this introduction and the verse is I–vi–ii–I in D, with two measures for each chord. A tenor saxophone growling in the high register takes over from the solo guitar and plays a simple melody over two cycles of the chord changes.

Li Yihan begins to sing an even melody in the subdialect spoken on Nan'ao Island:

> The beach party is about to begin,
> The beach party is about to begin.
> Neon party lights flicker,
> The karaoke machine belts out Minnan melodies,
> A round of applause.
>
> Sea birds riding on the waves sing along,
> The full moon shines round and bright.
> Drinking beer, barbecuing chicken wings,
> Mingling together.

One the third verse, a chorus of four other voices responds to some of the lines (indicated in parentheses):

> Come, come, come, come on, let's dance! (Come on, let's dance!)
> It's okay if you make a wrong dance move,
> Sounds of merry-making drift over,
> Warming your hearts.
>
> A guy sees a girl he fancies (Oh!)
> And invites her to dance,
> She sees ruddy faces all around,
> And fireworks light the skies.

Moving to an interlude, the drum set and strummed guitars drop out, one guitar plays fingerpicked arpeggios in a high register, and the bass plays a walking bass line in half time, with a simple rhythmic accompaniment on a cabasa. The harmony shifts to the IV, and the dialogue between solo lead vocals and the chorus continues over a IV–I–ii–I chord progression:

> Friend, come over for a drink! (Cheers!)
> The cool sea breeze fans the face,
> Destiny has brought us together,
> Let's drink up! (Bottoms up!)
>
> Call out to the sea! (Come on and shout!)
> Don't let bad vibes enter your dreams.
> Listen to the laughter ripple on the sandy shore,
> Happiness will always be yours.
>
> "Haibian de wuhui" ("Beach Party"), lyrics and music by Li Yihan, performed by Wanju Chuanzhang, copyright 2012 Li Yihan

After this interlude, the tenor saxophone and guitar trade solo phrases over the I–vi–ii–I chord changes for two choruses, and then the entire verse and interlude are repeated. The song fades out on an extended saxophone solo, with the sounds of the waves and distant voices returning.

"MISTER CURLYHAIR"

Set to a blend of flamenco, reggae, and rock, "Mister Curlyhair," the first track on Wanju Chuanzhang's 2016 album *Ching Chun Photo Studio* (*Qingchun zhaoxiangguan*), uses a fictional character portrait of a comic figure to tell a story about multiple waves of migration that are changing Nan'ao Island, obliquely narrating the social and geographic consequences of China's rapid development.

The recording begins with the sound of a moped sputtering to a stop, footsteps echoing, and a door squeaking open. A ska figure in D-flat minor then breaks in at a brisk 160 beats per minute—the bass plays a disco-like octave-jumping bass line with the guitar's skanking rhythm on the "and" of every beat punctuating the high notes in the bass. Horn hits played by a tenor saxophone and trumpet set up a rapid descending harmonic movement—the so-called Andalusian cadence—that returns to another eight bars of this introductory figure.

The song moves on to the verse, which uses the same harmonic figure—vi–V–IV–III—extended to two measures per chord, replicating a very conventional chord progression associated with flamenco music but widely used in pop music since the 1950s. The drum set plays a ska beat, heavy on the hi-hat, over which a set of bongos adds rhythmic variety. Li Yihan sings in a low register to a percussive melody that traces the downward harmonic movement, still played by the skanking punches of the guitar:

Mister Curlyhair, who lives next door,
He's a barber from another province.
So stylish with his suspenders and colorful coat,
Some people love to come and get their hair cut.
Some people love just to come and have tea.

Hee hee ha ha, he can hold his own in a squabble.
He speaks the Yun'ao dialect,
And he sounds like a bird learning to talk.
A big red "For Rent" sign in the window,
And mosquito traps spinning around on the ceiling fan.
The bridge is being built, which will be convenient for the island.
Unfortunately, it brings with it alarming rent hikes.

He sits in the barber's chair, his curly hair blowing every which way in the wind.
The wind blowing through his hand as he holds scissors,
I ask him, "Where do you want to go?"
He says, "This year, I'm thirty-seven. Where's my wife? Where's my wife?
Where I can find her, that's where I'll settle down."

"Juanmao Xiansheng" ("Mister Curlyhair"), lyrics and music by Li Yihan,
performed by Wanju Chuanzhang, copyright 2016 Guangdong
Xingwaixing Wenhua Chuanbo Youxian Gongsi

The lyrics are a fictional character portrait of a man called Mister Curlyhair, a barber and longtime resident of Nan'ao Island who is originally from elsewhere in China. He has integrated into the island life; he is beloved for his sense of humor and his fluency in the local dialect—even if he "sounds like a bird learning to talk." As a barber and small business owner, he sought to make a life and have a family on Nan'ao Island. However, rent increases brought about by the development of the island are forcing him to relocate, as he can no longer afford to live and do business on Nan'ao.

Up until 2014, Nan'ao Island could only be reached by a forty-five-minute ferry ride from the mainland. In 2014, a ten-kilometer bridge was completed that links the island directly to the city of Shantou. As the lyrics explicitly discuss, anticipation of this bridge's completion radically drove up rent prices, and the island underwent major development as it braced for an influx of tourists. Many of those whose roots are on the island own their homes and places of business, and this development continues to enrich them. However, for earlier migrants to the island from other parts of Guangdong, Fujian, and provinces further afield, the influx of wealthier tourists as well as the business owners and employees who will cater to them is pushing them out. Therefore, the local Nan'ao islanders bid Mr. Curlyhair farewell; in the chorus, the same chord progression is played in a driving rock rhythm with distorted guitar ringing out chords while a chorus of Li and two female backup singers sing:

> Farewell, farewell, Mister Curlyhair.
> Farewell, farewell to his salty jokes.
> Farewell, farewell, Mister Curlyhair.
> Farewell, farewell to his salty jokes.

After the chorus, Li plays a solo on the diatonic button accordion that lasts through three cycles of the chord progression. The solo is a measured single-note melody that mimics the contours and rhythmic timing of flamenco guitar solos over this common chord progression. At the end of the third cycle, there is a stop-time break, and the accordion slows down dramatically to 120 beats per minute. The band reenters with a slow reggae feel, with the trumpet and saxophone playing a melody that goes back and forth between harmonized long tones and unison eighth-note figures. Li sings another snippet of the verse, and then another break comes; in the recording, it is a lo-fi sample of the rhythmic footsteps of a flamenco dancer. In live performances, all band members clap a clave rhythm in unison, with Li leading with hands raised high and the dramatic flair of a flamenco dancer. This break leads back to a repeat of the verse, and the song fades out on the chorus.

"A SECRET IN THE BOTTOM OF THE INCENSE BURNER"

"A Secret in the Bottom of the Incense Burner" mixes lush vocal harmonies reminiscent of 1960s North American folk revivalists with tumbao conga rhythms and catchy pop ballad songwriting. The title is a riddle that is slowly revealed through the song, which uses a tragic tale to narrate the personal and familial repercussion of a neoliberalizing economy where migrant workers move far from home in search of economic opportunity.

The song begins with a fingerpicked acoustic guitar playing a solemn ten-bar chord progression of I–vi–I–vi–I–vi–V–vi–V–vi in C. Two voices enter; Li's, singing a melody that follows the roots of each chord, and a female voice that harmonizes the melody in thirds in a higher register, beginning in parallel motion but departing to a more distant contrary motion for the second line:

> Man; man against man. Man; man against man. Man; man against man.
> He lives inside, but no one knows.

On the last line, the guitar drops out and the voices slow down and hold out the last word. A pair of congas enters, playing an altered tumbao rhythm at

122 beats per minute. After four bars of solo congas, the band enters. The bass plays an ornamented tumbao bass, emphasizing the 3–3–2 rhythmic ostinato but occasionally also playing on the third beat of the measure and on the "and" of four as well. The guitar strums open chords on the first beat of every measure. The drum set plays a standard eighth-note feel pop-rock pattern. Li sings multiple verses set over a simple chord movement between G major and A minor chords. Verses are separated by a martial horn interlude with snare drum rolls and later an accordion solo set to the chord progression of the intro and chorus. The lyrics slowly develop a story told from the point of view of a migrant worker who is serving as intermediary between a fellow migrant worker from the same village and this friend's family:

> The sea breeze blows. It is not he that doesn't miss home.
> Every year I return to our village at Lunar New Year, and he has me send his regards and regrets.
> He deceives his parents, saying he's too busy working to come home for the holidays.
>
> Ten years away from home, from the time he turned fifteen until now.
> Everyone in the village loves to gossip about how those who left to find work and make their fortunes are doing.
>
> I beg him to return to our hometown together,
> But everything I say goes in one ear and out the other.
>
> I am part of his deception; I bring home cartons of the best cigarettes for his father, and say they are gifts from A Xiong.
>
> The front page story in today's newspaper is about my friend.
> It reports that he was installing an air conditioner in an office building.
> As the rain fell, his feet slipped, and he called for help to no avail.
> A bird, flying all around, sung his name.
> My heart throbs in pain—this year, what lie can I possibly tell his parents?
>
> His ashes are in the bottom of the incense burner.
> On New Year's Eve, his family waits to see if he will come home.
> Deceiving his mother, I only tell her to put this incense burner in their home,
> And that it will bring blessings and protection upon their family.
>
> "Xianglu midi" ("A Secret in the Bottom of the Incense Burner"),
> lyrics and music by Li Yihan, performed by Wanju Chuanzhang,
> copyright 2016 Guangdong Xingwaixing Wenhua Chuanbo Youxian Gongsi

The song tells a story of migrant workers, pressure from family, and a geography of inequality, set in Nan'ao Island or perhaps the broader Chaoshan region, where many young men leave home to find work in other provinces. Known as China's "floating population" (*liudong renkou*), workers such as the main characters in this story travel wherever short-term construction or factory work takes them. Most of these workers see their families only once a year, at Chinese New Year, a week-long national holiday during which nearly all business and industry shuts down, and people from throughout China return to their hometowns.

"Man against man," the first line of the chorus, is meant to evoke the comparisons made by parents and family members of how successful their sons or husbands are becoming far from home; as a later line expands, "Everyone in the village loves to gossip about how those who left to find work and make their fortunes are doing."[7] The narrator of the song speaks about a friend from his hometown who left at fifteen and who hasn't been back since. Every year, the narrator implores his friend to return to their hometown together for Chinese New Year. His friend does not go with him because he is embarrassed that he has not become financially successful; he refuses to return home until he has progressed beyond the short-term construction work that has employed him for ten years. Every year, the narrator makes excuses for his friend to his family and delivers gifts of expensive cigarettes that he buys himself.

One year, the narrator's friend dies in a construction accident. The narrator cannot bear to tell his family, so he gives them an incense burner with his friend's ashes inside so that he may be reunited with his family.

WANJU CHUANZHANG'S MUSIC AND NAN'AO ISLAND

These three songs are fairly representative of the unity and diversity of Wanju Chuanzhang's oeuvre in terms of both musical style and lyrical content. Lyrically, all three songs are centered around narratives of lives connected to the island. While "Beach Party" paints an idealized and almost caricaturized picture of beach life, the other two songs narrate simple stories about Nan'ao filled with complexity, darkness, and tragedy. Looking back from Guangzhou to his hometown on Nan'ao, Li Yihan composes nostalgic lyrics about places, people, and ways of life he has left behind but that are still very much a part of him; thus, many of these songs focus on lives in motion. The island Li describes is not an idealized and universalized island that lies outside of time and place—a chronotope (Bakhtin [1937] 2004) like the *furusato* (hometowns) Yano (2002) describes as a common theme in *enka* music in Japan—but rather a hometown undergoing changes connected to China's broader transformations, a place to which he feels enduring but dynamic connection. Li conceptualizes his bond to his hometown through his and others' movements to and from it and explores not only his own mobility but also the mobilities of others—the migrant worker, the singing child, the barber from another province—who travel through the same spaces but experience them differently.

It is important to consider the work being done by musical style in this process. The three songs draw on rhythms, instrumentations, harmonic and melodic conventions, and timbres associated with a wide variety of styles or genres: pop-rock, contemporary folk, flamenco, bossa nova, cha-cha-cha, reggae, surf rock, and Taiwanese Minnan-language popular music, just to name a few. As Li explains in a statement quoted earlier in this chapter, "elements of Nan'ao and the music style (*leixing*) that we want to express actually coincide." In Wanju Chuanzhang's music, articulations and disjunctures between lyrical content and musical style are generative of new ways of thinking about the local and situating it in the world. These frictions serve to perform the local in a way that brings attention to the local's ongoing construction; its connection to regional, provincial, national, and global scales; and to reconfigurations of these scales tied to China's broader transformations. This is not a case of a particular genre being transplanted into a new social context and largely retaining its cultural meanings—a mobilization of reggae as social protest outside of Jamaica, for example. Rather, musical style, cultural meanings, and ideas about place articulate in new and sometimes unexpected ways, as I discuss in the next section, expanding the observations begun at the outset of this chapter.

Haiyang Minyao (Ocean Folk) and *Lading Yinyue* (Latin Music): Putting a Genre on Top of It

After signing to the record label Liuzhen Yinyue in 2014, Wanju Chuanzhang underwent rebranding under the guidance of the record label in a process that was similar, though not nearly as profound, as the transformation of Mabang discussed in the previous chapter. Up until that point, they had referred to their music, as Mabang had, as *minyao* (folk). In 2014 they began to refer to their musical style as *haiyang minyao* (ocean folk).

Li reflected on the origins of this name:

> The ocean is maybe something, a theme, that has been with Wanju Chuanzhang since the beginning. The nature of these stories about the seaside and the nature of the music we make surge together. It is about warmheartedness.

> It's connected to the music styles of many coastal areas in other countries. Like Brazil, or like reggae, the music we are really liking these days. I think that it's a special characteristic of coastal areas. I think that there is a unique temperament [*qizhi*] that is special to all of these places. These are all musics of places on the ocean, and they are symbolic of this. We are also making music about the sea, but we center on these kinds of themes through the aspect of musical style. (Personal communication, December 14, 2014)

Li draws a connection here between music, narrative, temperament (*qizhi*), and place that invites further reflection on the affective dimensions of musical cosmopolitanism and the stability of musical genres on the move.

The signifying processes of Li's musical cosmopolitanism differ considerably from those in Chinese rock music, which has attracted outsized scholarly attention. Focus on rock in Beijing has inadvertently obscured the cultural importance of other kinds of popular music in China and has informed understandings of the localization of transnational popular culture under globalization in ways that tend to romanticize resistance. Contrasting "authentic" rock in Beijing with "commercial" pop in Hong Kong (scare quotes and the critical skepticism they imply in the original), De Kloet (2010) borrows Appadurai's concept of a "hard cultural form" as something that "come[s] with a set of links between value, meaning, and embodied practice that are difficult to break and hard to transform" (Appadurai 1996, 90)—Appadurai's own example is cricket in former British colonies throughout the world, which is not only constituted by the same practices wherever it is played but, Appadurai argues, has the same meanings for participants. For De Kloet (2005), rock's mythology, fashion, and attitude have a similar "sonic sturdiness." To varying degrees, all three English-language monographs about popular music in the PRC (Jones 1992; Baranovitch 2003; De Kloet 2010) look to rock in such a way and understand it as a form of resistance to government hegemony that is connected to a broader global youth subculture. This approach to musical genre as hard cultural form is tenuous even when applied to rock music, as De Kloet demonstrates, but it is an especially uncomfortable fit when applied to the syncretic musicking in southern China that this book takes as its focus.

Though Wanju Chuanzhang draws on rock, reggae, ska, salsa, and bossa nova, elements of these musical styles do not function for them as "hard cultural forms" but rather as musical elements and tools that may be recombined, strategically holding on to certain values, meanings, and embodied practices while discarding others. Cultural and geographic associations of musics are particularly malleable, and elements of diverse styles may evoke particular places in China, feelings about them, and connections to other places in and outside of China.

This malleability is in part a result of the particular histories of circulation of foreign popular musics into China. As I discuss at greater length in other chapters, access to global popular music in China occurred through chaotic and unpredictable circuits well through the 1990s. Now, streaming platforms, social media sites, and smartphone apps,[8] as well as record labels like Xingwaixing, offer extensive and easy access to music from throughout the world with information that deeply contextualizes the music for interested listeners. These forms of access and new ways of listening have also spawned new forms of musical creativity. Drummer Dao Jianghua put it this way:

> We, the newer generation of musicians, have started to understand the broader world, have started to have opportunities to come into contact with more things. From all different sorts of new musical languages we can then inform our own musical understanding. From many different understandings, then coming back, there's a merging, a collision that happens with our own lives. This kind of music doesn't depart from the seed of one's own music. Its soul is moving along the same line. But the technique of expressing it is new. There's reggae inside, some music is starting to incorporate ska, and some music is starting to incorporate jazz. But that's just a style. What the musician wants to express is still his own life. (Personal communication, June 27, 2012)

Dao understands musical genres not as "hard cultural forms" but rather as expressive techniques related to "the seed of one's own music." Diverse musical styles function as creative resources for personal musical expression, and the "merging" or even "collision" with geographically and historically emplaced musical subjectivities is at the heart of the creative process.

Dao's statement dovetails with perspectives on musical meaning and genre as soft, malleable, and dynamic; as Holt (Holt 2007, 5) observes in his monograph on genre in popular music, "musical meaning is highly contingent, and . . . the ontologies of the semantic codes that form the musical basis of generic categories are fragile." This perspective is supported by ethnographic work on popular music in a variety of contexts, which complicates any understanding of the relationship between cultural practices and social formations as isomorphic and stable. Discussing indie pop in Indonesia, for example, Luvaas (2009) describes intertwined processes of aesthetic deterritorialization (Deleuze and Guattari 1977) and reflexive place making (Giddens 1991) that result in "a conception of 'local' reinvented and reimagined . . . a 'local' dissociated from the classificatory schema of nation-state and colony, and built instead from the tropes and typologies of transnational popular culture" (Luvaas 2009, 248).[9] A similar process is at work here; Wanju Chuanzhang and Mabang are not localizing transnational genres but instead redefining the local through the selective use of elements from these genres.

In conversations with members of Wanju Chuanzhang about each member's listening habits and how the band came to play in the style they do, several band members described long-standing personal affinities for *lading yinyue* (Latin music), a broad descriptor used to describe everything from salsa to solo flamenco guitar. *Lading*, though it corresponds to the English "Latin," articulates a particular understanding of generic categorization that neatly aligns neither with categorizations used in the regions being described nor with the conventional generic understanding of the terms *latin music* and *musica latina*. In band members' expositions, *lading yinyue* is not a linguistically defined category—as music sung in Spanish and Portuguese languages. Nor is it a category defined strictly through geography—as music deriving from the Spanish Caribbean and Iberian Peninsula. Though no doubt indirectly influenced by actors such as Academia Latina de la Grabación and the Latin Grammys, it also does not exactly align or connect to the corporate-influenced "genre culture" (Negus 1999) of "Latin music."

Instead, the category of *lading yinyue* is understood by Li and others as a broad and porous assemblage that encompasses various Afro-Caribbean derived popular musics traditionally associated with the English term *latin music* as well as Jamaican reggae and flamenco-pop fusions such as the Gypsy Kings. Rather than strict stylistic or musical definitions, the category is constituted through a perceived temperament (*qizhi*) related to place; sounds are thus mapped to affective geographies through flexible ideas about genre. This conceptualization of *lading yinyue* and of genre more broadly supports Novak's (2008, 16) assertions about musical genre that emerge from his study of experimental music practices in Japan: that genres are centrally constituted through listening, which must be conceived of as a creative and subjective practice of interpretation, contextualization, and conceptualization.[10]

Lading yinyue is thus related and connected to—but importantly, not conterminous with—*haiyang minyao*, the band's self-categorization of their style. Li Yihan conceptualizes this connection—both listening preference and the resultant musical borrowing—in terms of an affinity of place. In his logic the pace and ways of life that he imagines in Caribbean islands are similar to those of his own childhood in Nan'ao Island. Put as simply as possible, he likes the music he does because of who he is and where he comes from; he plays the music he does because he likes it. As Novak (2010, 40) observes elsewhere, "acts of cultural borrowing channel emergent forms of cosmopolitan subjectivity." It is almost unremarkable, then, that musical expression of Nan'ao Island should be in a style reminiscent of the Caribbean that he imagines through cosmopolitan listening practices.

Music as signifier may point in multiple and ambiguous ways. Ethnographically dissecting the local meanings attached to mainstream country, rock, and reggae on the San Carlos Apache Indian Reservation in Arizona. Samuels (2004) uses the term *feelingful iconicity* to refer to the way a cultural form might come to have an iconic signifying relationship to group identity (or place) without a long-standing connection between the two. Musical sounds may come to feel and sound as if they resemble places, identities, and sociocultural formations through repetitive acts of listening and performance. It is in a related way that for these musicians and these listeners, certain sounds become connected to certain places—*Lading yinyue* (Latin music) comes to signify Nan'ao Island through a shared trope of "island culture," and a new genre category, *haiyang minyao* (ocean folk), can link Nan'ao, the Andalusian cadence, tumbao rhythms, the Nan'ao dialect of Chinese, the Caribbean, and southern Spain through chains of feelingful iconic signification.

In southern China, the negotiation of the local within the global ecumene is not a top-down process controlled from Beijing, or any other center, but a complex, multilayered process that happens in part through circulations of music and practices of listening. The music of Wanju Chuanzhang and Mabang is embedded in the shifting contours of a Chinese postsocialist modernity that is distinct yet fluidly connected to both local and transnational processes. Singing in local languages on top of fusions of transnational genres and local sounds, these and other bands perform alternative visions of space and place that connect their hometowns—through Guangzhou—to transnational and cosmopolitan imaginaries. These musicians express the local by, spinning David Samuels's (2004) words, "putting a genre on top of it."

4

Singing in Dialects No One Understands

Ye Honggang adjusted the volume of his guitar, looked up into the audience that filled Xiwo, a popular music venue in Guangzhou, and in simple and perfectly accented Mandarin yelled, "Dàjiā hǎo, wǒmen shì Mǎbāng Yuèduì!"—"Hello! We are Mabang!" The words and cadence of the sentence mimicked nearly every self-introduction spoken by bands and performers on stages large and small throughout China. After some encouraging shouts from the crowd, he yelled "Zou kilai!" Everyone knew what he meant: "Zǒu qilai" in standard Mandarin, a lesser-used exclamation meaning, more or less, "Let's go!" But the replacement of the "ch" initial sound of "qilai" with the hard "k" of "kilai" marked his speech as some variety of nonstandard Mandarin, probably from the southwest, where the phrase itself is more popular. Ye launched into a set of songs sung in Guiliuhua, the southwestern subdialect of Mandarin spoken in his hometown Liuzhou.

A table of two sat in the back; Ye's good friend (and one of the band's biggest fans) was also from Liuzhou. He sang along with the intricate poetic lyrics and understood most of them. Others furrowed their brows but moved along to the music, only able to understand the most basic gist of the lyrics. At a large table between the stage and the bar, a group of ten friends spoke loudly in Cantonese, playing a drinking game while emptying a tall tower of beer. People walked past on the way to the bar, where everyone ordered their drinks in standard Mandarin.

After Mabang played for some time, and after a short DJ interlude of reggae in Jamaican English, Wanju Chuanzhang took to the stage. "Dàjiā hǎo, wǒmen shì Wánjù Chuánzhǎng!" the lead singer yelled into the microphone, once again in perfectly accented Mandarin. They proceeded to perform songs in the southern Min subdialect spoken on Nan'ao Island.[1] Besides the increasingly exuberant Cantonese-speaking friends by the bar, most of the tables were filled with groups chatting in standard Mandarin. One table in the back held a group of friends conversing in Chaozhouhua,[2] a southern Min dialect spoken in the cities of Chaozhou and Shantou but very common in Guangzhou and the rest of Guangdong Province. Office workers hailing from Shantou, just across the bay from the island that is the subject of most of Wanju Chuanzhang's songs, they understood much of what the lead singer sang, but some phrases were hard to catch. When Wanju Chuanzhang played their biggest hit, much of the bar sang along. "Hiantai, le genglai homa?" ("Brother, how are you?") they sang, mimicking to the best of their ability the Min subdialect but often sounding more like Mandarin: "Xiōngtái nǐ jìnlái hǎo ma?"

Wanju Chuanzhang's set wrapped up and was followed by another interlude by reggae DJ Wang Dong. Then a third band, San Duojiao, took the stage and launched directly into a set of reggae-tinged covers of folk songs from Lancang Lahu Autonomous County in southern Yunnan Province. A song or two was sung in the Yunnan dialect of Mandarin, but most of the lyrics were in a variety of minority languages from the region, which no one in the audience understood.

On this night at the music venue Xiwo, three different bands played music sung in a variety of different languages that were largely incomprehensible to most of the audience. Among the eighty or so audience members that filled the bar, there were a handful from Shantou who could understand most of Wanju Chuanzhang's lyrics. One table of Ye Honggang's friends from Liuzhou sat in the corner; they understood Mabang's lyrics perfectly. Other Mandarin speakers could understand Mabang's lyrics in simpler songs and associated the sounds of the language with the southwest but could not follow the more complex lyrics of several of the songs. The minority languages that the band San Duojiao sang in were not even fully understood by its lead singer, a member of the Bulang minority who was raised speaking Yunnan dialect, standard Mandarin, and some Bulang.

As Mabang finished their set, Ye Honggang unplugged his guitar and stepped down from the stage to rejoin the audience. A man approached him and complimented the music. "What dialect was that you were singing in?" the man asked, and Ye explained. The man, who was from Xi'an, about a thousand miles north of Liuzhou, said he couldn't understand much of what was sung but that it nonetheless reminded him of home.

This chapter investigates the intersecting aesthetic and political dimensions of the use of *fangyan*—alternatively translated as dialects, local languages, or topolects—by an expanding cohort of musicians in southern China, and it explores contemporary forms of articulation between music, language, listening, and place. The production, circulation, and consumption of music in local dialects challenges the symbolic power of standard Mandarin by aligning local languages with alternative spatial and social imaginaries and articulates translocal geographies of southern China that stand in contrast to nationally sanctioned ways of imagining space and the isomorphic relationships between dialect, culture, and music they assume. Examining the implications of this multilingual musicking in a rapidly changing PRC also provokes broader consideration of the ways language functions in popular music. Processes of composition, rehearsal, performance, and listening in a polyglot setting marked by uneven linguistic competencies reveal ways the sounds of language in popular music—even when only partially understood—communicate notions of place and articulate cosmopolitan social formations.

Linguistic Diversity and the Politics of Language in Contemporary China

In several media interviews I participated in with the band Wanju Chuanzhang after festival performances, one of the first questions every interviewer asked was why Wanju Chuanzhang sings in the Min Chinese subdialect spoken on Nan'ao Island instead of in standard Mandarin. Li Yihan would respond:

> The most important reason to use the Nan'ao dialect in performance is as a record of what is being lost. One time, I was speaking with a fellow islander who mentioned that the central kindergarten now has less than one hundred students. This is because many young people from Nan'ao are unwilling to live like their forefathers, fishermen in life, ghosts of fishermen in death. So they choose to leave the island, first going away to study and then starting a career and raising a family. We may reject working as fishermen, but we may not reject that we are the next generation of fishermen. We use music as a record of the local language, a few fragments of the lives of fishermen, so that the generation after us, through the window of our music, can more deeply acknowledge the history of their own native place.[3]

In this response Li ties together several common themes in public discourse about local languages in China. First is a close association of local languages with local cultures and local histories; the language itself is framed by Li as a record of ways of life associated with Nan'ao: in particular, the fishing culture that has all but vanished from the island. Second is an anxiety about the loss of local language and a conscious association of this loss with a broader

TABLE 4.1. Major dialect groups of Chinese

Dialect group name	*Number of speakers as a first language in Mainland China*	*Prominent example of a dialect in this group*
Mandarin (Guanhua)	959 million	Beijing Mandarin
Wu	81 million	Shanghainese
Yue	77 million	Guangzhou Cantonese
Min	56 million	Hokkien
Xiang	37 million	Changsha dialect
Gan	22 million	Nanchang dialect
Hakka (Keyu)	36 million	Moiyen Hakka

Numerical statistics adapted from Ethnologue: Languages of the World, 23rd Edition (www.ethnologue.com).

homogenization of culture in China tied to new forms of mobility and widespread internal migration. Third is a recognition of a link between the erosion of local languages and economic development.

Against this backdrop, an overwhelming majority of popular musicians in the PRC, from the biggest pop stars to independent bands in smaller cities, sing in standard Mandarin. However, Wanju Chuanzhang and Mabang are among more and more bands in China's diverse popular and independent music scenes who choose to sing in local dialects and who foreground this choice as central to their musical identities. While fans of these bands include many who are fluent in the dialects sung, a significant portion of listeners are urban transplants from other regions who have varying degrees of semantic understanding of the lyrics. In order to understand this polyglot cosmopolitan context and to situate the discussions that follow, it is important to give an overview of China's linguistic diversity, political policies framing language use in the public sphere, and public discourse about local languages versus Mandarin.

Contemporary China is extraordinarily diverse linguistically. Linguists and Chinese dialectologists most often divide the Chinese spoken language into seven major language groups that are mutually incomprehensible, as outlined in table 4.1 (Yan 2006). "Dialect" is often used as a translation of the Chinese term *fangyan*, which more literally translates as "regional language," "local language," or "topolect." Translating *fangyan* as "dialect" is problematic in part because of the high level of mutual unintelligibility of these seven branches but also because of the malleability of the scale at which *fangyan* might group together languages (Kurpaska 2010). Furthermore, there is significant variation within each of these seven broad dialect groups. While the linguistic categories outlined in table 4.1 all may be described as *fangyan*, the term may be applied to subcategories within each of these categories as well. Even within the Mandarin supergroup that stretches from Beijing to southwest China, regional variation is so strong that a Mandarin speaker from Beijing would have only basic comprehension of the Mandarin subdialect that Mabang sings in, Guiliuhua, which has much in common with the Tai-Kadai languages spoken by the Zhuang minority surrounding Guilin and Liuzhou. Relatedly, the Min subdialect used by Wanju Chuanzhang is similar to the more common Chaozhouhua spoken in Shantou but is distinct and is related to but only minimally mutually intelligible with the Hokkien dialects spoken in Xiamen and Taiwan.[4]

While PRC government policies have continually promoted the use of standard Mandarin (Putonghua) in the public sphere, local languages are spoken by a majority of Chinese in their daily lives and are linked to strong regional identities (Duara 2000; Gunn 2006; Liu 2013). The friction between government language policies and the realities of a multilingual China is especially salient in Wanju Chuanzhang and Mabang's adopted home of Guangzhou, a linguistically diverse but traditionally Cantonese-speaking city that also is home to China's largest population of migrant workers and a large population of educated workers from other provinces. This friction is an important context for understanding musical production in local languages.

The poster seen in figure 4.1 is a good example of public efforts to promote Mandarin use and also highlights some of the ways Mandarin and dialects are presented in binary distinction in public discourse guided by the state. The large text reads, "Please speak Mandarin." Underneath it, a notice reads, "We can all communicate by speaking Mandarin." In the foreground, a young urbanite in a baseball cap and designer sunglasses exclaims, "Where ARE you all FROM?" Behind him, four faceless individuals in the shadows announce themselves in what can clearly be read as local languages: Shanghai Wu (signified by the use of the first person singular pronoun read as "aklak" in Wu and conveyed by its standard inscription 阿拉), Cantonese (signified by the use of the verb "to be" read as "hai" in Cantonese and inscribed with the character 系 and by the use of traditional characters used in Hong Kong, Taiwan, and Overseas Chinese communities to write the place name Guangdong), and nonstandard subdialects of Mandarin spoken in the southwest and the northeast.[5]

This stark juxtaposition of colorful young urbanite speaking standard Mandarin and shadowy figures speaking dialects expresses binary divisions of Mandarin versus dialect as cosmopolitan/provincial, global/local, urban/rural, educated/ignorant, modern/antiquated. In addition, the contrast in skin tone between the white-skinned Mandarin speaker and dark-skinned

FIGURE 4.1. Poster promoting Mandarin use originally uploaded in 2008 to the image-sharing website nipic.com by user Yi Lu and available for download and printing on many image-sharing websites including 58pic.com and cxtuku.com.

speakers of local dialects taps into discourses of skin color in China that prize white skin as beautiful and as a marker of cosmopolitan, modern subjectivity contrasted with tanned dark skin associated with rural workers and a preindustrial past (Mak 2007).

It is important to note that the realities of dialect usage contradict or at least complicate the various binaries embodied by this poster; many dialects are themselves transnationally prominent languages with wide circulation, such as Cantonese, Hokkien, Teochew (Chaozhouhua), and Shanghai Wu, and they continue to be important in the articulation of transnational Chinese cosmopolitan formations outside the configuration of the PRC state (Yang 2002). The perspective embodied in this poster—which is exemplary of wider state-guided public discourse—thus not only prioritizes mutual intelligibility and national integration but also minimizes the realities of cosmopolitan circulations of non-Mandarin dialects. The political goal of achieving a unified national culture and assimilating alternative subnational and transnational linguistic communities is promoted through an appeal for practicality ("We can all communicate by speaking Mandarin"), but this appeal is packaged with a perspective whereby local dialects are derided as backward and as impediments to becoming a modern cosmopolitan citizen.

This contrasts with the perspective held by Li, articulated in his media interview response discussed at the outset of this section. For Li, local dialects are important bearers of local cultures and ways of life, and promoting local dialects does not inherently contradict being a globally engaged Chinese citizen.

In China, as elsewhere, language and hegemony are closely intertwined (Gramsci 2000; Ives 2004), and language functions as a form of symbolic power (Bourdieu 1991). While linguistic standardization in China has been central to national integration (Anderson 1983; Hobsbawm 1990),[6] regulation by the state has not only promoted Mandarin use in the service of national integration historically but also continues in the present to restrict the use of dialects in a way that directly affects musical production. In 2001 the Ninth National People's Congress passed "The Law of the People's Republic of China on the Standard Spoken and Written Chinese Language." Articles 12 and 14 declare Mandarin the primary language of the mass media, while article 16 severely regulates the use of local dialects in the public sphere.[7] While explicit exceptions are written into the law for the arts (traditional opera is the example given), these regulations reinforce a self-governing linguistic choice made by most musicians who aspire to reach a mass audience and who hope to be broadcast on national airwaves controlled by the state.

The law has been selectively implemented and became an especially sensitive issue in Guangzhou, the traditionally Cantonese-speaking city that Wanju Chuanzhang and Mabang call home. In July of 2010 the provincial government advised Guangzhou Television to switch prime-time broadcasts to Mandarin and drastically limit broadcasts in Cantonese. This was met with widespread public outrage and an unprecedented large public protest, and the proposal was eventually rescinded. In Guangzhou and southern China more broadly, for both speakers of Cantonese and other dialects with less transnational currency and symbolic power than Cantonese, this protest points to an anxiety about the increasing saturation of Mandarin into all areas of life and more broadly about a cultural grayout tied to China's economic reforms.

In such an environment, language choices in media, arts, and expressive culture necessarily mediate political, geographic, and economic structures and ideologies. Examining the use of local dialects in contemporary literature and television, Edward Gunn (2006) demonstrates how choices about language perform and negotiate broader structures of power and how local language use in the public sphere supports local, regional, and transnational communities and economic structures as alternatives to a hegemonic national imaginary.[8] Building on Gunn's work, Liu (2013, 267) argues that "local languages help to articulate marginalized and unassimilated identities in postsocialist China, to enable those on the periphery to criticize the center and comment on the failure of modernity, to foster a strong sense of a distinctive local community that challenges any monolithic accounts of Chineseness, or to provide youth with a noninstitutional language that allows them to explore an alternative cultural space."[9] In recent years, music has emerged as an important example of such an alternative cultural space; the intersecting political, aesthetic, and affective workings of music in local dialects thus warrant close ethnographic attention.

Musical productions in local dialects, such as those by Wanju Chuanzhang and Mabang, may be understood as forms of resistance to linguistic hegemony, as challenges to the assumed symbolic power of standard Mandarin, and as self-conscious correctives to monolithic portrayals of Chineseness that maintain the PRC state as master signifier. It is especially noteworthy that these bands are based in Guangzhou, where questions of linguistic self-determination have been of great concern in recent years. It is also significant because of the central role Guangzhou and the broader Pearl River Delta region have played in China's economic reforms, the relatively liberal cultural atmosphere of the region, and the connections the city has to various "transboundary formations" and cosmopolitan imaginaries (Cartier 2001). Wanju Chuanzhang, Mabang, and other bands based in Guangzhou who consciously avoid singing in standard Mandarin preserve and promote the sounds of local dialects in an urban cosmopolitan context where standard Mandarin is preferred, and they thereby perform alternative understandings of Chinese urban modernity and cosmopolitanism that challenge or at least nuance monolithic nationalist narratives.

As the drummer Dao Jianghua put it in an interview, "These three bands are all working with our own cultures, with dialects. Within China's multicultural situation, this used to be very difficult. Everyone could just hear erhu, pipa, Beijing opera, Mandarin. But China actually has thousands of dialects, and thousands of kinds of music. Every place has its own airs, so we can't forget them." Dao's reflection here mimics Li's interview response at the outset of this section; language, sound, and culture are viewed by both Dao and Li as intimately connected. Furthermore, there is at once a sense of anxiety surrounding the loss of local dialects (and by extension, local cultures and musics) and an excitement at newfound possibilities for expressive culture that might not only deploy but also reinvigorate an appreciation of China's intertwined linguistic, sonic, and social diversities.

It is within this context that these bands perform cosmopolitan music in dialects, destabilize the binaries promoted by language ideologies privileging Mandarin, and offer an alternative vision of the role of the local in China's modernity. Compared to other media and expressive forms, music is an important medium for the promotion of local dialects precisely because of the ways it promotes attention to an aesthetic appreciation of the sounds of language. The complex intersections of linguistic and musical sounds in the multilingual setting of Guangzhou are what I turn to in the next section of this chapter.

Performing the Local in Polyglot Cosmopolitan Guangzhou

An underlying assumption in the analysis of popular music has been the understanding of song lyrics as social texts (Frith 1989). As a result, close readings of lyrics inspired by literary analysis, as well as an understanding of the total pop song as "text" with sung lyrics as a central element (Middleton 2000) have been key strategies for understanding how popular music articulates social formations. English-language studies of popular music in China are no exception, and analysis of song lyrics has been a central methodology of all three monograph-length English-language studies of popular music in the PRC (Jones 1992; Baranovitch 2003; De Kloet 2010). Even when sung language in popular music is understood as "verbal art" (Bauman 1984) or is analyzed under related frameworks drawing on vocal anthropology (Feld et al. 2005) that pay attention to voice over text, little attention is given to commonplace situations involving partial or total incomprehension. It is worth noting that in J. L. Austin's (1962) work, which has inspired so many branches of theorization about performance, any sort of misunderstanding would be a "misfire": a hollow performative with no force.

What, then, about polyglot cosmopolitan settings such as the one I describe at the outset of this chapter, where listeners (and even performers) have varying degrees of comprehension of the lyrics? This is in fact hardly unusual; as Szego (2003, 292) observes, "transnational music markets and culturally plural colonial and postcolonial societies makes this a quotidian reality." In writing about the experiences of students and listeners not proficient in Hawaiian learning songs in the language, Szego argues that nonreferential aspects of language might still have a communicative function: "Listener references to the temporal and timbral characteristics of language sounds, such as flow and sweetness, actually point to gestalt experiences that fused language with musical sound. Sung utterances, then, can constitute meaningful sonic streams whether or not they achieve denotative resonance" (306). Linguistic sounds, particularly when sung, communicate to listeners through domains other than the purely referential, affectively express notions of place, and articulate social formations.

In an interview with drummer Dao Jianghua, I asked him what he thought about the fact that audiences often could not understand the lyrics at Wanju Chuanzhang and Mabang performances such as the one I describe above. His response echoes this same "gestalt experience": "Me, I don't think it's important. I don't understand English, but look at what I'm listening to." He gestured toward a bookcase full of CD cases with English, French, and Arabic on their spines. "Good music doesn't just use language to express," he continued, now addressing me: "Say you listen to some really weird English, Jamaican English. You don't *understand*, but it doesn't keep you from *feeling* the music." Dao's contrast of understanding (*tingdong*) with feeling (*ganjue*) as well as his slippage between the object of listening being music versus language both point to the affective power of language sounds one does not understand and offer an entry point for thinking through the ways that sung language may affectively communicate notions of place, even when the communication of semantic content is disrupted by uneven linguistic competency characteristic of polyglot cosmopolitan settings such as urban China.

When they are not understood (or are only partially understood), song lyrics lack semantic content and become nonreferential, and the boundaries between musical sounds and linguistic sounds are blurred. The resulting misalignments may be understood as productive mediations between music and language where sounds—vocal and instrumental—function and signify in multiple ways at once with their ambiguities deployed as purposeful aesthetic strategies. Such an approach pushes both with and against Steven Feld and his students, who adopt a semiotic approach to music and language as "phenomenally intertwined and socially dialogic" (Feld et al. 2005, 340) and who look to "music and language as variably constructed distinctions in a total semiotic field" (Faudree 2012, 520).

Both Szego's argument and Dao's reflection focus on the phenomenology of listening and lend credence to the aforementioned framework in which the sounds of music and the sounds of language are intertwined. It is the "temporal" and "timbral" elements of language *as part of song* that make the listener "feel" the music.

The specific ways that language and music are intertwined yet distinct may be drawn out through reference to linguist Roman Jakobson's communication model, which divides speech into six factors and six corresponding functions (fig. 4.2) and has been drawn on by many scholars of music and language (e.g., Middleton 1990, 242).[10] For Jakobson (1960, 352), language is a unified linguistic code that exists across a speech community as well as a "system of interconnected subcodes." Jakobson emphasizes that the speech functions are not mutually exclusive; although one function may have the largest influence on the structure of a speech event (e.g., the prominence of the poetic function in verbal performance), speech functions work together to supplement one another in different configurations. In everyday speech,

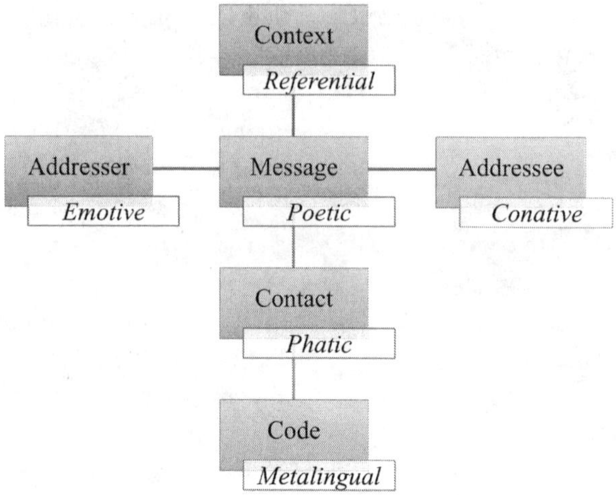

FIGURE 4.2. Jakobson's model of communication: six speech factors (large boxes) and six corresponding functions (italicized), superimposing two diagrams from Jakobson (1960, 353–57).

although messages dominated by the referential function are most common, even these often involve "accessory participation" (353) of the other functions.

At the bottom of this diagram, the "code" factor corresponds to the "metalingual" function of language and marks the particular linguistic code being used by an addresser and addressee competent in the code. In cases of musical performances in Chinese dialects where the audience has minimal comprehension of the lyrics, it is this code factor and corresponding metalingual function of language that is overwhelmingly dominant. The metalingual function stands in for both the poetic and referential functions, and the sound of the code itself indexically references notions of place. Furthermore, returning to Dao's contrast of understanding (*tingdong*) with feeling (*ganjue*), this is an affective mode of reference rather than a semantic one.

In Wanju Chuanzhang and Mabang's music, the referential content of the lyrics often describes local ways of life, but the expression of the local to audiences happens less through *what* is sung and more through *how* it is sung. In the case of performances by these two bands in front of audiences with limited comprehension of the message itself, it is primarily the sound of the code rather than the referential content that communicates a deterritorialized notion of the "local." Returning to the ethnographic sketch that began this chapter, the audience member from Xi'an commented that the sound of the dialect in which Mabang performs reminded him of home even though he could not quite tell what dialect was being sung or where it was from. The dialect was in fact different from the dialect spoken in his hometown. Thus, the use of dialects by these bands serves to express the local not as a particular place but as a nostalgic feeling of home connecting multiple locations and experiences in southern China through the cosmopolitan hub of Guangzhou. When I asked Ye Honggang about the man who approached him after the concert, he reiterated Dao Jianghua's point that the exact meaning of the lyrics wasn't important. The important thing, he said, is that "we sing about our home, and use the music to express that *feeling* of home."

When they are not understood (or are only partially understood), linguistic sounds lack semantic content and become nonreferential. In such cases, linguistic sounds—especially song lyrics—communicate through their metalingual function and may be composed and received in ways more similar to musical sounds. It is this process of composition and rehearsal of linguistic sounds as musical elements that I turn to in the next section.

Inscribing Local Sounds

In fall of 2014, Wanju Chuanzhang was cooling down from a busy summer consumed by work with their new record label. June had seen a south China tour, and the rest of the summer had been filled with nearly weekly performances on the major music festival circuit. Late fall would bring another round of major performances, and unlike the band's summer engagements, which had Wanju Chuanzhang flying to cities throughout China, most of the fall performances would be in the Pearl River Delta. When transportation costs weren't an issue, it was much easier to bring a larger band. With a few weeks of down time before another round of performances, it was the perfect time to try something new.

In addition to the original four core members of Wanju Chuanzhang, the band was already touring with a conga player and three horn players, including myself on saxophone. In preparation for fall shows, the band decided to employ three backup singers as well. All three were from Guangzhou and were native Cantonese speakers bilingual in Mandarin. All spoke English to some extent, and one had studied Italian, French, and German pronunciation for the opera work that frequently employed her. None, however, had any proficiency in Chaozhouhua, or especially in the Chaozhouhua subdialect spoken on Nan'ao Island that they would have to sing in. All, however, were professional singers, comfortable with reading sheet music and used to linguistic challenges singing in languages that they only partially understood.

Some months earlier, I had prepared the horn arrangements for two saxophones and trombone using the music notation software Sibelius. The lead singer Li Yihan asked me to prepare backup vocal arrangements for the three singers using the same software. With only weeks to go before the first performance with the new backup singers and with limited rehearsal time because of the difficulties of coordinating the schedules of eleven band members, Li Yihan believed sheet music would expedite the rehearsal process and serve as an authoritative guide to the correct singing of the backup vocal parts in case the chorus members ever had to change. Some songs would feature the three singers in unison, while others would feature newly written three-part harmonies. I would be in charge of the harmonies but would require significant assistance in preparing the lyrics for the sheet music.

In the liner notes to the band's 2012 recording, the lyrics were included in standard simplified Chinese, following the common practice of writing dialects in the standard Chinese characters that correspond to the spoken word. These liner notes included annotations to the lyrics with footnotes that offered definitions of terms in the lyrics that were written with standard Chinese but that did not mean the same thing in Mandarin. Reading these lyrics allowed any literate Chinese speaker to understand the meaning of the lyrics and to follow along as the Nan'ao dialect was sung. However, these lyrics written in standard Chinese offered no guidance to the nonspeaker of Chaozhouhua as to how to pronounce the words. Li Yihan believed that only including this version of the lyrics would be insufficient in offering the singers a guide to the proper pronunciation of the lyrics. Therefore, he provided two additional sets of lyrics.

The first he completed by himself. Called *xiangshengzi*, this set of lyrics followed the common practice of inscribing non-Mandarin dialects, minority languages, or even foreign languages with characters that, when read in Mandarin, more or less approximate the sound of the target speech. However, Nan'ao dialect includes many phonemes that do not exist in Mandarin; therefore, Li Yihan wanted to include another guide that would make learning and remembering the lyrics easy for the singers. The Nan'ao subdialect has no official standardized romanization system, and romanization systems for the closely related Chaozhouhua dialect are only used by experts and would be difficult to decode for the layperson.[11] The standard romanization system for Mandarin, Hanyu Pinyin, is understood by most educated Chinese speakers (especially those who have studied Mandarin in school as a second language, as all the chorus members had, being native Cantonese speakers). Therefore, Li Yihan decided to use Hanyu Pinyin as a departure point for an easy-to-read romanization system for the Nan'ao dialect. Though it wouldn't include all the important information and it would be devoid of tonal information, it would go a long way in preparing singers to sing in a pop ensemble singing style where tonal nuance wasn't crucial.

I sat with Li Yihan and Xiao Budian, a singer who had recorded backup vocals on the 2012 album and who was now an employee of their record label, to prepare the sheet music. We went through the lyrics word by word, and Li recited each word individually while Xiao Budian offered advice as to how best to capture the sound for a singer with no proficiency in the dialect. The results may be seen in figure 4.3, with the altered pinyin romanization system on top, the xiangshengzi in the middle, and the standard Chinese record of the lyrics on the bottom line.

The second line of lyrics in figure 4.3 demonstrates the varieties of inscription systems used to describe the lyrics. The bottom line inscribes the lyrics in standard Chinese and can be translated as "She isn't a swallow perched atop the powerlines, always back in time for spring." If read in Mandarin, this line would read "Yī bùshì diànxiàngǎn de yànzi zhǔnshí fǎn lái guò chūntiān." Apart from the third-person pronoun, 伊yī, the meaning of the sentence is completely clear when read and understood in Mandarin; however, the pronunciation as sung is entirely different.

The middle line of lyrics approximates the sound of the lyrics in the Nan'ao dialect with xiangshengzi; when read in standard Mandarin, this would read "Yī ènshì diànsànbù tiào yē yàn jiào zhǔnshí dēng lái guò chūntiān," and is largely nonsensical.

The top line alters the pinyin of the xiangshengzi in several strategic ways in order to offer a guide for pronunciation. "Yī èn shì diàn sàn bù tiào yē yàn jiào zhǔn shí dēng lái guò chūn tiān" is thus replaced with "Yi m xi dian san bu tiao e ng jiao zhun shi deng lai guo chuntian." The second syllable, the negative adverb "不" rendered in xiangshengzi as "èn," is rendered in the altered pinyin as "m," a sound that does not exist in Mandarin but that is similar to the Cantonese pronunciation of the negative adverb. The verb "to be" (是) is rendered also as "shì" in the xiangshengzi; in the altered pinyin, it is rendered as "xi," which more closely approximates the Nan'ao dialect reading of the word. The xiangshengzi "耶燕叫," which would be read as "yē yàn jiào" in Mandarin, is rendered as "e ng jiao" in the altered pinyin, as the sound "ng" as an initial does not exist in Mandarin.

After completing sheet music like this for six songs that Wanju Chuanzhang would perform with the newly added chorus, it came time to rehearse. As the other band members prepared the equipment and sound system for rehearsal, I sat with Li Yihan and the singers to go over the new sheet music. I first played the recordings of the songs on the bar's sound system, and everyone looked along on the sheet music. Then Li played the guitar and sang the lead vocals while coaching the singers on the pronunciation of the backup vocals. Each singer made notations on the original sheet music in

FIGURE 4.3. "Xiongtai, ni jinlai hao ma?" ("Brother, How Are You?") sheet music for unison chorus prepared in advance of a rehearsal with backup singers. Lyrics and music by Li Yihan, performed by Wanju Chuanzhang, copyright 2012 Li Yihan.

FIGURE 4.4. Backup singer's annotations on the sheet music for "Ni de heli shi yishou ge" ("Your Gift Is a Song"). Lyrics and music by Li Yihan, performed by Wanju Chuanzhang, copyright 2012 Li Yihan.

order to memorize the sounds of the lyrics. Figure 4.4 shows the sheet music for "Your Gift Is a Song," as marked up by one backup singer, Elizabeth.

After our rehearsal, I sat with Elizabeth and asked her to help me understand her various annotations. In the third line, above the characters 钟声, "the sound of the bell," which had been rendered in all three versions the same (zhong sheng), she had written 征 (a character with many meanings used in a variety of compound words) to be read in Cantonese as "zing," followed by 虾 (shrimp) to be read in Mandarin as "xiā". For the word 听, "to listen," the sheet music offered the xiangshengzi 田 (field), read in Mandarin as "tian," and offered the same in pinyin. Li Yihan had coached the singers to elongate the diphthong "ia" rather than the elided pronunciation of Mandarin; he had also emphasized that the final sound "n" should be accentuated only barely. Above the word, she had written "tia," as in the Spanish for aunt, a word she was familiar with through having sung many operas in romance languages. In the next line, 背影, "view from behind" is written in xiangshengzi as 贝影 and in pinyin as "beiying." This is another word that Li Yihan had spent some time coaching the singers on; he emphasized that the first syllable should be read with a nasal tone and a round vowel sound. The second word's vowel sound was halfway between the "i" written in ying and an "a" sound. Elizabeth had then written "boy" in English above the first word, and "yang" in pinyin above the second.

The diversity of techniques that Elizabeth and the other backup singers used in order to learn the lyrics points to the broader issue that I am using this example in order to illustrate. Rather than meaningful linguistic units, diverse languages are used as sonic palettes to approximate the sound of the local dialect. Singers with no proficiency in Nan'ao dialect learn the meaning of the lyrics by reading them in standard Chinese. While the sounds of the lyrics are very difficult for nonproficient singers to reproduce, the sounds of language are key musical elements in the song. Even though the lyrics are sung by those not proficient in the language they are singing, and even though an overwhelming majority of audiences cannot understand the lyrics that are sung, the precise sounds of the dialect spoken on Nan'ao Island are crucial in sonically expressing the place through music.

Sung language may affectively communicate senses of place even when the referential content is not understood semantically. By extension, music's affective power functions not only through sounds we historically consider musical but also through linguistic sounds. As these examples demonstrate, linguistic sounds, which for many listeners and even these backup singers, are nonreferential, may be composed, rehearsed, and received in ways more similar to musical sounds. Rather than separating "musical" and "linguistic" domains of sound, attention must be paid to creative misalignments between the two, which reveal music and language to be a "unified framework of sound" (Feld et al. 2005, 340).

Making the Local Comprehensible

Wanju Chuanzhang and Mabang make important acoustic-affective gestures in their choices of language, intentionally disrupting an assumed isomorphic referential relation between language, music, culture, and place. An important part of this process is techniques surrounding guided listening that are deployed to help audiences understand—or at least feel—the lyrical content of their songs. From simple, repetitive phrases to lyrics sheets handed out at shows, the bands employ various strategies to make their lyrics somewhat comprehensible to diverse cosmopolitan audiences. But offering linguistic guidance is about more than just directing an understanding of the meanings of words—it is about guiding audiences to follow along and aesthetically appreciate the sounds of an unfamiliar dialect in order to feel a connection to the places being sung about. The affective communication of place—and, by extension, the disruption of spatial hierarchies that mirror political ones—occurs through such directed listening to the sounds of local dialects.

Tuohy (2003) observes that local promoters of hua'er, a genre of folk song from Northwest China, have understood language comprehension as a major impediment to successful distribution on the national level and have encouraged linguistic choices that balance comprehension with local distinction. As a result, some singers who use local dialects standardize their pronunciation and delimit their use of specialized vocabulary in order to increase comprehensibility. Songs in standard Mandarin incorporate the selective use of dialect vocabulary and pronunciation in order to "flavor" their standard speech. Wanju Chuanzhang and Mabang make related linguistic choices in their music but accomplish a different goal. Many songs incorporate simple, repetitive language in a calculated linguistic tactic to make the dialect, and the local, comprehensible to a wider audience. One song by Mabang is a particularly good example.

Ye Honggang originally wrote "Yiqie hui guoqu" ("Everything Will Pass") in 2008 as a memoriam to the victims of the Wenchuan earthquake in Sichuan Province. The disaster, which killed seventy thousand people and injured hundreds of thousands more, inspired outpourings of support and sympathy throughout China. China Central Television (CCTV) held a telethon-like fundraising program that raised CNY 1.5 billion and featured many major stars. At a more local level, many benefit concerts and other events were held in Guangzhou to raise money for the Red Cross Society of China. This song was originally written for and performed at one such event at the Guangzhou venue Xiwo, the same venue discussed previously, but it became one of the band's favorite songs, often inserted in the middle of more energetic sets as a melancholy interlude.

The song begins with a *bawu*, a free-reed aerophone made of bamboo and played horizontally like a flute. The instrument's timbre is similar to the more common *hulusi*; a dark tone with a prominent high frequency buzzing, the sound lies somewhere between that of a clarinet and a harmonium. The instrument has a strong association with minority cultures of the southwest, though it is prevalent throughout China. The bawu plays a slow melancholic solo melody in a D minor pentatonic scale. After about ten seconds, a Buddhist prayer bowl is struck, the pitch an A, matching the fifth above the tonic of the bawu melody.

The tone sustains at a constant volume, achieved through a circular motion of the striker on the outside of the bowl. After several more phrases on the bawu, the melody ends on the tonic, and the prayer bowl is struck one more time.

The guitar then enters with a simple strumming pattern, playing a repeating cycle of two bars in B-flat major followed by two bars in F major, the simple I–V chord progression continuing throughout the song, with bass line outlining the tonic and fifth of each chord on the one and three of each bar. After one cycle, the bawu enters once again, playing a melody that hovers around F, thus accentuating the switch to the major key. The prayer bowl is struck every two bars and now functions as a pedal on the major seventh degree of the B-flat major and the major third of the F major.

Ye Honggang then begins to sing a short four-line phrase, a simple sentiment rendered in simple vocabulary that, when sung in Guiliuhua, is immediately comprehensible to any Mandarin speaker but that sounds like a heavily accented standard Mandarin.

Lyrics in Chinese:
一切欢乐会过去，
一切痛苦也会过去。
一切灾难会过去，
一切的一切也会过去。

English meaning:
Every happiness will pass,
Every suffering will pass,
Every disaster will pass,
Every everything will pass.

Lyrics in pinyin, as would be read in standard Mandarin:
Yīqiè huānlè huì guòqu,
Yīqiè tòngkǔ yě huì guòqu,
Yīqiè zāinàn huì guòqu,
Yīqiè de yīqiè yě huì guòqu.

Lyrics in altered pinyin, as sung in Guiliuhua:
Yiqie huanluo hui guoke,
Yiqie tongku ye hui guoke,
Yiqie zainan hui guoke,
Yiqie de yiqie ye hui guoke.

"Yiqie hui guoqu" ("Everything Will Pass"),
lyrics and music by Ye Honggang, performed by Mabang,
copyright 2015 Guangdong Xingwaixing Wenhua Chuanbo Youxian Gongsi

These four lines of text are repeated throughout the six-minute song. Ye uses Guiliuhua pronunciation, for example rendering "guòqu" as "guoke" and "huānlè" as "huanluo." Each iteration of the verse is followed by a chorus of rhythmic octave unison vocables and then the bawu melody. A second verse repeats one additional line four times in a row: "Yīqiè ài yǒngchuíbùxiǔ" (Every love will never be forgotten). Like the first verse, this verse is simple, repetitive, and comprehensible to Mandarin speakers.

This entire cycle repeats a total of three times, making for a fairly long song. After the third time, the other instruments drop out, and we are left with only the guitar, still strumming the I–V progression that has formed an unshakable foundation for the entire song. Ye Honggang then speaks the lyrics one more time, this time in standard Mandarin, well enunciated and with the tonal structures of the speech almost exaggerated in the style of a public announcement. No translation is needed at this point, but Ye offers one nonetheless, as if to clarify any question about the content of the lyrics.

In this song, both the use of simple language in the dialect, recognizable to any Mandarin speaker, and the recapitulation of the lyrics in standard Mandarin at the end of the song are significant in the ways they articulate together a particular relationship between the linguistic sounds of the local and the linguistic sounds of the national. In the years since the Sichuan earthquake, questions of ownership and self-representation in public mourning of this tragedy have been fraught with political overtones, often relating to a tension between the local and the national. For the tenth anniversary of the earthquake in 2018, many local commemorative events in Sichuan were stifled by government officials, who sought to maintain control of the narrative surrounding this tragedy (Buckley 2018). In a melancholic but hopeful song that sympathizes with this widespread tragedy, Ye enacts an alternative subnational space where the local (in this case, the southwest) is performed as cosmopolitan and as a voice that can and should be understood alongside nationally sanctioned performative mourning conducted in standard Mandarin and broadcast on state-run television. This example from Mabang's music serves to illustrate how simple lyrics in unfamiliar dialects become familiar to listeners through repetition and how the sounds of the lyrics become entwined in the melodic and rhythmic elements of the music to serve as part of a sonic whole.

However, songs by both of these bands often incorporate complex and poetic language in local dialects. Wanju Chuanzhang, whose lyrics are in a dialect as different from Mandarin as English is from German, has employed a different tactic, which I turn to in the next section.

Guiding Tactics of Listening

In summer of 2012, before Wanju Chuanzhang signed with a major record label, I traveled with the band on a short tour with stops in Xiamen, Shantou, and Quanzhou. Unlike later tours once Wanju Chuanzhang signed to Xingwaixing Records, which were promoted with flashy and professional posters and marketing material, the 2012 tour was promoted with a self-conscious DIY aesthetic; the poster for the tour showed a cartoonlike drawing of our "tour bus," Dao Jianghua's beat up Volkswagen Santana sedan (the same as many older taxis in China) with everyone piled inside the car and a trunk that cannot close.

The same artist who prepared the poster for the tour also prepared an illustrated lyrics booklet. Photocopied on both sides of standard A4 paper, the paper was cut into three columns, and then folded like an accordion to form a booklet. We folded these in the hotel each night, and every attendee of the shows was given a booklet upon buying a ticket at the door. Xiamen, Quanzhou, and Shantou, the three stops on the tour, are all traditionally southern Min-speaking cities. Hokkien is spoken in Quanzhou and Xiamen; Chaozhouhua in Shantou.

More than anywhere else in China, audiences in these cities were primed to understand many of the lyrics in the Nan'ao dialect, but subtle differences in dialects, as well as the usual difficulties understanding lyrics in a live performance, made intelligibility somewhat limited. The aim of the lyrics booklet was to supplement intelligibility. In addition to writing the lyrics in standard Chinese, footnotes on the lyrics translated particular local vocabularies. During our performances in these three cities, I was surprised to see that many in the audience held the booklet in their hands during the performance, occasionally cross-checking the lyrics as they were sung.

In this case, the sonic stream was not enough to convey referential content; it was supplemented by a text that was meant to accompany and guide the experience of listening. Audience members could choose whether or not to make the additional effort necessary to understand the lyrics. In performances, however, lead singer Li Yihan repeatedly referred to Nan'ao Island and explicitly mentioned their efforts to preserve both the culture and the dialect of Nan'ao, furthermore relating this to a broader effort to capture Chaoshan in sound—a desire that was felt sympathetically by many of those in the audience.

While the strategies of comprehension I have discussed in the previous two examples differ in both their basic functioning and in their intended effect, what they share in common is an explicit desire by the artists to be understood on their own terms though local languages. By avoiding standard Mandarin, the Chinese nation is decentered as master signifier, and alternative translocal communities are realized through sound. In a sense, effort must be made by listeners to meet these musicians halfway; even if 100 percent intelligibility is impossible, the code of the message (and the metalingual function of the lyrics) is centrally important to not only the referential content of the lyrics but also to a broader affective sense of place communicated through sound. One final example further illustrates how circulations of musics in local dialects articulate alternative spatial and social imaginaries through this affective sense of place communicated through the sounds of language.

In preparation for tour stops in Xiamen and Quanzhou on a band tour in 2014 sponsored by record label Xingwaixing Records, Wanju Chuanzhang rehearsed a special surprise encore song. "Ai pin cai hui ying" ("You Have to Love to Fight If You Want to Win," or "No Pain, No Gain") is a popular film song in a 1989 Taiwanese film by the same name by director Chu Yen-Ping. In each stop on the tour, we performed a reggae cover of this song, with the drummer responding to calls for an encore with the standard slow and deliberate rhythm that begins the song on the floor tom. As soon as the first few drum hits were played, everyone in the audience cheered; the song is recognizable enough that a drum set imitating a slow timpani immediately evokes the song. Inevitably, the audience would sing along, intimately familiar with the nuanced lyrics. Sung in Hokkien (another southern Min dialect), the song is beloved by many and is a prominent example of the reach of transnational Min media industry centered in Taiwan.

Throughout the Chaoshan region of Guangdong Province and much of Fujian Province, the sounds of Taiwanese pop music sung in Hokkien (especially from the 1980s) are ubiquitous. Thus, it is important also to understand the music of Wanju Chuanzhang within larger circulations of music and media in other Min dialects and to attend to the ways these musical circulations enact translocal connections between Min-speaking regions of mainland China, Taiwan, and Chinese diasporic communities.

Yang's discussion of the effects of transnational media on shifting Chinese subjectivities offers insight into these circulations. Focusing on film, television, and popular music in the Shanghai Wu dialect and in Cantonese, Yang (2002) explores how spontaneous networks of circulation "decentralize information sources" (294) and lead to a deterritorialized transnational Chinese subjectivity. By discussing "the reemergence of a transnational Chinese global media public and its effects on the modernist project of the nation-state" (287), Yang argues that "transnational media have enabled the detaching of Chinese subjectivity from the state and its mobilization across imaginary space to link up with alternative Chinese subjectivities far away" (311). It is in a related way that Wanju Chuanzhang attempts to both access and consolidate a deterritorialized Min-speaking media public through their music.

While based in Guangzhou, Wanju Chuanzhang has reached a fan base largely through social media, including Weibo and Weixin. Many, though not a majority, of these fans are speakers of Min dialects. In this way, the circulation of Wanju Chuanzhang's music through social media, music-sharing websites, and actual tours through the region enacts a translocal imagined community of southern Min speakers that connects Guangzhou, pockets of Guangdong and Fujian, Taiwan, Hong Kong, Southeast Asia, and overseas Chinese communities throughout the world.

"We sing in dialects even as we wander far from home"

> While the hulusi sounds, we sing together.
> The songs of our hometowns are the best provisions.
> We sing in dialects even as we wander far from home,
> Seeking treasures amidst old stories.
>
> "Mabang wuqu" ("Mabang Dance"), lyrics and music by Ye Honggang, performed by Mabang, copyright 2015 Guangdong Xingwaixing Wenhua Chuanbo Youxian Gongsi

The lyrics of this song by Mabang highlight and tie together many of the issues that this chapter has explored. Mabang and Wanju Chuanzhang are only two of many bands in China's increasingly diverse independent music scene that choose to perform music in local dialects instead of in standard Mandarin. Against a historical backdrop wherein music played an outsized role in linguistic standardization and nation building in China (Jones 2001; Hung 1996; Liu 2013), the significance of new musical cosmopolitanisms based on complex language interactions is not only a linguistic issue—it is rife with musical, aesthetic, social, and political significance.

As the process of notating and rehearsing Wanju Chuanzhang's music with backup singers not proficient in the Nan'ao dialect demonstrated, the sounds of dialects are deployed by these bands as sonic elements in a broader music-language mix wherein phonemes rather than morphemes function as sonic signifiers of the local in realms other than the directly referential. Against a historical backdrop of linguistic standardization wherein music played a large role—and dialects were contrasted with standard Mandarin as backwards, but nonetheless important, bearers of local culture—singing in local dialects is a way of "seeking treasures in old stories" and preserving the sounds of local Chinese cultures against a perceived cultural homogenization tied to China's economic development. Various strategies of comprehension, from the repetition of simple language in dialects to the distribution of lyrics written in standard Chinese at performances, bring attention to how these musicians view understanding the local and understanding local dialects as connected. At the same time, the increasing prominence of musical productions in dialects such as Guiliuhua, which have far less transnational reach than Cantonese or Hokkien, points to a plurality of local identifications in contemporary China. This plurality highlights the importance of spatial imaginaries and social configurations that decenter the nation as master signifier in China and demonstrates ways in which communities other than the national—transnational as well as translocal—are imagined through the sounds of music and the sounds of language.

New modes of translocal belonging result in a disruption of isomorphic ways of linking dialect and place and inspire creative reflection on the movements of people and spatial reconfigurations at the heart of China's broader transformations. In the polyglot settings that arise from such a situation, the sounds of language become a medium for contemplation and expression of these changes, and dialects are deployed in creative new ways for linguistically diverse audiences by these musicians who "sing in dialects even as [they] wander far from home."

5

Musical Lives: Mabang

Mother, mother, tell me where to go.
I see a kind of true independence,
Unceasingly gazing forward,
and passing through the void.
Mother, mother, tell me where to go.
Mother, mother, kneading our only flour into soft songs.
In two thousand years, when the last rain is falling,
The first will arrive at daybreak.

"Tuwei" ("Breaking Out"), lyrics and music by Ye Honggang, performed by Mabang, copyright 2015 Guangdong Xingwaixing Wenhua Chuanbo Youxian Gongsi

Raising a crumpling plastic cup filled with Coke, Xiao Dao proclaimed "Yinyue shenghuo!"—"Music life!" We all echoed the sentiment from the rickety wooden stools where we sat around a tarp-covered table at a roadside restaurant in rural Yunnan Province, our Toyota minibus parked on the pavement next to us. We had driven for much of the day and still had a few hours ahead of us over bumpy mountainous roads before reaching our destination, where we would perform the following day. "Music life"—I first heard this pithy phrase uttered at this table in 2007 by Xiao Dao before it became his mantra and a popular toast among his circle and the musicians at the center of this book. The words can mean a number of things—they can celebrate an exceptional performance or lament an unexpectedly long journey; entreat someone to join a new project or laugh off an empty wallet. They proclaim an ideal—a life lived through music and for music—that the following two chapters explore.

Examining musical lives in contemporary China means unraveling intersections of personal histories, national histories, cosmopolitan formations, and musical creativity. These intersections offer insight into the role of individual agency and expressive culture in broader cultural shifts and into the lived and subjective dimensions of cosmopolitanisms and mobilities that are self-reflexively grappled with in part through listening to and producing music. Anchored around detailed biographies of seven musicians, these chapters are about *yinyue shenghuo* and explore musical lives on the move.

Practice theory and the anthropology of subjectivity (Ortner 2006), as well as ethnomusicological work in the past decade that has reinvigorated and reimagined the role of biographical writing in the discipline (Rees 2009; Feld 2012; Guilbault 2014), provoke closer attention to the musical dimensions of subjectivity and the subjective dimensions of musicality. Building on calls for "subject-centered musical ethnography" (Rice 2003; Ruskin and Rice 2012), *yinyue shenghuo* may be examined not just as musical *lives*, but as musical *subjectivities*. Reworking Ortner's most concise definition of subjectivity, musical subjectivities encompass the "ensemble of modes of perception, affect, thought, desire, fear, and so forth that animate acting [musical] subjects" as well as the "cultural and social [as well as musical] formations that shape, organize, and provoke those modes of affect [and forms of creativity]" (Ortner 2005, 31). Musical subjectivity must, then, be examined "in its relations to (changing) forms of power, and especially . . . the subtle forms of power that saturate everyday life, through experiences of time, space, and work" (46). By proposing such an approach to musical subjectivity, I mean to highlight the ways that China's broader cultural, political, and economic transformations have affectively shaped the musical outlooks of my interlocutors and to focus on the perceptions, desires, and struggles that brought these individuals from diverse backgrounds to careers in music in Guangzhou. Understanding music as a "technology of the self" (DeNora 2000), I mean to take seriously the ways that listening to music—from *tongsu gequ* (state-sanctioned popular music in the 1980s) to the Hong Kong rock band Beyond—shapes musical lives and ways of being in the world.

As Helen Rees (2009, 9) summarizes in the introduction to an influential collection of biographies of Chinese folk, traditional, and popular musicians, "'writing lives' in Chinese music has never been more timely." In addition to these broader disciplinary developments, examining musical lives in China today is important because of the dynamic cultural shifts they reflect and refract. These shifts revolve around a transforming notion of the individual as a creative and desiring self. Music offers unique insights into these transformations. Xiao Dao's toast to *yinyue shenghuo* is an expression of desire for a particular way of living—and making a living—through art in a privatizing China where creativity is commodified in new ways. Desire takes many forms, and as Rofel (2007) demonstrates, expressions of desire in postsocialist China are intertwined with neoliberal subject formation. Economic privatization and the broader political and economic transformations since Reform and Opening Up have instigated a fundamental transformation of Chinese subjectivities;

FIGURE 5.1. Members of Mabang in a publicity photo used in the liner notes of their eponymous 2015 release on Xingwaixing Records. From left: A Fei, Xiao Dao, A Gang, Fan Feng. Photograph by Yan Ming.

as Zhang and Ong (2008, 16) observe, "techniques associated with neoliberal governmentality unleash powers of the self." Under a political rationality where elements of neoliberalism mingle with socialist rhetoric, rather than a liberal public sphere, the "social" in China is still a space severely intertwined with state policies, and powers of the self are contained by and framed within the power of the state. Ethnographic focus on musical subjectivities offers an important window into these particularities of China's political rationality, its connections to global capitalism, and the lived experience of China's political and economic transformations in recent decades. Exploring the sonic and aural dimensions of China's transformations, I mean to contribute to these broader discussions about subjectivities in China and to listen critically to some of the ways in which powers of the self are claimed through music.

The current chapter introduces the members of the band Mabang (fig. 5.1);

chapter 6 introduces the members of Wanju Chuanzhang.[1] While I discuss several themes that emerge through the juxtaposition of these seven *yinyue shenghuo* at greater length at the end of chapter 6, one particularly important theme central to the broader themes and theoretical goals of this book is that of mobility—in different ways, each of these musicians has led a remarkably mobile life. These mobilities often intersect with major policy initiatives of the state, which have variously entailed or curtailed citizens' mobilities. Actual mobilities are in turn intertwined with vicarious mobilities; in each biography, a particular geographic, educational, and class background shapes opportunities for coming into contact with various musics, ways of thinking about music in relation to the world, and approaches to making music. Taken together, the biographies explore the process of becoming a musical cosmopolitan in contemporary China as one that is structured by political, economic, and cultural factors but that is nonetheless profoundly personal and unique to thinking, feeling, reflecting, and listening individuals.

Xiao Dao

Drummer of both Wanju Chuanzhang and Mabang, co-owner of Xiwo and Tutu, manager of Liuzhen Yinyue

This book in many ways has grown out of a long friendship with one man: Dao Jianghua.[2] He goes by many names—some people still call him Ainuo, his given name in the Dai minority language, a name he went by in the 1990s. Now, people most often call him Dao Zong, a respectful address that merges his Chinese surname with a word for boss: "Boss Dao." I still always call him Xiao Dao, the nickname he went by when I first met him in 2006. It's a nickname that follows a common formula of preceding one's surname with "little," but that, with his unusual sinicized Dai surname (Dao, literally, "knife"), sounds even more like it fits him: "Little Knife." With a piercing presence and power that make him stand out in a room, Xiao Dao has lived an *yinyue shenghuo* that makes him one of the most respected figures in music circles in southern China.

Xiao Dao was born in 1970 in Mengla County, a rural county in southernmost Yunnan Province that shares its southern and eastern borders with Laos and its western border with Myanmar. His family lived near Mengla Township, which is about eighty miles from Jinghong, the seat of Xishuangbanna Dai Autonomous Prefecture. Like many of Mengla's residents, Xiao Dao is Dai, one of China's fifty-five recognized ethnic minorities. Though *Dai* as an umbrella category is arguably a Chinese creation of the ethnic classification project of the 1950s, the term refers to speakers of various Tai-Kadai languages who practice Therevada Buddhism, who are spread throughout southern Yunnan, and who have strong cultural ties to groups in Thailand and Laos.

I traveled with Xiao Dao to Mengla three times from 2006 through 2009 and stayed for about a week each trip with his younger brother Ham. The first year we went, Ham was working, like many local residents, in the rubber industry, tapping the rubber trees spread throughout the surrounding tropical forest to collect their sap. That year we stayed in Ham's house, which was a traditional Dai structure raised a full story above the ground that he shared with his wife and son. The next year, Ham had moved into a larger house with multiple rooms and modern amenities built in a similar traditional style on an adjacent lot—Xiao Dao had built this house on his family's land and left Ham to run it as a guesthouse. The third year, Ham had moved to Guangzhou and was working at a bar that Xiao Dao had recently opened, so he traveled both ways with us. On each visit we met what seemed like an unending roster of Xiao Dao and Ham's extended family members. Each of his parents had upwards of ten siblings, and Xiao Dao has scores of cousins he calls "brother" and "sister."

In Xiao Dao's earliest years, China was in the throes of the Great Proletarian Cultural Revolution (Wuchanjieji Wenhua Dageming, 1966–1976). During that time, many young urban intellectuals and others perceived as bourgeois and/or capitalist were "sent down" (*xiafang*) to work in rural areas as a part of a program known as the Up to the Mountains and Down to the Countryside Movement (Shangshan Xiaxiang Yundong). Southern Yunnan was a destination for such urban transplants, as memorialized in Zhang Nuanxing's 1986 film *Qingchun Ji* (Sacrificed Youth). Inspiring the plot of Zhang's film, some of these "intellectual youths" (*zhishi qingnian*) made lives for themselves in ethnically Dai areas of Yunnan's countryside. One of Xiao Dao's uncles had been studying music in Shanghai before relocating to Xishuangbanna and marrying into the Dao family. This uncle took Xiao Dao under his wing: "He taught me how to read notation, and other things about music. From a young age, I loved music and dance, and he really influenced me," recalls Xiao Dao.[3]

Dao's musicality was nurtured by this uncle and his parents. In 1982, at the age of twelve, Dao was admitted into the Xishuangbanna Ethnic Song and Dance Troupe (Xishuangbanna Minzu Gewutuan) for training. A state-sponsored institution presenting highly choreographed performances of local minority folk musics and patriotic songs, this was considered an excellent career path for an aspiring performing artist. Xiao Dao moved to the prefectural capital Jinghong to attend the troupe's boarding school and began to focus on percussion: "The teachers recognized that I had a good feel for rhythm [*jiezou gan hen hao*]. They could play a very long rhythm"—he imitates an intricate drumming pattern—"I'd listen once, and I could repeat it. So, they said, 'Eh? His rhythmic feel is especially sensitive. This kind of person should study percussion.' So, they enrolled me in the percussion program." During his early teenage years he studied a wide variety of music but focused on western percussion with a specialization in the timpani. After a year in Jinghong, his teachers sponsored his application to study percussion in the more selective Kunming Song and Dance Troupe (Kunming Gewutuan), which brought him to the provincial capital several hundred miles away. He studied a broad curriculum of music theory and western classical music there, but when I ask him about the most memorable parts of his training in these years, he launches into a medley of the first lines of political songs of various minorities that have become part of the national canon. "If you want to hear more minority songs, I can keep going for days," he jokes.

While in Kunming as a teenager in the early 1980s, Xiao Dao was exposed to western pop music for the first time, an experience that would change his musical life. Popular music from Hong Kong and Taiwan, referred to in Chinese collectively as *gangtai* music,[4] was beginning to be heard in mainland China's major coastal cities more and more. However, it had far less reach into provincial capitals and rural areas: "You couldn't hear *gangtai* music," says Dao. "In 1985, you might hear a tiny bit. For popular music, it was really just *tongsu gequ*," the dominant state-produced popular music, often with political themes.[5] Academic and popular narratives of the spread of western popular music to China usually elevate the role of *dakou die* (cutout media),[6] but they, too, were not yet a significant phenomenon: "No way, no way [were we listening to dakou die]. This was the early 1980s, a very early time. There's no way there could be these kinds of things. No one would dare to import or smuggle [*zousi*] dakou die. Some of the senior students from Shanghai had brought cassette tapes from relatives abroad. It was not easy." Through listening to cassette tapes shared with him by older students who had cosmopolitan connections in China's major coastal cities, Dao developed a taste for a music that was wholly unfamiliar to him before moving to Kunming: European and North American contemporary pop.

Dao describes hearing this music for the first time as a feeling of suddenly having his eyes opened (*maosedunkai*): "The music sounded marvelous and intriguing [*qimiao*]. There was this kind of music? It sounded like a completely different way of making music. I had listened to classical music, or to *tongsu gequ*. They weren't as powerful. At that time, Madonna and

George Michael were really the best music in the world. Its influence on me was huge. I listened, and I just wanted to listen to more." At roughly the same time, the beginnings of rock and roll in China were brewing; while this was most significant in Beijing, it to some extent also reached and influenced interested musicians throughout China. In 1986 Dao heard Cui Jian's first televised performance of "Yi wu suo you,"[7] and came to be aware that there were other musicians in China who were interested in and working with pop and rock music from outside of China. These experiences all contributed to Dao's thirst for learning more ways of making and thinking about music from beyond Yunnan.

These desires led Xiao Dao to abandon his studies and a reliable career in an Ethnic Song and Dance Troupe in 1988 at the age of eighteen. "I wanted to know the world outside [*waimian de shijie*]. To understand more music, to get to know the most modern culture [*zui xiandai de wenhua*], civilization, the 'fine life' [*meihao de shenghuo*]. In Kunming, I couldn't find these things. I guess it's like the way people in North Korea look to South Korea now." At the time, China was undergoing the first years of rapid economic transformations as part of Deng Xiaoping's Reform and Opening Up. The state established five original Special Economic Zones (SEZs), all in southern China. The largest among them was Hainan Island, a thirteen-thousand-square-mile island off of the southern coast of China that had been administratively part of Guangdong Province until its elevation to province and SEZ in 1988. Dao moved to Hainan that same year.

When I ask him why he selected Hainan over other SEZs such as Shenzhen or Shantou, he replies, "At that time, Hainan was much more open [*kaifang*] than the other SEZs. The central government made all sorts of special policies just for Hainan that made it convenient. So, everyone thought that Hainan was full of hope. It was more capitalist, more free. The economic policies were more free. So, it was flooded with people, especially young college graduates." Dao recalls the painful four days he spent on the road to get to Hainan but also the relative ease of moving there versus other places. "There were no problems related to the *hukou*.[8] No one had a *hukou*. Everyone was the same. No one had an ID [*shenfenzheng*]. No one asked to see any sort of ID either."

When he first arrived in Hainan in 1988, Dao was among many musicians who busked in the streets. With several other musicians, Dao formed a collective called Sahala Yedi Gezu (Sahara Wilderness Music Group). "It wasn't a band, we just played together," he stresses. In addition to percussion, Dao played guitar and sang. "We'd play *gangtai* pop, and foreign music. There were no bars or hotels to play in. Maybe a restaurant occasionally. But mostly we just played in the street, and earned enough to live on that way." This was comparatively lucrative; he was able to make more money in Hainan than many of his family members were making back in Mengla.

Dao spent three years busking in Hainan and met many other musicians, including several with whom he'd later collaborate. He also met a singer who became his girlfriend and who would be the impetus for moving away from Hainan. In 1991 Xiao Dao first moved to Guangzhou with her because she got a job in a new music venue in the city.[9] Xiao Dao reflects on the venue and Guangzhou's music scene in the early 1990s: "It was just a very large place for performances. Very similar to today's live houses.[10] But it was all pop music. Guangzhou at that time was the place in China where popular music was developing the most. It influenced all of China." Xiao Dao goes on to describe the '94 Xinshengdai ('94 New Generation), a term used to refer to a cohort of pop stars who emerged to national fame in 1994, many of whom worked with Guangzhou-based record labels and grew out of this scene of which Xiao Dao was a part.

In the mid-1990s Xiao Dao moved on from Guangzhou to Shenzhen and played drums for a series of bands. In 1999 Xiao Dao joined a band that would come to be one of the most well-known rock bands out of southern China. Headed by Wang Lei (whom he had met in Hainan as part of the busking collective), the band was called Beng (a Chinese loanword from English meaning, and sounding like, "pump") and included Xiao Dao's future wife, Xu Ying, on keyboards as well as Wang Dong, who still works in Xiao Dao's bars as a sound engineer. Pump played electronic rock that was synth-heavy but drew on diverse genres of electronic music. Shortly after releasing a well-received album in 2002, Pump began to develop an affinity for dub reggae and started working with a Swiss man living in Guangzhou who went by the Chinese name Ma Ti. Xiao Dao recalls their expanding love for reggae: "The first band we loved was Hightone," the French dub band from Lyons. "It sounded like real fusion [*ronghe*] music. We really, really, really liked it. Because inside, it had Eastern [*dongfang*] elements. There were western elements. We had finally found a way to use the language of music to express the best parts of China, and a way of fusing it all together. We had found a road."

Beginning in 2003 the band began to draw heavily on reggae. Through Ma Ti, they invited Rico Rodriguez, one of the best-known trombonists in reggae, to come to China for a handful of performances and, most importantly, to spend time teaching them about reggae. They rented an apartment together and rehearsed all day for a whole month. Rodriguez taught them his own songs and played with them as he coached each member on developing a reggae feel. In the coming years, Wang Lei and Pump played several well-received concerts, including several alongside Hightone on a China tour. Wang Lei traveled to France to collaborate and record an album with Hightone, *Wangtone*, released in 2005. At around the same time, Wang Lei was struggling with mental health issues and began to exhibit irrational and violent behavior that would eventually alienate him from many of his friends and collaborators. Pump disbanded in 2005.

Throughout this time, Xiao Dao was also involved in several business ventures. Beginning in 2003 he was part of an arts collective and creative space in Guangzhou's Haizhu District. Originally called Park19 (named for its location on the nineteenth floor of an apartment building), the collective put on a series of music and arts events in their large loft. The next year, many of the visual artists involved in Park19 established forty studios on three floors of an older apartment building near the Guangzhou Academy of Fine Arts (Guangzhou Meishu Xueyuan). In the center of the middle floor was a large communal space curated and run as a café and bar by Xiao Dao and his wife Xu Ying, who lived in a small loft on the same floor. While the café originally served as a meeting place for the artists who worked and sometimes lived on these three floors, it often put on special events and came to be a popular hangout for students at the Academy of Fine Arts and at nearby Zhongshan University as well as for young professionals working in creative industries. Many identified as *wenyi qingnian*, "art and culture youth."[11] It is here that I first met Xiao Dao.

In 2006 I moved back to Guangzhou after leaving the company that had first brought me there when I graduated from college. I was working a nightly jazz gig at an expensive western restaurant in the downtown district of Tianhe playing three forty-five-minute sets during the dinner hour six nights a week. We finished at ten o'clock, and most nights, I would head to Loft345 afterwards for a drink, a snack, and often informal free music making. Xiao Dao played drums in these jam sessions, and the style often drew on long-form reggae and dub vamps with simple chord progressions over which a variety of singing, instruments, and electronic effects were layered. Several musicians became regular fixtures of these jam sessions, and Xiao Dao proposed starting a band; these members and I coalesced in late 2006 as San Duojiao (Three Step), named after a traditional social dance of several minorities in southern Yunnan. Many songs were derived from Yunnan folk songs that Dao and the guitarist, Zhou Tianhai, brought to the band. Xiao Dao considered this band both a continuation of his work with Wang Lei, which had disintegrated, and a new exploration of his own musical heritage. He had long desired to form a band that drew on the Yunnan minority musics that he had been exposed to as a child and that he had been trained in professionally throughout his teenage years.

At the same time, Loft345 was exploding in popularity and was so full of people most nights that it began to attract the attention of the police. Since it was operating without the correct official license, problems began to arise, leading Xiao Dao and Xu Ying to seek a new location. In December of 2006 they moved into what had been a café in a building that was largely an entertainment complex housing several restaurants, a karaoke club, a massage parlor, and mahjong rooms. Xiao Dao and Xu Ying took on a business partner who, in addition to infusing capital into the business, promised to alleviate any potential police problems through his own connections as a former fire marshal. While Loft345 stayed open, it ceased hosting live music events and attempted to convert its clientele into customers of the new bar.

The bar was called Xiwo, which can be translated as "nest of happiness."[12] The bar was decorated with a pan-African color scheme with red, green, and yellow fabric behind the stage and posters of Cui Jian, Bob Marley, Wang Lei, and Rico Rodriguez on the walls. The menu was handwritten and illustrated by Xiao Dao's wife, Xu Ying. Electronic dartboards filled the back of the bar. Outside was a large courtyard with lush tropical plants and an artificial waterfall that hid the outdoor bathrooms beneath it. Our band, San Duojiao, played nightly in hours-long sets that provided a background to activities that spilled outside into the courtyard.

Xiwo became a hugely popular nightlife spot within several months. Even though large bottles of beer were priced at a modest 15 RMB (US$2), the bar regularly took in upwards of 20,000 RMB (US$3000) in a single night, even on weeknights. At the same time, San Duojiao began to regularly play outside of Guangzhou and to meet minor critical acclaim within independent music circles. Hoping to build on these successes, the band went in together on investing in a second location in Shenzhen that spring. Taking over Genjudi (Base Bar), a popular Shenzhen music venue with a long history, Xiao Dao, myself, and the other band members split our time between the two cities.

Over the next three years, Xiao Dao devoted his time to the intertwined tasks of developing the bar business and developing our band. We traveled to Yunnan for several weeks each year, spending time in the hometowns of both Xiao Dao and guitarist Xiao Hai (Zhou Tianhai), and traveling extensively through rural villages with the help of Xiao Hai's father, who was a cultural official for the county. Through these trips we developed a roster of original songs and covers of local folk songs that we performed at Xiwo and Genjudi.

In 2009 we ceased playing regularly for a number of reasons—two band members had children, limiting time and availability, and the bassist entered a graduate program in pharmacology. In addition I moved to Beijing with the intention of spending a year there while applying to PhD programs back in the US.

Nonetheless, Xiwo continued to grow as a preeminent center for independent music in southern China, becoming an essential stop on tours for both Chinese and international acts. Xiao Dao's involvement in the business brought him financial success and cemented his position as an important figure and gatekeeper in Guangzhou's music scenes. He opened two more music venues, Tutu Kongjian (T:Union) and Yuefu (Imperial Music Bureau) in the years that followed. With San Duojiao abandoned, he started to work with and develop the two bands that are at the center of this book. By the time Xiwo finally closed its doors for good in 2014, Xiao Dao was playing drums in both Wanju Chuanzhang and Mabang, was part owner and creative director of two other music venues, and was beginning to work as principal of Xingwaixing's sublabel Liuzhen Yinyue.

A Gang

Lead singer, composer/songwriter, and guitarist of Mabang

Ye Honggang was born in 1979 in a steel-mining area outside of Liuzhou in Guangxi Province. His given name, Honggang, consists of Hong, a generational name (*zibei*) shared by his brother and cousins and determined in a family roster generations ago, and his given name, Gang, "steel," which reflects his birthplace and the metal that brought his family its livelihood. His parents are both from Guilin, another medium-sized city in Guangxi Province that is a major tourist destination because of the karst peaks and minority villages that surround the city. They moved to the mining area for work before A Gang was born. There, while his father worked as a lathe operator in the foundry, his mother ran the household, and supplemented her husband's income by growing corn, sweet potatoes, and pumpkins on a small plot near their home. "Where I was born was about as far from Liuzhou as Dongguang is from Guangzhou"—he describes the distance to me in terms of Pearl River Delta cities—"but the only way into Liuzhou was by *lupi huoche*." *Lupi huoche*, literally "green skin trains," are the iconic green railcars that dominated China's railway system before the 1990s, giving way to the *gaotie* high-speed railway system that links more and more of China's cities. The railway, which A Gang describes as impossibly slow, was specially constructed by the state-owned enterprise and purposely designed to link the mining area to the city a few hours away, transporting both steel products and the workers that produced them.

The mining area itself was located in a remote part of the hills in what was once a largely minority area populated by Zhuang, Yao, and Bai villages. On outings arranged by his elementary school and later independently with friends, A Gang would often venture outside of the confines of the mining area into the hills that surrounded for hikes and picnics. He recalls being fascinated by the horse-drawn carts that traveled the dirt roads zigzagging the mountains and being drawn to the sounds of singing by the people who walked the roads to and from market. In his recollections, he often uses a word, *yuanshi shengtai*, or *yuanshengtai*, that directly translates as "original ecology." A semantically slippery neologism widely used in Chinese popular and academic discourses over the past decade to refer to local cultural forms, especially music, it evokes notions of cultural authenticity, primitivity, and connections to the land.[13] One of his songs, "Gan xu," is about the weekly country fairs that he attended with his family growing up—the simple lyrics and sung vocables evoke the sounds and sights of the fair:

> Searching, searching, searching,
> Searching around the country fair.
> Listening, listening, listening,
> Listening to the country fair.
> Listening to mountain songs until my nerves go numb.
> Oh-oh-oh, A-yi-yo lie-lie-lie!
> Oh-oh-oh, A-yi-yo lie-lie-lie!
> The road is long, the mountains high, but the sound of
> her song carries through the valley. Her hair in the wind,
> her dress fluttering, she stands on the hillside.
>
> "Gan xu" ("Country Fair"), lyrics and music by Ye Honggang,
> performed by Mabang, copyright 2015 Guangdong Xingwaixing
> Wenhua Chuanbo Youxian Gongsi

When A Gang was in elementary school, he recalls being notorious among his teachers for having a very loud voice and an abrasive personality to match. While his temperament led to reprimands from most of his teachers, his physical education teacher put his piercing voice to good use and had him lead the whole class in calisthenics and marching exercises. Under the same teacher's guidance, he excelled at track and field, especially the high jump and the long jump. However, he was falling behind in his academic classes. He continued to draw the ire of his other teachers and developed a bad reputation among them by middle school. School administrators put him in a "special class." He explains, "They gave up on us. They said, 'Fine, you don't want to study? Then sit in this room. Everyone else is preparing for the *zhongkao*,[14] and you are a bad influence.' So, in the second and third year of middle school, there were ten of us who just sat in that room and smoked cigarettes and messed around, and the teachers left us alone." During that same time, his elder brother graduated from middle school, and at the age of sixteen went to work in Liuzhou. Their mother followed him there to take care of him, and his father, in ailing health, soon followed to look for new work in the city center, which was more suitable for his advancing age.

A Gang reflects on his independence as a teenager left to his own devices: "I was pretty skilled for a thirteen-year-old. I could cook, and if there was no meat, I could go catch frogs or sometimes even steal a chicken with a few of my classmates. In little towns like that, you grow up fast. We got drunk, we chased after girls. I even had a girlfriend, and when I brought her home, everyone was jealous. We were bad kids really. But I think it was also the happiest time in my life." He tells many stories of his youthful escapades, from conspiring to forge his teacher's signature on a receipt in order to avoid paying his entire year's tuition for eighth grade to vicious fights with older kids that landed him and others in the police station and in the local newspaper. "I got the 'bad' out of my system. That's why I'm not now," he summarizes.

After middle school, A Gang's test scores weren't good enough for academic high school (*gaozhong*), but he was accepted into vocational secondary school (*zhongzhuan*), where he began to study welding, expecting to be able to work in one of the many jobs in the metal industry in and around Liuzhou and perhaps fulfilling the destiny his name had laid out for him. The vocational school was in Liuzhou City, and it was there that he met new friends, including several who introduced him to the groundbreaking rock and folk music that was being produced in Beijing in the mid-1990s. Like many musicians of his generation, A Gang vividly remembers the transformational experience of seeing a televised concert by Moyan Sanjie ("The three heroes of Moyan Records": He Yong, Dou Wei, and Zhang Chu) in December of 1995 at the Hong Kong Coliseum. "I saw that concert," he says, "and I was just amazed. Before, I had just listened to Beyond, you know, and whatever pop music, Jacky Cheung, that kind of thing. I didn't understand. I didn't have any sort of my own concept." From there, he started listening to Nirvana, The Eagles, and then Bob Dylan, and of course Cui Jian, and he bought his own guitar and started playing and studying with his friends in the evenings as he studied welding during the day.

A Gang recounts how he got serious about music: "As I started studying welding, I became more serious about everything. I'm actually a very good welder even today. Even hard welds, double-joints, I can make look clean and beautiful on both sides. And I suddenly started to think, if I really put my mind to studying and learning something, then I can master it. So, why not study music? And if I know I can rely on temporary work welding, then why not try a little harder and do what I really love? From training for the long jump and the high jump in middle school, I knew how to really practice something, how to train the body. From then on, I was diligent in everything I did."

After graduating from vocational school, A Gang worked for two years in Liuzhou as a welder and formed his first band, Jingzi Yuedui ("Mirror Band"), which performed original ballads and love songs. A Gang describes the name: "In a mirror, you can see yourself. But you don't know what your true self is really like, or whether you're ugly or not, or see inside your heart, your understanding." A Gang also developed a relationship with a guitar teacher during those two years. He recalls, "He took me on for free. We went all around together, having fun. He was a reckless guy, loved to gamble, smoke, drink. We went everywhere together on his motorbike. Out to the villages to pick up girls. I helped him enroll new students at the local schools. He was an amazing classical guitarist, and I learned a lot from him."

It is through his friendship with this teacher that A Gang got his first few gigs at a small bar in Liuzhou called Heibao Jiuba (Black Panther Bar[15]), substituting when his teacher was away. He played solo classical guitar, sang a few pop songs, and was paid 30 RMB (US$4) a night. "I was very excited. I did it about six times, and made nearly 200 RMB (US$25). I thought, 'Wow, there's hope! I can make money doing this?'" A Gang started to seek out more paying gigs; to this end, he bought a bass and found occasional work in cover bands in Liuzhou nightclubs.

One of A Gang's classmates had moved to Shenzhen in search of work in the construction boom there and saw an ad that Genjudi (Base Bar)[16] was looking for solo performers for early sets at the bar. Adjacent to Hong Kong, Shenzhen was the first SEZ established by Deng Xiaoping as part of Reform and Opening Up, and at that time it was going through a rapid and dramatic transformation from sleepy town to one of China's major urban centers. The friend pleaded with A Gang to come to Shenzhen and give it a shot. A Gang recalls deciding to move to Shenzhen for the first time: "So I set out boldly, by myself, with my bass on my back. It was the first time I had left Liuzhou, the first time I had traveled so far from home. I just told my job I needed a little break, but I didn't really care. My brother scolded me, told me to come back home. I didn't have any money, but those friends [that had invited me] took me in, and I lived with them, ate their food. They had a drum, so I taught them how to play, how to play bass, and keyboard, and we learned a few pop songs. We played at an event at their company, and an agent saw us and hired us to play at an outdoor festival, small events like that." A Gang hung out at Genjudi, watching and learning from a more established cohort of musicians based in Shenzhen, including Wen Feng, who is still an in demand drummer in China's jazz and folk circles, and Chen Chusheng, who went on to fame in Beijing for ubiquitous pop songs including "You meiyou ren gaosu ni."

A Gang and his friends from the Liuzhou vocational school auditioned for a gig at Genjudi and played covers ranging from Taiwanese pop songs like "Bu rang wo de yanlei pei wo guoye" by Qi Qin to hard rock songs by He Yong. A Gang was hired but played there only a total of ten times over a month before being fired. "They said I sang badly. But I wouldn't give up. I must have walked through every street in Shenzhen looking for a gig. Everywhere I saw a neon light, I went in and asked if the manager was in. 'How much will you pay a night,' I asked, but kept running into brick walls. I had no experience, and no success."

Defeated, A Gang returned to Liuzhou in 2002 and reformed his band Jingzi Yuedui. For two years, he was unsettled. He stayed mostly in Liuzhou but frequently made trips to Shenzhen to try his luck once again. He worked odd jobs welding and picked up restaurant and bar gigs here and there. He saved his money and bought a blue Yamaha acoustic guitar, which he uses to this day. Along with the last remaining friend from Jingzi Yuedui, he studied MIDI production through online tutorials and prepared backing tracks with keyboard and drums for a long roster of Chinese and western pop songs. His friend played electric guitar, and A Gang switched off between bass and acoustic guitar. "With the MIDI setup, we started to get lots of gigs in Liuzhou, so that we wouldn't have to worry about starving so quickly. Finally, we had enough work to live on." Things were looking better, and they soon got a call from an agent in Shenzhen and once again moved there to take over a gig at a small bar. As had happened many times before, the job didn't last long, and they were once again left in Shenzhen without work or the prospect of finding it. At that point, A Gang decided to move to Guangzhou to see how life there might be different from Shenzhen: "We never played original music in Shenzhen, and I thought it might be possible in Guangzhou. I always felt that Shenzhen, the spirit of the culture there was a bit weak. But Guangzhou seemed different."

They came to Guangzhou in 2004 and rented a small room in Linhe Cun, a small urban village near Guangzhou's East Railway station that has since been demolished for new development. The room cost only 300 RMB (US$36) a month, but performance opportunities were scarce because of the ongoing SARS epidemic. They spent most days busking near Exit H of Guangzhou's East Station in a constant cat-and-mouse game with security guards there. "This was the most miserable time in my life. We could barely afford to eat. We would buy one *kuaican* and share it between the two of us, and buy two *mantou* [steamed bread] to supplement it.[17]" He compares his life at this time to San Mao, a popular Shanghai cartoon about child vagrants.

One day while busking, an agent approached them. "You guys are real professionals," A Gang recalls him telling them. "He asked us if we'd be interested in a gig in Zengcheng. 'Is that in Guangzhou?' we asked. 'Yeah, it's Guangzhou,' he told us. We had no idea we had been duped until we were in the car, traveling three hours away. There was no highway to Zengcheng at that time." They made 100 RMB (US$12) each a night, and lived comfortably in the small satellite city for three months. Afterward, working with the same agent, they secured shorter gigs in other small developing cities in the Pearl River Delta until they returned to Guangzhou.

Back in Guangzhou, A Gang started part-time work teaching children at a music store so that he wouldn't need to travel. With his friend, he got a gig at Peace Bar in Huaqiao Cun (Overseas Chinese Village), which at the time was the epicenter of Guangzhou's nightlife. "300 kuai a night for two people, awesome. Play for ten days, and you can buy a new cell phone," he recalled.

It was 2007, and A Gang met Liang Jun, another musician from Liuzhou who was somewhat established in Guangzhou's folk circles. Along with Liang Jun and an older stalwart of the folk movement there, Ye Lang, their newly formed band played a very well-received show at Liufang Yuan, a bar run by a music promoter from Hunan who goes by the name Lao Tian. After the show they decided to form a permanent band and called themselves Nanman Yuetuan (The Southern Barbarians). With the name recognition that Ye Lang brought, the band played several small festivals, performed regularly at an Urban Folk Night (*chengshi minyao ye*) at Liufang Yuan, and at the 2007 Beijing MIDI Festival, China's most significant and large-scale music festival. A Gang recalls that it was in this band that he felt that he had finally become successful as a musician: "Going to MIDI, we rode the train [as opposed to higher profile bands who were bought plane tickets], and we weren't paid anything, but I was so excited to just be there. Even if we weren't playing my songs, just to go there and see so many bands and such a big stage. I had never dared imagine I could play a show like that." He tells me excitedly about all of the details of that first time in Beijing—the artists he met, the lamb he ate, the beer he drank.

At the same time, A Gang was also working on a repertoire of his own songs in a style he said was drawn from his work with Nanman Yuetuan. He was playing more Chinese woodwinds, including *xiao*, *hulusi*, *dizi*, and others. His goal was to release his own CD. "I was determined to realize my cherished dream before I turned thirty. My wife and I had just got married, and I needed 5000 RMB (US$735) to record my album. My wife was livid. 'Do you want me, or do you want this album?' she asked." A Gang recorded the album, and had five hundred pressed. He sold them as he continued to perform at music festivals and events outside of Guangzhou with increasing frequency.

At around the same time, he started coming to Xiwo, the bar owned by Xiao Dao and described in the previous section. It is here that A Gang's path and my own first crossed. On New Year's Eve of 2010, A Gang played some of his solo material in a late-night jam session at the bar, and Xiao Dao sat in on drums. Afterwards, Xiao Dao said, "Not bad. Come back after you rehearse a bit." A Gang was refining his sound playing weekly at 191Space, another smaller venue in Guangzhou, with the musicians who would eventually become Mabang. Then, one day, A Gang was riding the 802 bus in Guangyuan Xincun, and Xiao Dao happened to be riding the same bus. "Have you been rehearsing?" asked Xiao Dao. A Gang assured him that they had been doing nothing but, and Xiao Dao said he'd have them play at Xiwo sometime soon. When Gao Fei (guitarist of Wanju Chuanzhang) sprained his ankle playing soccer one day, Xiao Dao called A Gang to substitute. A Gang, Fan Feng, and A Fei took to the stage, and after a few songs, Xiao Dao interrupted his game of darts to join in on the drums.

From that gig in spring of 2010 forward, Xiao Dao took an interest in the band, and rehearsed with them when he could. It was then that they started using the name "Mifen Yuedui," and they soon played their first major gig together at the Beishan World Music Festival in Zhuhai. They continued to develop as Mifen Yuedui, and then as Mabang, which I write about in depth in chapter 2.

A Gang summarizes: "Now, I've played MIDI Festival a few times, I've played Strawberry Festival, I've traveled to Macau, to Hong Kong, to Malaysia. It all feels like a dream."

A Fei

Woodwind player and backup singer of Mabang

After knowing A Fei (given name Huang Hui) for many years, I felt like I understood him far less than the other musicians I have worked with. Like myself, A Fei is shy. He has a serious countenance and always seems measured in his interactions with others. He is reserved, and in meetings and social settings speaks far less often than others. He has long hair, which he sometimes wears in a tight ponytail and sometimes wears free. His style of dress is nondescript—usually jeans and a T-shirt, a style that blends into a crowd. He doesn't open up in groups, but in a one-on-one setting, he is engaged and open. I realized this when we had our first serious conversation on a follow-up trip after my full year of fieldwork. It was years after I had first met him and well after a period during which we were regularly spending days and weeks at a time in close proximity.

It was August 28, 2015, and we were in Xiachuan Dao, a small island off the southern coast, for a commercial music festival. We had traveled about six hours to get to the island; first a few hours in the car, then a wait for the ferry, and finally a forty-five-minute boat ride. When we arrived on the island in the late afternoon, we went straight to a hotel in a touristy beach area on the south side of the island. Everyone was exhausted except for A Fei and me. I was rooming with A Gang, who was napping, so I left him in the room in peace and darkness and came outside. The hotel felt like an American roadside beach motel, with doors to each room opening onto a shared balcony that also served as the hallway. At the end of the balcony was a small area with two park benches and an ashtray. I went there to sit and smoke, and A Fei soon came out of his room as well.

It was early evening, and the full moon had just come out. The seventh full moon of the lunar year, it marked Zhongyuan Jie, the Chinese Hungry Ghost Festival, a traditional holiday where ghosts and ancestors come back to the world of the living to roam the streets. A Fei came and sat down beside me and asked me what I knew about the holiday. I admitted that I knew very little. I knew people burned paper offerings to their ancestors in the streets and burned other things to ward off hungry ghosts that could bring bad luck. I also knew that for our own present purposes, the holiday was an excuse for the music festival, the reason we were there. A Fei complained that people in Guangzhou didn't care about the holiday any more, and he wistfully started telling me about how it was celebrated in his hometown growing up—about the genuine fear and dread he had about the hungry ghosts as a child and about the excitement and wonder he had felt making offerings to the dead. It was important for him that I understand all of this, and he was both nostalgic and joyful as he told me details. His sincerity in telling me all of this reminded me of my own feelings over the years when passing important holidays in China, far away from family, surrounded by those for whom what I considered a special day held no significance.

A Fei was born in 1981 in a rural area of Nanxiong, a county-level municipality in northern Guangdong Province, about 160 miles northeast of Guangzhou in an area abutting Jiangxi Province. The closest urban area is the prefecture-level city Shaoguan, which lies about fifty miles to the west and administers Nanxiong's government. When I ask him about his parents, he says simply and directly, "They're *nongmin*," letting the word stand in for a more detailed description. *Nongmin* describes China's agricultural peasant class, farmers who accounted for a majority of China's population throughout the twentieth century. "When I was growing up, my family was extremely poor [*pinkun*]," he continues. "The life of a peasant is hard. Because at that time . . ." He trails off and interrupts himself. "So, my own childhood was rough." A Fei attended elementary school in his village but left before graduating from middle school to work in agriculture. A Fei was the oldest of four brothers. He wanted to study Chinese medicine, but his family was too poor to send him to school. "We were poor, and when someone was sick, we didn't have money to see a doctor. So, I wanted to become a doctor."

Ironically, it was his family's poverty that inspired an early interest in music. "As a kid, there wasn't anything fun to do in the village. We didn't have toys. But there were a few instruments. A *dizi*, a harmonica." In addition, his parents were amateur singers and avid lovers of traditional theater. A regional theater form called *caichaxi* that is native to Jiujiang Prefecture in Jiangxi Province was popular in his hometown, which abuts Jiangxi. His mother loved attending *caichaxi* productions and loved singing them at home. "That is, until we got a TV," he laughs. "Then, she would sing the theme songs to soap operas." When he was around fourteen (in 1995), A Fei remembers starting to hear some *gangtai* pop music. He was immediately a major fan of Beyond, the famous Hong Kong rock band. He mentions a few other pop artists including Alan Tam and Samuel Tai as favorites during his teenage years.

At eighteen (in 1999), A Fei left home to come and work in Guangzhou having never left his hometown or ridden a long-distance bus before. Arriving in Guangzhou, he found a city he had difficulties adjusting to and fell ill. He was unable to work jobs that required great physical strength, and he couldn't find other work. An uncle was in Kaiping, a city of about a million people, one hundred miles southwest of Guangzhou, so he moved there in 2000. There he worked alongside his uncle selling fruit in a wet market and earning a meagre salary. It was in Kaiping that he had his first opportunity to see a live band concert—a cover band playing Beyond songs. He also made friends with a man who sold audio equipment and instruments and got his first guitar.

He reflects on the time: "I was trapped [*buneng ziba*] because I was uncultured [*wenhua shuiping bu gao*]. I thought music might be a way out." So A Fei practiced guitar by learning Beyond songs and decided to come to Guangzhou in 2002. Several members of his extended family had moved to Guangzhou for work by that point, and A Fei thought it might be a good place for him to earn money as well. Furthermore, he thought that a larger city might be better suited to his personality.

In Guangzhou he quickly found work in a factory. He worked there for a year until he reached a breaking point: "In 2003, I decided, once and for all, I wouldn't work in the factory. I thought, 'this isn't the life I want for myself.' I wanted to get out. At that point, Guangzhou already had a subway system. In the stations, there were singers, buskers. So, I thought to myself, I can already play guitar pretty well. And I can sing. And music is what I love. So, of course it wasn't for the money. It was for *freedom*. I imagined myself as Wong Ka-kui, the lead singer of Beyond, writing my own songs. That was my dream."

A Fei describes a transformation into a vagrant (*liulang*) lifestyle, playing in subways and in the street, as he met other buskers and made friends, sometimes performing together. A Fei himself played only songs by Beyond, but he started to hear other buskers performing a wider repertoire, and also noticed that buskers who took requests from passersby made a lot more money than he did. Requests were most often for older Taiwanese and Hong Kong pop stars like Chyi Chin and Lo Ta-yu. "These older pop songs, that's what moved people, and that's what earned money."

In 2004, he met a musician friend named Ji Zai who also sometimes played in bars. Ji Zai arranged a gig for A Fei in a bar in Guangyuan New Village, a mixed-use development in the northern part of the city. He was to work with another guitar player, Li Yongtao, but on the very first night, Li came close to refusing to play with him: "I had no sense of rhythm or song structure," recalls A Fei. "I had only ever played solo. I started singing when I wanted to and stopped when I wanted to. It was difficult for me to play in a duo." Despite the difficulties of working together, Li liked A Fei's voice and asked him to form a band together, with A Fei as lead singer. "There were a lot of things I didn't understand. But I learned them slowly. And Yongtao was also a good businessman. He could find gigs at bars, at restaurants, for events. And he knew he could pay me less than he would have to pay other singers. But I'm still extremely thankful for the opportunity. We played all over. Shenzhen, Jiangmen, Taishan. All of the little cities around Guangzhou, we played them all. Sometimes it would be for a single night. Sometimes for a month contract. And sometimes we'd show up for the first night of a month contract, and they'd"—he makes an axing motion—"'this singer can't bring atmosphere [*qifen*]. The singer needs to speak, to interact with the audience, make the guests happy. It's not about the singing, it's about the atmosphere,' they'd yell at me, and we'd be fired. And, other times the gig would work out."

In 2005 access to the internet was changing the music that A Fei was playing and listening to as he continued to expand his repertoire. He was playing more mainland pop, including Dao Lang and Hei Long. "Whoever was popular that year, I'd sing that. The next year, it would be someone different.

Pop music is like that. This year, for example, it's "Xiao Pingguo" ("Little Apple"). Wherever you go, you hear that. And if you're playing in a bar, then you play that song, and everyone loves it. If you're a musician, you need to know this music. You need to study it. You need to be able to play it."

In 2005 A Fei met Fan Feng playing in the subway, setting the stage for the formation of what would eventually become Mabang. While A Fei liked Gangtai pop, Fan Feng was playing folk (*minyao*) and playing djembe in various folk groups. Fan Feng introduced A Fei to several artists in Beijing's alternative folk movement that he liked, including Wild Children (Ye Haizi) and Guangzhou's own Zhu Fangqiong. A Fei and Fan Feng became friends and also roommates. A Gang himself was playing a steady gig with another band in Panyu when he asked for a few days off to visit his home in Guangxi.[18] An agent called A Fei and Fan Feng to sub for the band while they were gone and invited them for a trial run on one of the nights before A Gang left. It was on this night at a small bar in Panyu that the three original members of what would become Mabang met for the first time.

While A Fei continued to get by playing music, he felt unstable and unhappy. In 2007 and 2008, he abandoned music altogether. "I was confused and wallowing," he says of the time. He became a devoted gambler, playing *liuhecai* (mark six), a popular lottery game from Hong Kong. "The odds were forty-two to one. So, if you bet one hundred kuai, you can win more than four thousand. When I was growing up, we were poor. I always hoped, hoped that maybe I'd suddenly become rich. So, I thought that the only way to do that was the lottery. I'd pick the numbers very carefully. Sometimes I'd win. But as everyone knows, in the lottery, in the end, everyone loses. So, for those two years, I didn't play music. I just drifted along aimlessly [*hun rizi*]. I didn't have any great ideas. I just thought, well, if I can just make a little bit of money, that's okay, that's enough."

"And musically, it bothered me that I didn't have any training. I taught myself. And I saw all these other musicians with real training, some even graduating from Xinghai Conservatory [in Guangzhou]. If they can afford that tuition, I thought, how can I compete? Music is a system, and you need to study the system and to be a part of it. So, I also thought, if I only had a little bit of money, I could go and really study music."

"And right around that time was when the internet singer [*wangluo geshou*] phenomenon was just starting. So, I saw A-Do. He's from Singapore. He's a worker, a construction foreman. One day, he's wearing a construction hat. And the next he's a star. But he loves to sing, and he enters a competition and wins it. But then, I thought, you need money even to get to the competition, to enter the competition. So, I thought if I could just have a little bit of money, then I could pursue music again."

A Fei met his wife during this time as well. "I'm a very earnest and serious person. I didn't want to agree to spend my life with just anyone. But we thought the same way. And she turned me around." His wife worked in an electronics factory, and he was still without work. His wife suggested all sorts of work for him—selling things in the street, or opening a small store. And he felt pressure from their parents to have a child. But she was supportive of pursuing music as a career if he did so seriously. So, in 2009 he returned to music.

In 2009 he got in touch with Fan Feng again. Fan Feng was playing djembe with a folk guitarist in a nightly gig at an outdoor late-night barbecue restaurant. Fan Feng invited him to join him on the gig at the restaurant. A Gang was playing in Nanman Yuetuan and Mimi Houyuan at the time but also played a similar gig. He also was playing in his own band with Fan Feng and another man from Guangxi named Suo Li playing wind instruments. A Fei went to 191Space to see them perform.

A Fei had played *dizi* (Chinese bamboo flute) as a child, but in his words, "never Chinese music. Just pop songs." When Suo Li had to return to Guangxi, A Gang asked A Fei to sit in with the band and to play bass and sing backup vocals. In 2010 he officially joined the band, which still wasn't playing under any name other than Ye Honggang and His Band. While A Gang had wanted A Fei to play bass, A Fei had little interest but mentioned that he played *dizi* and *erhu* as a child. A Gang invited him to try out those instruments with the band. "So, A Gang also taught me to play other instruments: *hulusi*, *suona*, *bawu*. You're a wind player, so you know," he says, addressing me. "There's a commonality in all of those instruments that makes it easier to learn once you can play one. A Gang is my teacher. He is also my friend."

Since 2010 A Fei has played with A Gang, Fan Feng, and Xiao Dao. Throughout these years, he has also often played a six-night-a-week solo gig in a western-style cafe restaurant where he plays a mix of classic *gangtai* pop music and contemporary hits. This, he notes, is steady work that he still can't give up even though he'd like to be able to. But his hope is that Mabang will become as successful as his earliest musical heroes Beyond, and he works hard toward that goal: "Keeping a band together for this long really isn't easy. Because a band is a collective effort, not the work of one person."

Fan Feng

Bassist and percussionist of Mabang

Like A Gang, Fan Feng is from Guangxi Province. He was born Li Yechang in 1982 in Teng County, a rural county under the administration of Wuzhou City, in easternmost Guangxi, straddling the border with Guangdong. Whereas residents of the area A Gang grew up in speak the Guiliuhua subdialect of southwestern Mandarin, residents of Teng county speak the Wuzhou dialect of Cantonese and have stronger ties to Guangdong Province.

Like A Fei, Fan Feng recalls a rural upbringing far different from that of urban residents: "I grew up in the country [*xiangcun*]. Our home was at the foot of a mountain, where it meets the fields. In our village there were less than a hundred households. It's not like in the city, building after building full of people."

There was an elementary school in his village, but he traveled to another county for middle school, which he attended for only one year. "When I was fifteen I quit school. I still really believe the educational style there had deep problems. It's called a school, but fundamentally, it's not a school. We'd have tests, and everyone in the class would score forty or fifty percent. Very rarely did anyone score above ninety. I thought I could do better for myself by leaving than staying there."

So, only fifteen and without a middle school diploma, Fan Feng left home to find work in Guangdong Province. He first went to Jiangmen, a smaller city in the Pearl River Delta about one hundred miles southwest of Guangzhou that is home to a large manufacturing industry. There, he was able to find work quickly. "I've worked in all sorts of factories. The first one was a toy factory—it made all sorts of things for kids, superhero action figures and the like. Then a metalworking factory that made pots and pans and that sort of thing." Seeing his and others' success in Pearl River Delta cities, his parents moved there as well to find better-paying jobs.

In the factory, Fan Feng met a few friends with similar interests, and he started to play music with them casually. "At that time, there was a lot of western music first coming into China. Nirvana, Bon Jovi, those kinds of bands. I started listening to this kind of music in 2000, buying dakou die [cutout media] on the streets." Soon, Fan Feng was inspired to buy a guitar with the money he had been earning in the factory, and he started to learn to play some of the songs he liked to listen to. Apart from the western rock and heavy metal that he liked, he also came to like many Chinese independent rock and folk bands. His favorite Chinese bands included the leaders of the Beijing folk movement, Ye Haizi (Wild Children), as well as the godfather of Chinese rock, Cui Jian.

In 2002 Fan Feng formed a band with a few friends with whom he worked at the factory in Jiangmen. He played guitar, as did the lead singer A Zi, and a third member played hand drums. They called themselves Na.[19] When the third member had to leave Jiangmen to return home, Fan Feng took up the hand drums.[20] Soon, they started making plans to leave Jiangmen: "When we were working, we felt that . . ." He paused. "Doing factory work or manual labor wasn't the way. It wasn't the life we wanted. . . . We thought we should start a band. But, starting a band in a small county town won't work. You can't make that last. So, we said, let's move to Guangzhou! So, that's how we got here."

He goes on about the move: "We had all sorts of problems. At the start, it was a lot of back and forth. When we first came to Guangzhou, we didn't really have any money. Working at the factory in Jiangmen, we made some money, but it wasn't much. Then we came to Guangzhou and had to rent a place to live, and we had normal day-to-day expenses. We were living in Guangzhou for a few months without any sort of income. We didn't have any jobs, but we were trying to make some money busking. Then came the day when we ran out of money. So we didn't have any choice but to go back to Jiangmen and work in the factory again. We did that for a few months, then we came to Guangzhou again!" Fan Feng laughed as he recounted several more times back and forth between working in the factory in Jiangmen and running out of money in Guangzhou. This cycle repeated until 2004.

At that point, Fan Feng and his friends decided that they would come to Guangzhou and not abandon their hopes of making a life there no matter what. This time they found work in a factory in Guangzhou to soothe the transition, and to have an income to fall back on. Even with the factory jobs, they were just getting by. "In Guangzhou, the salary for working in a factory is very low for living in the city. After just paying rent and eating, you don't have any money left. It felt pointless, and I thought I could make as much money busking as working there."

To supplement his income, Fan Feng started a small business buying and selling dakou die. "At that point, the internet was not so developed. There weren't too many people with computers. Everyone listened to CDs. Or even cassette tapes still. So, there were a lot of people like me selling dakou die. Now that the internet is developed, people just listen to music online." But, at that point, if one had good taste and a good eye, one could make decent money scouring the boxes of dakou die in the electronics markets and reselling them on the street.

In those first two years in Guangzhou, Fan Feng also became connected to the folk music circle that was emerging, in particular the two bands (Nanman Yuetuan and Mimi Houyuan) that A Gang was working with. "At that time, there weren't many people playing hand drums in Guangzhou. So, sometimes, people would ask me to play with them. Each performance was a little bit of money. So slowly, I resolved not to return to the factory." He went on about the flowering of the folk scene in Guangzhou in the mid-2000s and its current decline: "At that time, the folk circle in Guangzhou was actually much more extensive than it is now." Fan Feng recalls that there were a lot of musicians playing original music and also doing creative things with Chinese music, even more than in the rock scene. "Now, many people have either started businesses or returned to their hometowns and don't play anymore."

In 2008 Fan Feng took a job at a music shop and continued to play with Mimi Houyuan, Nanman Yuetuan, and various singers. He enjoyed working in the music shop more than working in the factory. But, as he was getting more gigs, he also felt that working in the shop kept him from rehearsing. In 2009 he began playing full time with A Gang in what would become Mifen Yuedui and later Mabang. Since then, Fan Feng has played with Mabang and also continues to operate a small business selling CDs and other music memorabilia online and to friends.

6

Musical Lives: Wanju Chuanzhang

Xiao Li

Lead singer, composer/songwriter, guitarist, and accordionist of Wanju Chuanzhang

Li Yihan, who goes by Xiao Li, was born in 1985 in Yun'ao Township in the southeastern part of Nan'ao Dao, a small island off of the southeast coast of China. Once accessible only by ferry from Shantou, the fifty-square-mile island is now connected directly to the mainland by a recently completed six-mile-long bridge. The island has a population of around seventy thousand people, most of whose families have lived on the island for generations and speak a Min subdialect related to Chaozhouhua.

In 2013 I traveled with Xiao Li and the members of Wanju Chuanzhang (fig. 6.1) to Nan'ao for a performance at his elementary school. From Guangzhou, we drove about eight hours northeast to get to Shantou, one of the five original Special Economic Zones (SEZs) established in the early 1980s. Shantou looks like many other midsize Chinese cities, full of low- to mid-rise buildings built in an unadorned style typical of the 1980s with bustling businesses on the ground floor. Several large new apartment complexes and high-rise office buildings dot the cityscape, evidence of economic development in the city that is substantial but that lags far behind first-tier cities and behind other original SEZs like Shenzhen and Xiamen that have transformed into major metropolises. In Shantou we spent a good deal of time in the secondhand markets, a legacy of the region's role from the 1980s as a major receiving port for electronic and other waste from throughout the world. Outside of Shantou are many sorting centers and villages where waste is sorted and resold. The best of these items end up in the city's secondhand markets. We were searching for old records, undervalued audio and recording equipment, and knickknacks to decorate everyone's apartments.

FIGURE 6.1. Members of Wanju Chuanzhang in a photo from their 2016 release *Qingchun zhaoxiangguan* (*Ching Chun Photo Studio*) on Xingwaixing Records. From left: Xiao Dao, Gao Fei, Xiao Li, Zhou Yi. Photograph by Baiye Zhaoxiangguan (White Nights Photo Studio).

After spending some time in Shantou, we headed to the ferry port. A long line of cars snaked for about a mile from the port, portending a several-hours wait. Our trip was sponsored by the prominent newspaper *Southern Metropolis Daily* (*Nanfang Dushi Bao*) and its parent media company, so the videographer and reporter traveling with us walked to the front of the line and convinced the security guards to allow us to move to the front via the VIP and government vehicle lane because of their press credentials. We got on the next ferry.

The ferry ride was about forty-five minutes. Arriving at the port, we passed through a waiting area filled with food stalls and shops selling dried seafood and various souvenirs. During this trip, the island was already well on its way to becoming a major beach tourist destination. From the port, we looked out at the bridge, which was simultaneously being built from the island and from the mainland. The two sections, each unimaginably high and long, had nearly joined in the middle of the sea. Leaving the port, we drove into the island through lush green forests and mountains covered in huge wind turbines; the island was also a key testing ground for China's embrace of alternative energy sources. We also passed a secure military complex; the island's strategic location in the Taiwan Strait against a context of historical tensions between the mainland and Taiwan also position it as an important military site.

Xiao Li recalled his own childhood spent between these same mountains and sea before the rapid development had begun: "When I was little, we played with animals. In the mountains, we would catch birds. On the shore, we would catch crabs that scurried along the stones." He often talks of his childhood fascination with the fishing culture that has all but disappeared from the island and laments the development that has brought with it so much change.

Like many on the island, Xiao Li's parents are the descendants of families who have lived and worked on Nan'ao for generations. For them, economic development and the island's transformations have also employed them and brought prosperity; Xiao Li's father is a highway engineer working on the many new roads that crisscross the island and on the bridge that now connects it to the mainland. His mother is retired; she worked as an accountant in the tax bureau. Both were civil servants with skilled jobs that afforded their family a comfortable middle-class lifestyle. Their family home, in Yun'ao township, is a large apartment in a low-rise building. It is both spacious and gleamingly new, appointed with fine furniture.

On my visit to Nan'ao with Xiao Li, we spent several hours on the shared rooftop terrace of his family's apartment building. From there we could see out to the township, a small conglomeration of similar low-rise buildings, between which there were glimpses of the sea. In the evening, we went to a fair in the township right along the coast. There was a Chaozhou opera troupe performing on a medium-sized stage that had been erected for the event. Old people sat on plastic stools watching the opera attentively for hours as children ran around them and played. *This* was the Nan'ao that Xiao Li remembered from his childhood, he told me, as we sat next to a barbecue stand eating chicken wings and drinking freshly made fruit ices. One of his songs, "Kan laoxi" ("Watching a Chaozhou Opera"), describes a similar scene to the one we witnessed:

> Carrying a stool to the side of the opera stage,
> There's going to be an opera tonight.
> Grandma leads me there,
> Early birds get the best seats.
> A street hawker pushes his cart,
> Selling his fragrant rice and groundnut cake,
> When the little ones see him, they'll flock to him,
> He's got his own show at the bottom of the stage.
> A huge crowd gathers at the stage's bottom,

Some are alert, while some are yawning.
Grandma's fanning her paper fan,
She says her eyesight is not so good.
My eyes can barely be kept open,
Grandma tells me to take a nap,
Wait a while longer, just a while longer,
See what the finale is like.

"Kan laoxi" ("Watching a Chaozhou Opera"), lyrics and music by Li Yihan, performed by Wanju Chuanzhang, copyright 2012 Li Yihan

While Xiao Li romantically reminisces about falling asleep to Chaozhou opera as a child, the primary music that captured his interest when he was younger was pop music from Taiwan sung in Taiwanese Hokkien. It was the close (albeit unofficial) ties between Nan'ao and Taiwan that set the scene for the saturation of Nan'ao with Taiwanese music, as Xiao Li explains: "There are many fishermen here, and business people, who travel across the straight to Taiwan to sell fish or other things.[1] And many people from Taiwan who come here. So, illegal import/export and immigration was always very common. Those people would go to Taiwan to buy quality electronics—washing machines, that sort of thing—as well as cassette tapes and such, and sell them here." Xiao Li goes on to explain that music from Taiwan was the most popular music on Nan'ao not only because it was sung in a language close to the mother tongue of Nan'ao residents but also because the entire "life situation" (*shenghuo zhuangtai*) it embodied was closer to the lives of listeners than that of Mandarin or Cantonese pop music. He notes one singer, Chen Lei, as a particular favorite of islanders during his youth. Chen is also a good example of how popular music from Taiwan of that era has more in common stylistically and historically with Japanese enka, using melodies and singing styles drawn from traditional forms as much as from European and North American pop music.

In middle school, which he attended on Nan'ao, Xiao Li's favorite subjects were art and music. He had family members who were art teachers in a high school in Shantou, which he considered attending upon graduating from middle school—it was not uncommon for students on the island to attend boarding schools in cities on the mainland. In the end, though, he decided to go farther afield to Guangzhou to study music. "I had never seen a real piano in person, only on the television," he recalls. "No one on Nan'ao had a piano. So, to study music, you had to leave the island." Xiao Li auditioned for the school and was accepted in large part for his potential as a dancer.

Only sixteen years old, Xiao Li moved by himself to Guangzhou to attend Guangzhou Yishu Shifan Xuexiao (Guangzhou Arts Pedagogical School), a high school with a music and arts focus. Xiao Li recalls the breadth of the required classes: "Piano, dance, ear training, sight singing, erhu and Chinese instruments, chorus, all those kinds of things, because it was a pedagogical school [for preparing teachers in primary and secondary schools]." Xiao Li felt intimidated by other students, who already were skilled musicians knowledgeable about music, but also inspired by the atmosphere: "My heart never stopped racing. So I developed a habit of spending a lot of time in the library." In addition to reading assigned works, Xiao Li also was a voracious reader of music magazines, which the school's library stocked extensively. It is through these magazines that Xiao Li came to be interested in Chinese rock music, most notably Cui Jian, and foreign music, most notably the Beatles and Bob Dylan. Near the school were many stands selling dakou CDs and cassettes; it is in these stalls that Xiao Li sought out the music he read about in these music magazines.

In the second year of high school, his school merged with the Guangzhou Waiyu Shifan Xuexiao (Guangzhou Foreign Language Pedagogical School), and the newly merged school was renamed Guangdong Waiyu Yishu Zhiye Xueyuan (Guangdong Professional School of Foreign Languages and Arts). "So, when we tell people where we went to high school, they think our English will be very good. But we studied music." He laughs. It is at the newly merged school and in this second year that he met Zhou Yi, Wanju Chuanzhang's bass player. They formed a band called "Jinhua" with a third friend and rehearsed various cover songs—in his words, "mostly Beyond and that sort of thing . . . a few pop songs. Some originals, but very few. It was a bit chaotic."

Xiao Li stayed in Guangzhou for college and in 2004 began attending Guangdong Wenyi Zhiye Xueyuan (Guangdong Professional Arts Academy), where he entered the popular music department. There, he took on a roster of classes including MIDI production, piano, sight singing, and composition: "It was preparing us to play in bands, so that's really what we did the most," he recalls. In college, he had a band that played *shijue* music, a genre categorization and fashion subculture that literally translates as "visual" and derives from the Japanese "visual kei" (*vijuaru kei*) movement, which shares some commonalities with British glam rock. Musically, many of the bands in this movement played heavy metal, but the style is most known for its visual aesthetic, consisting of "crazy makeup" (in Xiao Li's words) and exaggerated stage antics. Xiao Li's favorite band at the time was X-Japan, the famous Japanese rock and heavy metal band that is central to the visual kei movement.

Xiao Li graduated from college in 2007, and the band members he had played with moved to other cities one by one for work. For a short time, he worked at a record company as a low-level manager accompanying artists to performances and doing various tasks. The salary was comparatively low, so Xiao Li also supplemented his income by writing commercial music as a freelance composer and MIDI producer. He also taught guitar lessons to children.

In 2008 Xiao Li started what would become Wanju Chuanzhang with Gao Fei, who attended the same college but was two years behind him, and a female singer from the college who had studied ballroom dancing. He met Gao Fei when a mutual friend asked him to come to a rehearsal to give his opinion on their band. "In that band, there was only one rhythm player, Gao Fei. I immediately really liked this guitar player. The things he was playing were very simple, but he played them with great strength. The rest of the band was a mess." Xiao Li laughs. "So, when he left that band, I spoke to him and the ballroom dancer, whose voice I really admired, about starting a band."

In that configuration, Wanju Chuanzhang released their first self-produced CD, *Waiguo ke* (*Guest from beyond the Seas*). On the recording, one can hear the roots of their current style. Xiao Li plays both guitar and accordion, and several songs, such as "Guest from Overseas" and "Fisherman," explore themes related to those he writes about in later songs. These and a few other songs on the album are sung in the Nan'ao dialect. Others, like "A Guy I Met in McDonalds," are sung in Mandarin, and have tongue-in-cheek playful lyrics about love and relationships, in a light indie-rock style. The recording uses MIDI drums, bass, and some synth sounds with guitars and vocals overdubbed. Xiao Li reflects on this early iteration of the band: "When we started performing, it was still messy. I only had an electric guitar, and Gao Fei also only had an electric guitar. So, every time we played, we had to borrow an acoustic guitar with a pickup from a friend. After a few gigs that paid 200 RMB (US$29) per person, we bought an acoustic guitar that cost about 2000 RMB (US$290)."

In 2009 Zhou Yi returned from his travels abroad, and he joined the band (more details of this are in his own biography, below). In 2009 they played at a small folk festival at Tutu Kongjian and met Xiao Dao for the first time. And in March of 2010 they had their first show at Xiwo at the invitation of Xiao Dao. "It's not easy to get gigs. Especially at Xiwo. The first day we played there, Xiao Dao was there. I hadn't seen him play the drums, but I knew a lot of people said he was a great drummer. We asked him to play with us for the second set. He had only ever heard the songs one time, but he played fantastically. We had always been looking for a drummer, we had just never found one that worked for us. From then on, he played with us."

The performance at Xiwo turned into a weekly gig on Wednesdays. After about two months, Xiao Dao moved them to Saturday nights, the busiest night in the bar. "Soon, we were playing all the time at Xiwo," says Xiao Li. "Every Saturday, plus every Wednesday, as well as any time another regular band had to cancel."

In March of 2011 they began working with saxophonist Yu Zhenhai and recorded the first song, "Haibian de wuhui," of what would become their 2012 release. Peter Scherr, an American double bass player who had been employed by the Hong Kong Philharmonic Orchestra for nearly a decade and who was working to expand his own connections in the mainland with a company he started, Creative Music in China, brought equipment to Tutu to record the band. While Peter spent the next year occasionally having members overdub parts and mixing the record, Wanju Chuanzhang used preliminary mixes of the songs as a demo to seek out larger performances: "During this time, we had many concerts [*zhuanchang*; as opposed to *yanchu*, which refers to more informal gigs], and various sponsors and agents came to see us play and liked our music. So, when we officially released the CD in 2012, we started to get more opportunities to play in major music festivals like MIDI and Strawberry. It's because we had a CD. A CD is great promotion. But it was also because of Weibo.[2] At that time, we became pretty hot on Weibo. That really helped to popularize us. From the start, we relied heavily on Weibo and online platforms for promotion. That allowed many promoters and music festival organizers to hear our music."

Xiao Li goes on to speak about the progress they made. "At first, they would give us pretty bad time slots at the music festivals. You know as well, at this point we often get scheduled in pretty good time slots." Wanju Chuanzhang played the main stage at Beijing Midi Festival in the early evening in 2014; the only better slots are slightly later, which are usually reserved for major stars. He finished, "But this happened slowly."

In April of 2014 Wanju Chuanzhang signed with Xingwaixing Records. They had spoken as far back as 2012 with CEO Zhou Xiaochuan, who, perhaps in part because he is from Shantou and is quite familiar with Nan'ao, personally liked Wanju Chuanzhang's music. Zhou wanted to pursue a sublabel or side business that involved so-called independent music. When I ask Xiao Li why they wanted to sign to a record label instead of continuing to work independently, as they had for many years, he replied, "Producing a CD and doing promotion is not something that we can do ourselves. The company has money to invest in these projects, but even more importantly, it has resources that we don't have. And Zhou Xiaochuan has great experience and expertise as well as a desire to promote independent music. . . . It's still in the process of breaking in. The boss, he very much wants to get things done."

Xiao Li speaks about the music they are making eloquently and relates it to his own experiences getting to this point: "Even though our music's starting point is coming from Nan'ao Island and from the Chaoshan region, but in fact, we're really looking out at the entire world. Because these stories perhaps share a common state of mind [*zhuangtai*] with people in lots of places."

Gao Fei

Guitarist of Wanju Chuanzhang

Gao Penghui, who goes by Gao Fei, was born in 1986 in Xinhui, which he describes as "a very small third-tier city." Xinhui is officially an urban district of Jiangmen City (the same industrial town where A Fei and Fan Feng came to work in factories) and lies about sixty miles southwest of Guangzhou. It is one of many smaller cities that dot the Pearl River Delta region and is at the confluence of several rivers. Gao Fei's father worked in the maritime shipping industry, while his mother worked as a tailor in a dress shop.

Gao Fei started playing the guitar when he was thirteen, in the first year of middle school: "I started playing the guitar because of Beyond [the famous Hong Kong rock band], because of their lead singer. I though he was so handsome, people cheered for him, he could get all the girls." He laughs. "At that time, in middle school, that's how I thought. But later, I realized that this thing [music] isn't just for using like that. I discovered how music could touch [*gandong*] people."

When I tell Gao Fei how interesting I find it that so many people explicitly mention Beyond as the starting point of a lifelong love for music, he tells me more about his relationship with the band. "It's weird, actually. Before Beyond, I didn't really have any knowledge of Gangtai music, I didn't really care about it. Then one time, when I was very young, in elementary school, I was riding on the back of my [cousin's] bike,[3] and we were on the way to school. He sang this song, and I just thought it sounded so good. I told him how much I liked it, and asked him what it was. He just said, 'Beyond.' Back then, only his family had a CD player. So, every time I'd go to their house, I'd put that same CD in the machine and sit there and just listen, listen, listen, listen, listen until they couldn't stand it anymore."

Gao Fei attended a technical high school that focused on e-commerce. When I ask him why he chose to study e-commerce, he responds, "Actually, at that time, I didn't really have any sort of goal. You could choose the type of high school you wanted to go to. I thought about an English high school, but I wasn't good enough at English. And, I figured that I at least had a little bit of interest in computers. I looked at a music high school, but the tuition was too high for my family, so I didn't choose that one."

After graduating from high school, Gao Fei took a gap year and came to Guangzhou in 2006 to attend college at Guangdong Wenyi Zhiye Xueyuan, the same college that Xiao Li attended. He had wanted to study music, but his test scores did not gain him entrance into the program. Instead, he entered the college as an environmental design major with the hope of switching majors once he was already in the university's School of the Arts. "Then, once I got there, they wouldn't let me switch majors. So, I ended up studying environmental design all the way through graduation."

Even though he was unable to transfer into the music program, he continued to play music and to seek out others with similar interests. His music tastes shifted—"I liked Hardcore, Metalcore, and Emo," he says, using the English for each genre name. Gao Fei listened to relatively obscure bands. One of his favorite bands was Saosin, a posthardcore band from California. "I listened to a lot of bands like that then. But that's the only name I remember. All the names were long, and I couldn't pronounce them anyways."

Gao Fei formed his first band in college. It started out under the metal-sounding name Modeng Baobiao (Modern Bodyguard) but later changed its name to Yila Guan (Pop-Top, referring to the kind of soda can with a tab that you pull to open): "The idea of the name was that we wanted to make music that was easy for people to like." Gao Fei describes the band as primarily "pop-rock" (*liuxing yaogun*).

It was through this band that Gao Fei ended up meeting Xiao Li and eventually forming part of the core of Wanju Chuanzhang: "I met Xiao Li in my second year of college. He had already graduated, but he came back to watch my band rehearse. Our drummer was a friend of Xiao Li's from the popular music program. He had asked Xiao Li to come by and give us some guidance, give his expert opinion." After this first meeting at Gao Fei's band's rehearsal, Gao Fei and Xiao Li stayed in touch. In 2009 Xiao Li asked Gao Fei to play guitar with him on a few gigs. Their first gig—and Gao Fei's first ever performance in front of an audience—was at 191Space that year. "I was very nervous. It was the first time I had been on a stage. At that point, I thought playing at 191 was really fucking cool. So, I was really excited but really nervous. Xinhui, where I grew up, didn't have any places like 191."

After graduating college in 2009, Gao Fei got a job that he did not enjoy but that drew on his major in design. His work consisted of cross-checking proposed logos of companies with registered copyrights. At the same time, he continued to play with Xiao Li and moved into a small house in a village on the southern outskirts of Guangzhou. His music tastes shifted away from the metal that he had loved in college: "I think every person's outlook really grows and changes with age. So, when I was younger, like a lot of people, I really liked very heavy music." He imitates the growl of a metal vocalist. "But after listening to that kind of music for a long time, you start to feel like it's boring, and just plain loud. So, I think everyone's always pursuing that next thing. When I was younger, I really didn't listen to folk or to reggae. I didn't think it was interesting. But, getting older, you don't just want it to be loud. You need it to have soul [*linghun*]. It's only good music if it has soul . . . Now, my favorite music to listen to is reggae and dub. I didn't even know anything about this kind of music until 2010. I went to Ping Pong [a bar in Guangzhou in a small arts compound in a converted factory] to play a gig with Xiao Li, and they were playing French dub, Hightone. I thought the music was great, and the rhythms were so strange. So, the next day, I called the manager to ask what the music they were playing was, but he didn't know. Then, later, I met Dao Zong [Xiao Dao]. He told me that this music is called reggae."

While he continues to discover more music and is an adventurous listener, Gao Fei speaks openly about a troubled relationship with music that has come about since Wanju Chuanzhang's success: "I think I haven't really seriously practiced the guitar in two or three years. In my heart, sometimes it feels like only when I have to work do I hold my guitar. Otherwise, I won't even touch it. It's almost as if I hate the guitar. It's because it's become my job. It's different than when it was my love, or my hobby. Work and play are forever separate. This is a change in my mentality, and I think I've only recently realized it. . . . I am age-phobic [*nianji de kongjuzheng*]. I'm almost thirty years old. How can I face my own age? When I was seventeen, my birthday wish was that I'd become a great guitarist. Here I am, eleven years later." Despite struggling to balance music as vocation and music as passion, Gao Fei's consistent and creative guitar playing has been central to Wanju Chuanzhang's sound and success, and he continues to grow as a musician.

Zhou Yi

Bassist of Wanju Chuanzhang

Zhou Yi was born in 1985 in Guizhou Province in southwestern China.[4] His father was from Jiangxi, and his mother from Shanghai, but they met and were married in Guizhou. When Zhou Yi was six years old, his parents were hired for jobs in Guangzhou, and they moved the family there. Both of his parents work in universities; his mother as a bookkeeper and accountant, and his father as a professor of western classical music. His father was an accomplished violinist who also worked as a choral director at several universities before coming to Guangzhou.

Zhou Yi reflects on the influence this background had on him: "From a very young age, I grew up under the strong influence of classical music. We would often go to concerts, and go to all sorts of performances that most kids don't really like. Symphony orchestras, opera, these kinds of things that we see as very precious [*zhengui*]." When I ask him if he liked attending these performances, he responds with a straight face, "Yes, I enjoyed them very much. My favorite part was the intermission," his dry sense of humor always on display. "I could run into lots of my friends, and in the gardens of the concert hall or opera house, we would play games."

Zhou Yi's parents started his musical training very young. At four, he started taking violin lessons, and at five, they added piano lessons as well. "It's because my father was a musician," he says, "so, perhaps, he hoped that music would nurture me as well. Now that I'm this much older, in fact, this method wasn't quite right. At the time, I felt that I was suffering. I looked at the piano and the violin with a heavy heart—they repelled me. I knew that there was half an hour set aside every day that I had to practice. I found it unbearable."

Aside from his music lessons, Zhou Yi was also pressured to excel at school. "School was high pressure, and I wasn't a very good student. I didn't really like theoretical things. I liked to play. So when it came time to select a high school, I had two top choices. One was a music high school. The other was a soccer school. In the end, for a lot of reasons, including my parents and my relatives, I selected music."

Upon entering high school, Zhou Yi recalls a very musical atmosphere. "It seemed like everyone had a guitar on their back," he says. When he was in the first year of high school Zhou Yi started playing other instruments, including guitar, bass, and drums. Despite his parents' influence, his own musical tastes veered toward popular music. His favorites were Jay Chou, Eason Chan, and Michael Jackson—he characterizes his musical tastes in high school as "very mainstream" (*zhuliu de*). I asked about Michael Jackson's inclusion in his top three. "Other than him, I really didn't listen to any foreign music. Maybe because he was so hot then [in China]. We all listened to Gangtai music. Very little foreign music. I hadn't even heard of the Beatles." This music he listened to on CDs that he and his friends bought in market stalls and music shops around their high school.

In this first year of high school, he met Xiao Li, and they formed their first band together. Whereas Xiao Li is very serious in telling me about it, Zhou Yi tells about the band comically and nostalgically. When I ask him what style they played, he laughs, "What style were we playing? I don't know! I don't think we knew. We played some cover songs . . . Beyond, and Nicholas Tse."[5] Zhou Yi started to play bass at this point, because, in his words "they needed a bass player."

In this high school, Zhou Yi received a wide-ranging training in music: "It was an arts pedagogical school. So, we had to study everything. Classical music, violin, piano, chorus. Dance, we even had to study. With dance, for example, it wasn't a specialized training, as a dance major would receive. We studied Chinese dance, ballet, popular dance. A lot of the students become teachers. So, anything related to music, we studied a little bit. But it's different from studying music in college. I really liked this high school." Zhou Yi also counts the time as transformational in giving him a sense of independence: "I think my independence [*dulixing*] really comes from there. For me, being an only child, I was very closely looked after by my parents. Everything was organized for me through my teenage years. My clearest memory that shows what I'm talking about is the first time I needed to do laundry at high school. I didn't know how to wash my clothes! What am I supposed to put in with them? A lot of funny things like that. Very regular things, I just didn't know. But I had to learn to live on my own."

Zhou Yi graduated from that school in 2004 and enrolled in a diploma program at Beijing City College (Beijing Chengshi Xueyuan).[6] When I ask him why he chose to go to Beijing for college, he responds quickly, "Parents." At the same time, Zhou Yi's parents also encouraged him to go abroad to study. He was strongly opposed to the idea, but eventually gave in. He had hoped to study music in New Zealand, but his English scores were not high enough to gain him entrance into a normal university or conservatory. "To study abroad, we have to take the IELTS or TOEFL. There was no way I was going to score high enough. So, I had to enroll in a language school, and then transfer into a 'foundation,' where I studied for a business diploma. In all, I spent a little over two years there."

Once again, Zhou Yi reflects on the experience largely in terms of his growing independence. "When I first went to New Zealand, my independence still wasn't that strong. In New Zealand, I completely changed as a person. My thoughts and ideas, including my mentality, in so many ways and so many directions, everything in me was overturned. In and outside of school, I was exposed to a lot of new things. With regard to education, but also just people, and the environment. It's also the first time I came to know Christianity. In China, Christianity isn't very prevalent. Buddhism, of course, is much more common. So, being in New Zealand, I just was experiencing so many things that were fresh to me. You see things that you had never even thought about. And everyone was so simple and straightforward and wanted to communicate, connect, and exchange. In China it's not like that, as you know. People are protective of themselves. You don't just strike up a conversation with someone you don't know. So I met all kinds of people. I also met people from all over the world. I had Korean friends, Japanese friends, Malaysian friends, Taiwanese friends. New Zealand is a multicultural country, so there are people from all over there."

While Zhou Yi was in New Zealand, his music tastes didn't change much. But he started to play more. He bought a Martin guitar, a very expensive and well-regarded model, and studied fingerstyle guitar with a close friend.

His parents wanted him to continue to study abroad and perhaps to transfer to a school in the US. "My parents didn't have strict requirements about my education, but they hoped that I could take in cultural experiences in more places. They figured I had spent enough time in New Zealand. I had already been to the US. I even toured some colleges. With my dad's connections, I had even met with some professors of music in the US. I went to Denver, New Orleans, and LA. My father has a colleague there, and the whole family went together. This colleague took me to a few colleges. It was all but set. But then I made the decision myself. I wanted to return to my own country. I wanted to stay in China. I wanted to play music. It's at that point that I joined Wanju Chuanzhang."

At first, Zhou Yi's parents were strongly opposed and wanted him to take advantage of the opportunity to study in the US. He jokes about their continued entreaties as a form of "ideological work" (*sixiang gongzuo*), invoking the Maoist term. But he was steadfast. When Zhou Yi returned from that trip to the US in February 2010, he reconnected with Xiao Li and joined Wanju Chuanzhang. "So, when I returned to China, it was a new beginning."

Zhou Yi had wanted to play guitar in the band. "I had just bought a Martin, for God's sake," he jokes. But he had played bass with Xiao Li in high school, and Gao Fei and Xiao Li both already were playing guitar, so Zhou Yi reluctantly joined as a bass player. "At that point, I still didn't really understand the bass. I didn't think it was important," he says.

He speaks eloquently of growing into his role as bass player, both technically and personally. "The first time that I really changed my understanding of the bass was when a friend of ours introduced us to a band called Primus. He said, 'your bass player's not bad. He should listen to this.' I hadn't heard of them. He sent me a link to their music. I was like, 'wow, how could a bass be played like THAT! Too cool!' Before, my conception of what the bass was . . ." He hums a melody: bum (dotted quarter) bum (eighth) bum (half), followed by the same thing a fifth above. He uses a phrase, *zhongguizhongju*, that can best be translated as "square," and implies conformity to norms above all else. "I had listened to far too little music and was far too limited in my taste. It was still all very mainstream pop music. It was only through expanding the music I was listening to that I could come to a new understanding of the bass. Les Claypool (Primus's bass player), that's the kind of bass player I wanted to be. And then Bob Marley's bass player. And now Victor Wooton. So, now I think the bass can be such a beautiful instrument. So, I've come to it step by step, and I love it more and more. So, why do I want to buy such a good bass now?"—at the time of this interview, Zhou Yi was waiting for delivery of a custom made bass from a luthier in Italy—"The first bass I bought was 400 renminbi [US$60]. That's because I didn't think it was important. Playing in this band, and getting to know people, especially Dao Zong [Xiao Dao], I've come to know more what a band is and what each person's role can be. People who don't understand, they just say, 'the lead singer is important. Because he's always singing.' So, even in some pop music, the other parts don't really matter. Now, I think I've come to understand what a 'band' is."

Since returning from studying abroad and joining Wanju Chuanzhang in 2010, Zhou Yi has devoted himself wholeheartedly to the band and to improving himself as a musician and as a person. When I ask him about the future of Wanju Chuanzhang, he invokes a Chinese saying, "Huangtian bufu youxinren," which may be translated as "Heaven rewards those with a good heart." He elaborates: "I think we're working so hard at this, and we've been doing it for such a long time, there has to be a good outcome. Along the way, we'll have ups and downs. We'll go through uncomfortable times. But in the future, we'll be successful. Since I've joined the band, I've learned so much. And I've changed a lot. It's a road. From New Zealand, back here, to America, to my decision to come back and live here, to starting Wanju Chuanzhang, from 2010 until now, this whole process has been enriching, and I've been happy. I have learned a lot. And I've come in contact with new perspectives. So, today, sharing this with you, I feel very comfortable. Reflecting on it, I feel like it's been an accomplishment. So, Wanju Chuanzhang has given me this. I don't care about the future, or the past, I care about the now."

Yinyue Shenghuo (Musical Lives) and Musical Subjectivities

Economic, political, and cultural formations shape lives lived through music, and affective experiences of these formations provoke desires, ideas, and new forms of creativity. Several significant themes that course through the *yinyue shenghuo* described in these two chapters offer perspective on how musical subjectivities are fulcrumed between these structuring forces and powers of the self.

"I SET OUT BOLDLY, BY MYSELF, WITH MY BASS ON MY BACK"—A GANG

As discussed briefly in the introduction to these biographies, one of the most noteworthy elements of all of these musical lives is their mobility. Each musician recounts a decisive initial move, usually made as a teenager and made alone, that set them on a different life path than if they had stayed in their hometown or village. For A Gang, who summarized the decision, its motivation, and the risks it entailed in the quote that headlines this section, this meant leaving Liuzhou, a career as a welder, and fledgling success as a bar musician in a minor urban center of southwest China for Shenzhen, a significantly larger city adjacent to Hong Kong that, as a SEZ in the midst of rapid expansion, offered broader economic and cultural opportunities. Nearly ten years before A Gang, Xiao Dao made a similar move from the provincial capital of Kunming to Hainan, another SEZ that was notable for its openness; bureaucratic matters like household registration were not obstacles in Hainan, and new opportunities attracted an exciting mix of young people from throughout China. A Fei and Fan Feng both left their rural villages to work in factories, while Xiao Li left his small island hometown to attend a highly regarded boarding school. All three were teenagers and all moved to Guangzhou or its satellite cities, even if the conditions under which they made the move were quite different (as I will discuss below).

In their own narratives, these initial moves are dramatic turning points that are told with details that highlight both the significance and the uncertainty of the moment. While A Gang paints a romantic and almost cinematic image of the moment he "set out boldly . . . with [his] bass on his back," Xiao Dao recounts at length the unpleasantness of the four-day bus ride he had to endure on the way to Hainan. But in all cases, the gravity of the decision is emphasized through these details; as they tell it, choosing to leave one's hometown at a young age begins a process of claiming ownership of one's own destiny.

This initial move away from home as a teenager set each on a path where their lives were shaped by further movements. "It was a lot of back and forth," observes Fan Feng, telling of a cyclical process of moving to Guangzhou to pursue music, running out of money, moving back to Jiangmen to work in a factory and save money, and then starting the process over again. A Gang ricocheted between Liuzhou and various Pearl River Delta cities in a similar fashion. For Xiao Dao, Hainan was just a stepping stone where he made personal and musical connections that soon brought him to another Special Economic Zone. For Zhou Yi, studying abroad in New Zealand widened his perspectives but also led him to decide that he did not want to pursue a future in the US that his parents envisioned for him and instead wanted to make Guangzhou his home.

While these narratives all share mobility as a defining feature, the conditions and experiences of this mobility vary greatly and bring attention to the ways that geographic mobility intersects with class mobility.

"THE LIFE OF A PEASANT IS HARD"—A FEI

There are stark contrasts in the class backgrounds of members of Mabang and Wanju Chuanzhang that influenced the paths members traveled to becoming musicians in Guangzhou. These contrasts and their implications speak to the evolving geographies of inequality (Sun and Chio 2012) in China in recent decades. Mabang's members A Fei and Fan Feng's parents were both rural peasants, and A Gang's father was a skilled worker in a state-owned enterprise. Wanju Chuanzhang's lead singer Xiao Li's parents were both educated civil servants, Zhou Yi's were a university professor and an accountant, and Gao Fei's parents were urban residents of a medium-sized Pearl River Delta city. These divergent backgrounds deeply influenced the opportunities each individual had and the paths that they followed to arrive in Guangzhou.

As rural residents in less developed areas of southern China, Fan Feng and A Fei both struggled particularly hard to persevere against a system where their most likely futures were as unskilled laborers in factories. Both left school to work in factories in the Pearl River Delta as teenagers. After several years of factory work, each reached a breaking point; both recount the precise point at which they consciously decided that they could not continue on the same path for the rest of their lives. As A Fei summarized, "I decided, once and for all, I wouldn't work in the factory. I thought, 'this isn't the life I want for myself.' I wanted to get out." For both, music, even if busking on the street, provided a better, if more precarious, future.

Zhou Yi's life represents another point on the class spectrum in China, and as a result, his mobility was of a different nature than that of Fan Feng and A Fei. He grew up in a major city, and his highly educated middle-class parents were very supportive of his education. His father's connections as a university professor helped earn him a place in a prestigious high school in

Guangzhou followed by years of studying in the national capital Beijing and abroad in New Zealand. Even though his parents wanted him to continue his studies abroad in the US and had the means to support him to do so, he chose to stay in China and to pursue music. His decisions were not motivated by experiences of economic precarity, and even though his parents were not as wealthy as many in Guangzhou, he was relatively well off; for him, his economic situation enabled mobility rather than necessitating it.

As all of these examples demonstrate, an important dimension relating to class background is educational opportunity and performance. Academic performance early on in school, and in particular on the nationally standardized *zhongkao* and *gaokao* exams, is a huge factor in determining the life path of each of these individuals. Recent media attention has focused on the tremendous pressures that these exams exert on Chinese students, how performance on these exams can determine a person's future, and how experiences of urban versus rural students are quite different (e.g., Roberts and Zhao 2016). The disparities between rural and urban educational systems are particularly apparent when comparing these biographies.

For A Gang, poor performance on the *zhongkao* meant attending vocational school instead of academic high school. Nonetheless, this vocational school gave him the skills to find decent paying work as a welder whenever and wherever he needed. For Fan Feng and A Fei, their rural schools left them feeling that education offered nothing to them, so they both quit before completing middle school. While it might seem that their choices significantly limited their economic opportunities, at the same time, the abundance of demand for unskilled labor in factories contributed to their decisions: why finish school when they could find a job without doing so?

For Xiao Li, Gao Fei, and Zhou Yi, relatively privileged backgrounds, better schools, and parents who were themselves highly educated led to educational experiences that supported their development as musicians. China's system of specialized schooling beginning in high school worked especially well for Zhou Yi and Xiao Li, who attended the same music and arts high school in Guangzhou. Both of them applauded the education they received there and count the quality of the school as instrumental in their development as musicians.

This educational gap continues to resonate for independent musicians in China. While some, like the members of Wanju Chuanzhang, have extensive musical training, from instrumental technique to composition, others are self-taught. As A Fei observed, "I saw all these other musicians with real training, some even graduating from Xinghai Conservatory [in Guangzhou].

If they can afford that tuition, I thought, how can I compete? Music is a system, and you need to study the system, and to be a part of it."

"THIS WAS THE EARLY 1980S, A VERY EARLY TIME"—XIAO DAO

Economic formations further entwine with political ones. Major policy initiatives of the state, from the Cultural Revolution to Reform and Opening Up, are the markers through which Chinese history is most often analyzed. These biographies offer examples of the far-reaching lived implications of these policies and their on-the-ground impacts for artists navigating shifting cultural-political fields. Noteworthy among these implications is how they variously entail and curtail new kinds of mobility within and beyond China.

While only one of these musicians—Xiao Dao—was actually alive during the Cultural Revolution, the deprivations and upheavals of this period form an important backdrop for much of what was to follow. The Up to the Mountains and Down to the Countryside Movement brought about the movement of nearly twenty million urban residents to China's countryside. While this movement is more often understood in terms of the effects on those sent down, it is interesting to think about the reverse perspective, that is, the effects on rural village life of an infusion of young urban cosmopolitan intellectuals. In Xiao Dao's particular case, a childhood relationship with an uncle from Shanghai resulted in a more formal musical education than he would have otherwise received as a rural resident of a small village far away from any urban center.

All of these musicians except for Xiao Dao were born in the first years of Reform and Opening Up and belong to the so-called post-80s (*balinghou*) generation. China's economic and political transformations beginning in the early 1980s deeply affected the opportunities afforded them, particularly because of southern China's outsized role in the implementation of these policies. For A Gang, the SEZ of Shenzhen drew friends from his vocational school who were trained as welders to work in a dramatic construction boom. For both A Fei and Fan Feng, it was the explosion of factories in the Pearl River Delta in the 1990s that drew them away from their hometowns for work. For members of Wanju Chuanzhang, economic reforms lifted their parents into China's rapidly expanding middle class and gave them opportunities to study music in faraway provinces or abroad.

In all of these cases, Deng Xiaoping's policy making and vision for southern China led to new mobilities and contributed to cultivating desires for mobility and economic opportunity. As they moved from their hometowns to larger cities, factories, and schools, these musicians met like-minded people and were exposed to new musics. Fan Feng's first band was formed with his workmates at a factory, and A Gang's was formed in a vocational school in the closest major city to the mining area where he grew up. The members of Wanju Chuanzhang met each other because they attended high school and college together in Guangzhou, far away from all of their hometowns. Zhou Yi's experience studying abroad in New Zealand exposed him to all sorts of new musics and new ways of thinking about musics.

The personal histories of all of these musicians resound through the music they produce; their mobilities intersect with national histories and cosmopolitan formations and inflect the creative processes explored in other chapters of this book.

"I JUST THOUGHT IT SOUNDED SO GOOD"—GAO FEI

Along the way, the musics that these musicians encountered—and the ways they encountered them—shaped them as musicians and as people. Drawing on DeNora (2000), De Kloet (2010) writes specifically about *balinghou* (post-80s) youth in China and looks to listening to popular music as a "technology of the self" (De Kloet 2010, 141). Through an ethnography of music fans, listening practices, and discourse about music, De Kloet demonstrates how "music is integrated into the fabric of everyday life, simultaneously pointing at the agency of the listener . . . as well as the structural power of sound" (139). In the musical lives discussed in the previous two chapters, music was integral to forging personal identities from a young age. At the same time, the historical moments, geographical locations, and socioeconomic positions in which the musicians grew up resulted in unique and varied experiences of access to popular musics from China and abroad.

For Xiao Dao, hearing George Michael and Madonna on illicit cassette tapes shared by his classmates at the Kunming Song and Dance Troupe boarding school "opened his eyes" and led him to imagine an "outside world" and a lifestyle far different from his own. Listening to the music was thus a form of vicarious mobility, where the auditory experience was intertwined with imagined travel. Relatedly, hearing Cui Jian's "Yi wu suo you" led him to imagine that he might meet like-minded individuals interested in making rock music in bigger cities within China. Together, these listening experiences inspired a major move that was only possible because of Deng Xiaoping's Reform and Opening Up and the new policies and practices in the Hainan SEZ that were central to reform. Thus, for Xiao Dao and others, vicarious mobility and actual mobility are woven together through their musical lives.

It is also interesting to note that two artists play an outsized role across several of these personal musical narratives: the Hong Kong rock band Beyond and the godfather of Chinese rock, Cui Jian. While Cui Jian's influence on the Chinese musicians who came after him has been widely discussed, Beyond is a far less acknowledged innovator that left a deep footprint not only in Hong Kong but throughout southern China and the Cantonese-speaking world. Beyond's music circulated widely in the 1980s and 1990s as part of a broader penetration of Gangtai music into the mainland. It was innovative musically and lyrically and was especially important for Cantonese speakers. Practically speaking, it was much more likely for someone living in a rural village or small town in southern China to hear Beyond than Cui Jian, or even more so, than western musicians such as Nirvana and Bob Dylan.

A Fei counts Beyond as his largest influence; he performed their songs exclusively in his first years as a performer and still couches his ideas of musical success in terms of comparisons to Beyond's lead singer Wong Ka-kui. For Gao Fei, Beyond played a similar role. He heard his cousin singing Beyond while riding on his bicycle and played their CD endlessly every time he visited his cousin's house. For A Gang and Xiao Li, performing covers of Beyond songs helped to develop their own songwriting abilities.

The centrality of a popular band from Hong Kong in all of these individuals' musical developments draws attention to South China as a transborder region where connections to Hong Kong and Taiwan are as important, if not more important, than connections to Beijing (Cartier 2001). This is also illustrated by Xiao Li's childhood saturated with Minnan-language pop music from Taiwan. He mentions the Taiwanese singer Chen Lei as a particularly large influence; growing up on an island separated from Taiwan by 200 miles of sea, neither Cantopop nor Mandopop were as significant for Xiao Li as music created in Taiwan that shared not only a language but in his words, a "life situation" (*shenghuo zhuangtai*) with that in Nan'ao.

Expanding outward from Cui Jian, Beyond, and other mainland and Hong Kong artists, these musicians came to listen to popular music from North America and Europe in evolving ways that reflect broader processes of integration with global culture as well as technological development. As discussed previously, for Xiao Dao, cassette tapes smuggled by relatives of well-off classmates introduced him to the music of Madonna and George Michael. For A Gang and others, moving from small towns to medium-sized cities gave them the opportunity to meet peers who were fans of western music. Thus, when A Gang moved to Liuzhou for vocational school, he heard and came to love The Eagles and Bob Dylan. Learning their songs was instrumental in teaching himself to play guitar and to compose music. Similarly, voraciously reading music magazines in college, Xiao Li developed a love for the Beatles; to this day, he can play and sing a broad roster of Beatles songs and recite the full lyrics from memory even though he speaks little other English.

Through the 1990s all of these musicians listened to these foreign musicians by buying dakou cassettes and CDs as well as pirated media in street stalls. While government regulations still required all foreign music to be approved for sale within China, *dakou die* circumvented this policy. However, it was still largely major pop stars that were available in these formats, and the peculiarities of chance led certain artists and songs to gain a stronghold among Chinese listeners. As a buyer and seller of dakou die, Fan Feng is a particularly interesting example. His success in the business was tied to developing a deep knowledge of Chinese and foreign music in order to recognize what was worth buying among boxes and boxes of discarded media sold in the electronics market.

By the mid-2000s the internet dramatically changed all of this. At this point the musical tastes and proclivities of each of these musicians moved toward the relatively obscure. Xiao Li's love of X-Japan and the visual kei movement is a good example, as is Gao Fei's passion for West Coast American emo rock. Xiao Dao's actual connections to Jamaican reggae through Rico Rodriguez evolved into a virtual connection to a reggae dub revival in Lyons, France, led by Hightone and other bands. The internet not only made a huge amount of music available but also made finding out information about this music much easier; unlike in earlier eras, music circulated into China in a much less chaotic and much more contextualized way. New modes of circulation and related availability of contextualizing information about music led to new vicarious mobilities that drew these musicians to Japan, Jamaica, France, Britain, and the American West Coast through experiences of listening.

"I WAS DETERMINED TO REALIZE MY CHERISHED DREAM"—A GANG

Music cannot be extricated from the economic structures of which it is a part. Though other chapters in this book focus on record labels and music venues as economic contexts and conduits for the music, these biographies bring attention to the shifting informal economies of which music is a part and to the economic precarity of devoting oneself to a life in music.

For many of the musicians, busking on the streets provided the first opportunity to earn money as a musician. Members of Mabang all began playing guitar as a hobby while working or training for other jobs and recount being surprised to discover that they could earn money doing it. The informal economy of busking was imbricated in Guangzhou's rapid urban development. A new subway system that served an increasingly affluent urban population provided a stage for many of these musicians, and unlicensed late-night outdoor eateries selling barbecue provided another venue. Busking was comparatively lucrative; A Fei and Fan Feng both mention that what they could earn busking was comparable to what they might earn working full time in a factory.

Busking led to more formal gigs in an expanding roster of nightlife establishments that featured live music. Western-style bars featuring alcohol sales, little or no food, dark lighting, and popular music played (often live) at a loud volume became increasingly popular in the 1990s in the region. Businesspeople in the many smaller cities in the Pearl River Delta that generated huge amounts of wealth as part of the region's industrial boom beginning in the 1980s opened establishments catering to local customers. Agents turned to Guangzhou to find entertainment for these bars. "We had no idea we had been duped until we were in the car, traveling three hours away," laughs A Gang, recounting landing a three-month gig in the nearby city of Zengcheng.

Band members formed part of a broader community of musicians, agents, and venue managers, and being a successful musician also meant developing a sense for the business. Of a friend who often called him for gigs, A Fei observed, "Yongtao was also a good businessman. He could find gigs at bars, at restaurants, for events. And he knew he could pay me less than he would have to pay other singers. But I'm still extremely thankful for the opportunity." Playing in these venues meant learning all the latest popular songs from mainland China, Taiwan, and Hong Kong and catering to evolving popular tastes: "If you're a musician, you need to know this music. You need to study it. You need to be able to play it," as A Fei observed.

Slowly, many of the musicians began to establish relative economic security through music. But this often entailed pursuing related side businesses. For Fan Feng, this was buying and selling dakou CDs. For several others, it involved working at music shops and sometimes teaching music lessons to children. And for Xiao Dao, this involved opening his own venues, gradually leading to opening the highly successful venues discussed in this book.

At the same time, the musicians all slowly developed desires to create original music. "I was determined to realize my cherished dream," reflects A Gang, recounting his decision to use a substantial sum of money to record and press a CD of original songs shortly after he was married. This involved self-reflexive creative processes, looking both inward and outward, and fusing diverse musics that the musicians had come to know through their mobile lives with musical styles, narratives, and dialects from their hometowns that they considered uniquely their own, as discussed extensively in the rest of this book.

To *Yinyue Shenghuo*

When I am on stage performing, listening to the music go by as I keep my reed wet and body ready, I have a habit of holding my saxophone up in front of me and staring into the reflection of myself, the other musicians, and the audience. Through the yellow brass, enlivened by scratches and patches of dull brown where the lacquer has worn away, refracted through the angular interruption of keys and mother of pearl, the stage folds in on itself to become all of the stages I have ever stood upon. I think of all the places that this brassy looking glass has brought me, of all the *yinyue shenghuo* intertwined with my own. I think of the chance encounters that guided me to Guangzhou when I was twenty-two, of the journey that has filled the ensuing years, of how my life became entangled with those with whom I now share the stage. As I inhale and bring the saxophone to my mouth, A Gang's singing voice reverberates:

> In order not to change the direction the river flows,
> I am willing to be like the moonlight,
> And write my dreams on the water's surface.
> In order not to change the direction the river flows,
> I am willing to be like a drop of water in the desert.
> After I evaporate, I will be carried away
> from the desert floating in a light breeze.
>
> "Bu gaibian heliu de fangxiang" ("Not Changing the Direction the River Flows"), lyrics and music by Ye Honggang, performed by Mabang, copyright 2015 Guangdong Xingwaixing Wenhua Chuanbo Youxian Gongsi

7
Sonic Infrastructures

In 2015 a young office worker in Shenzhen browses through genres and band names on her smartphone and streams a song by Wanju Chuanzhang. Hearing nostalgic lyrics sung in the dialect spoken in her hometown several hours away, she visits the band's page on the microblogging platform Weibo and begins to follow the band and their record label, Liuzhen Yinyue. Weeks later, she sees a post in her Weibo feed announcing an upcoming show by Wanju Chuanzhang at the live music venue B10, so she clicks a link to buy a ticket. On the day of the concert, she arrives to the venue after work and mingles with other audience members. Some, like her, are from Shantou, and have come to see a band that sings in the dialect spoken in their hometown. Others have followed Wanju Chuanzhang here from Guangzhou for the evening's events, spending just forty minutes aboard the newly opened high-speed rail that links the cities together and connects onward to cities throughout China that Wanju Chuanzhang will perform in on this tour organized by their record label.

In 1995 several college students listen to a cassette tape of George Michael in their dormitory. The cassette came to their boom box by way of a stall in a market in Guangzhou whose owner had in turn purchased it among several boxes of discarded tapes in secondhand electronics markets of Shantou, a Special Economic Zone (SEZ) a half day's bus ride away.

In 1965 a family is stirred from sleep by the sounds of the revolutionary song "The East Is Red" emanating from a speaker in the village square. The speaker is connected by copper wires to a local radio rediffusion station, where workers are preparing to spool a taped news broadcast delivered to them all the way from the capital of a young PRC.

Music changes alongside the mediums through which it travels. Today, Wanju Chuanzhang and Mabang's music is part of an emergent infrastructure of music venues, online platforms, record labels, and smartphones. Contextualizing these contemporary systems within a broader sonic archaeology of the PRC reveals how practices of listening are connected to political and economic rationalities and how the production of space occurs in part through infrastructural circulations of sound. By considering the music at the center of this book within a broader historical context while paying special attention to these infrastructures, this chapter argues that evolving modes of musical circulation and the listening practices associated with them reveal and contribute to broader transformations of state, society, and space.

By "sonic infrastructure," I mean to encompass and connect many things—the technical infrastructures that transmit mediated sounds, from copper wires to compact discs to online platforms; the political systems that contextualize and promote certain sounds; the informal social relationships that bring musicians and listeners together in new places; the corporate relationships that seek to influence what is heard, where, when, and by whom; and even the high-speed railroads that transport musicians on tour. I mean to suggest, furthermore, that the evolution and accretional layering of new and changing sonic infrastructures as well as the particular ways of listening that they bring about are interwoven with the layered economic, political, and cultural formations that have developed in China over the past half century.

Brian Larkin (2013, 328) defines infrastructures as "built networks that facilitate the flow of goods, people, or ideas and allow for their exchange over space." The anthropology of infrastructure, then, examines the "totality of both technical and cultural systems that create institutionalized structures whereby goods of all sorts circulate, connecting and binding people into collectivities" (Larkin 2008, 6). While Larkin's work demonstrates the utility of this approach to studies of media broadly, the particular media history of twentieth-century China highlights the value of such an approach when applied to sounding and listening practices in mediatized societies and brings attention to two strands I develop in this chapter that build on and nuance frameworks from both the anthropology of infrastructure and sound studies.[1]

From the top-down spatial hierarchy traced by wired radio in the 1960s to the translocal regional tours organized by Wanju Chuanzhang's record label in the 2010s, the materialities and spatialities of sonic infrastructures are embedded in and shaped by broader spatial formations that are in turn connected to economic and political rationalities. Inspired by Lefebvre (1991) and the geographers and theorists who draw on him—who remind us to see spatial reorganization as underpinning and bringing about higher-level economic and cultural reorganization—as well as a broader "spatial turn" in the humanities and social sciences (Soja 1989), many scholars have looked to issues of space, place, and scale as central to understanding and analyzing China's economic and political transformations (Cartier 2001; Duara 2009; Oakes and Schein 2006; Zhang 2001). Infrastructures undergird and reveal political rationalities and economic systems in which they are embedded (Collier 2011; Schnitzler 2008) and not only enable exchange over space but also the production of space (Graham and Marvin 2001). Sonic infrastructures are thus important windows onto intertwined political, economic, and spatial transformations in China. The spatial particularities of China, both its long-standing scalar system (Wang 2005, 9) and the rapid transformations it has undergone in recent decades, offer unique perspectives on the ways sonic circulations articulate with broader spatial formations.

Practices of listening also constitute subjectivities through the relational sensing of these spatialities. Understanding sounding and listening as important ways knowledge is constituted (Erlmann 2004; Ochoa Gautier 2014), my analysis is inspired by work that looks to practices and histories of listening in relation to intertwined questions of space, place, and self. Sensory experience and subjectivity cannot be extricated from questions of place; rather, as Casey (1996, 9) observes, "place is the most fundamental form of embodied experience—the site of a powerful fusion of self, space, and time." Feld's (2015) neologism of "acoustemology," which describes the "local conditions of acoustic sensation, knowledge and imagination embodied in the culturally particular sense of place resounding in Bosavi" (Feld 1996b, 90), not only highlights connections between sounding, listening, and knowing but also draws attention to ways notions of the self may be constituted in relation to the acoustic sensation of space and place.

Once again, the situation in contemporary China offers important perspectives on these issues. Many scholars link economic privatization in the reform era to a fundamental transformation of Chinese subjectivities and examine the ways socialist ideologies, authoritarian central control, and neoliberal elements commingle and reorient notions of the individual in part through spatial politics (Harvey 2007; Rofel 2007; Zhang 2001; Zhang and Ong 2008). In contemporary China, sounding and listening are important ways that "powers of the self" (Zhang and Ong 2008, 16) are articulated because of sound's ability to address simultaneously the economic, the political, and the affective (Hirschkind 2006). Thus, the approach to sonic infrastructures I am outlining addresses the underutilization of sound as an anthropological lens on these processes. In China and other industrialized and mediatized societies, culturally particular senses of place resound through culturally particular, historically constituted, and dynamically evolving sonic infrastructures.

Paying attention to issues of place, space, and scale, recent scholarship on regional Chinese media explores the ways in which the spatial configurations of media systems reflect and influence broader economic, political, and cultural formations (Sun and Chio 2012; Wang 2005; Zhao 2008). This scholarship focuses primarily on television, print media, and the internet and leaves the realm of the acoustic largely unaddressed. Sound—taken broadly to include both musical and linguistic sounds, as well as the soundscapes of which they are a part (Faudree 2012; Samuels et al. 2010)—has been historically central in the affective constitution of subjectivities, space, and nation in China (Tuohy 2001) and is an important dimension of these broader processes. Thus, the particular media history of twentieth-century China provokes an attention to the evolving ways in which sounds have circulated, circulations that have traced political and economic formations and the ways of imagining space they entail.

This chapter begins with discussions of two historical sonic infrastructures—wired radio in the Mao era and *dakou die* (literally "cutout discs," i.e., surplus CDs and other media) in the reform era—exploring the articulations of each with the political and spatial systems of the times in which they were most prominent. Through discussion of these two examples, I sketch some general observations about the material, spatial, and acoustic workings of sonic infrastructures. In the second half of the chapter, I apply this framework to a more extended ethnographic discussion of Xingwaixing Records, the company to which the two bands at the center of this book are signed. I discuss the ways that the various sonic infrastructures in which the bands participate reflect the modes of mobility and cosmopolitanism discussed throughout this book. I conclude by reflecting further on how the concept of sonic infrastructure nuances the more widely invoked concept of "soundscape" by attending to issues of mobility.

A key insight of scholars of postsocialism in China is that China's present does not mark a sharp break from the country's socialist past but rather a complex transformation from it (Zhang and Ong 2008; Zhang 2012). Since reform, sonic infrastructures in China have been reorganized by commercialization, new mobilities, restructuring of administrative hierarchies, and technological innovation. While wired broadcasting continues to exist only in small villages, state-run China Central Television (CCTV) still functions as an important mouthpiece of the state and is but one element, albeit a very important one, in a complex media landscape. The market stalls in Guangzhou that once exclusively sold dakou die now more often sell salvaged vinyl records to a new generation of affluent youth. Meanwhile, private sector corporations and local governments promote the burgeoning independent music scene of which Wanju Chuanzhang and Mabang are a part. Sonic infrastructures inevitably overlap and evolve, giving rise to new practices of listening and modes of musical circulation that reveal and contribute to broader economic, cultural, and political transformations.

Wired Radio

> The speaker wires stretch far and wide,
> They connect Beijing with our hearts. (Yu 1963, 11)

In 1963 this couplet, ascribed to farmers listening to a wired radio speaker in their rural home, introduced an article titled "Radio in the Villages" in *China Reconstructs*. The magazine was published in English, Chinese, Arabic, and several European languages and was circulated internationally as part of a major public relations strategy of the Chinese state. Depicting the underlying physical infrastructure of a media network (the speaker wires) as an affective connector between citizens dispersed throughout the nation and the capital in Beijing, this couplet encapsulates many dimensions of this most important sonic infrastructure in the first few decades of the PRC.

Building on what was already a robust radio network in the Republican Era, one of the first major media efforts of the Communist government was to centralize, consolidate, and expand nationalized radio broadcasting beginning with localized efforts in the 1940s in Yan'an and accelerating nationwide after the founding of the PRC in 1949. Private radio stations in major urban areas as well as stations formerly operated by the Nationalist government were commandeered to form the backbone of the earliest wireless broadcast network, the Central People's Broadcasting Station (Zhongyang Renmin Guangbo Diantai). A 1950 editorial in the *People's Daily* titled "All Levels of Leadership Ought to Effectively Make Use of Radio Broadcasting" (Geji lingdao jiguan yingdang youxiao de liyong wuxiandian guangbo 1950) summarized the importance the state placed on radio from the very earliest days of the PRC:

> Radio broadcasting is the single most powerful educational and propaganda tool for the masses. From its inception to today, the radio broadcasting undertaking has only spanned five years. However, owing to the people's mighty victory in the War of Liberation [between the Communists and Nationalists, 1945–1949], radio broadcasting has experienced rapid development in a period of little over one year. Nationwide, there are now fifty-one radio stations and a large audience of frequent listeners. . . . More than a year later, radio broadcasting has proved its worth and is an important educational and propaganda

> tool for the masses with outstanding potential. This is especially the case in places where transportation and communications are inconvenient; for the large number of illiterate people; and in cases where newspaper circulation is difficult to achieve. If we are adept at using radio broadcasting, it can become enormously useful.

Outlining potentials for future development, this article foreshadowed the central role that radio broadcasting would play for decades to come.

An even more important part of China's early radio infrastructure was a wired radio rediffusion network that was established in the early 1950s and rapidly expanded over the subsequent decades (Li 2012, 2014; Liu 1971). This wired radio network linked public address speakers in public spaces, homes, and workplaces throughout rural and urban China to sounds emanating from the national capital. Broadcasts from Beijing—political speeches, news, and musical programming—were distributed to local rebroadcasting stations and interspersed with locally produced content, including agricultural information, weather reports, and news commentary. This sonic infrastructure connected much of China's population though wired public loudspeakers that by official counts numbered over one hundred million by the late 1970s (Zhongguo de youxian guangbo 1988; Li 2007).

The importance of wired radio in early PRC efforts at national integration has been discussed by many scholars of media and communications in China (e.g., Chang 1989), who most often cite two factors as instrumental in its promotion. First, it was a media infrastructure that was relatively inexpensive and easy to install (Jan 1967, 307). It enabled prerecorded programs to be distributed throughout China's vast countryside while allowing for locally relevant content and local language programming to be interspersed with programs recorded in Beijing. Second, it reached an audience that in the 1950s was largely illiterate, as the *People's Daily* article I quote above notes. Thus, early efforts at national integration in China were based in sound more than any other sensory medium, and imagining the Chinese nation happened in large part through mediated listening practices.

Furthermore, music was one of the most important cultural expressions and political tools of revolutionary movements in China from before the establishment of the PRC well through the Cultural Revolution (Bryant 2007; Holm 1991; Hung 1996). While there were other means by which citizens listened to and learned revolutionary songs, wired radio was nonetheless a significant medium through which the sounds of this new form of song were not only heard but heard in particular technologically and spatially mediated ways that situated them as sonic expressions of the nation.

In a short nostalgic piece in *Suzhou Magazine*, Chang Xin (2014, 15) reflects on memories of the wired broadcasting system during the Cultural Revolution:

> During that time, our relationship with the loudspeaker was so inseparable you could say it was our alarm clock and our lullaby. At five in the morning, the broadcast would punctually begin, and the mellifluous sounds of "The East Is Red" would fill our dreams. Shortly thereafter, there was the agricultural program, the educational program, the weather forecast, and a summary of the day's news, and you'd listen as you struggled to get out of bed. In the evening, at 10 o'clock sharp, the day's programs would end, and the majestic sounds of the Internationale would hasten you to sleep.

This passage illustrates several points. First, the author highlights the radio's role in regulating the schedules of citizens; through wired radio, "time discipline" (Thompson 1967) was instilled through a central broadcasting system, and the state exercised power over citizens through regulation of work schedules crucial to China's rapid industrialization. As demonstrated by Corbin (1998) with reference to village bells in eighteenth- and nineteenth-century France, public sounds may regulate citizens' lives by structuring time and imposing a particular symbolic order. Second, the particular "soundmarks" (Schafer 1977) the author links to important times of day are musical; they are iconic revolutionary songs that are central to what Tuohy (2001) calls China's "sonic nationalism," forming part of "a monumental piece composed through the discourse and practices of twentieth-century musical nationalism that link them to each other within the organizational form of the Chinese nation" (107). Through the musical regulation of time, listeners were interpellated (Althusser 1971) as citizens of a young People's Republic.

In describing cassette sermons in Egypt, Hirschkind (2006, 2) writes, "the contributions of this aural media to shaping the contemporary moral and political landscape . . . lies not simply in its capacity to disseminate ideas . . . but in its effect on the human sensorium, on the affects, sensibilities, and perceptual habits of its vast audience." Understanding that media technologies shape culturally specific practices of listening that bind the political and the affective, it is also important to emphasize the particular ways that wired radio functioned to mediate between state and publics in China. Liu (1971) argues that radio was one of the most important tools of mass media in the socialist era because of practices of "collective listening" (120) that conjoined the sounds broadcast from Beijing with face-to-face interactions with local cadres in order to strengthen and localize national messages. A 1956 article in the *People's Daily* titled "The Peasants' Beloved Friend: Wired Broadcasting"

(Li 1956) lends credence to Liu's assertion and illustrates the intended modes of sociability that were associated with listening to wired broadcasting, describing scenes of villagers of all ages converging to listen to their village's loudspeaker together, singing along with musical broadcasts of revolutionary songs, and discussing the political messages being broadcast. Though the levels, modes, and attitudes of engagement by peasants with wired radio were no doubt more varied and complex than the idealized picture painted in an official newspaper, official accounts are nonetheless helpful in understanding the models and intentions behind this ubiquitous media system. The article ends with a short rhyming verse ascribed to Hou Dehe, a blacksmith and amateur opera singer in the village that is the subject of the article:

> Wired radio is all around,
> Old and young both love its sound.
> We can hear the nation's biggest news,
> We can hear [Henan opera star] Chang Xiangyu singing tunes.
> We can know when gales will blow,
> And when our seeds we ought to sow.
> Let's support our country's industrialization,
> And install wired radio loudspeakers throughout the nation!
>
> (Quoted in Li 1956)

In socialist era China, sounding and listening were central to how the nation and hierarchies of place subsumed under it were sensed. Returning to the short essay by Chang Xin (2014, 15) about wired radio during the Cultural Revolution offers a more personal view of wired radio and furthermore ties this discussion back to the broader topic of sonic infrastructures:

> Every day I woke up early to make a trip to the sports stadium before breakfast. At the first glimmer of light, with the dusky street lamps reflecting my own shortness of breath as I jogged, the program "A Song a Week" would begin, and the loudspeaker on every door of every house came on, suddenly loud and suddenly soft, causing these few little streets and little alleys to thread together and form one large surround sound stereo speaker. Running to the rhythm of the music, my mood soared upwards with the sound of song.

In comparing the interaction of multiple speakers to a "large surround sound stereo speaker," this passage points to some ways in which listening practices were embedded in the sensing of space. As a material infrastructure consisting of local rebroadcasting stations, copper wires, transducers, and loudspeakers visible in the home and the workplace, this infrastructure connected citizens to the nation's capital through the sensorium, functioning not only through the sounds it transmitted but also through its mere visibility. In addition, wired radio not only sonically encompassed the nation but also reinforced a particular way of thinking about space and of relating the local to the national. As Sun and Chio (2012, 13) have observed, like many media systems in the socialist era, it "mirrored and was metonymic of a spatial hierarchy" that was highly centralized and was formed along administrative boundaries and scales. The speakers that Chang described did, as he observed, form a massive surround sound system. And while the speakers in his neighborhood were networked together to form an unbroken soundtrack to his morning jog, they also connected to a central rediffusion station that was in turn connected to Beijing by wire, wireless transmission, or, more often, the physical transportation of prerecorded programs on audio tape. Thus, the speakers on doorways that Chang describes were nodes in a complex sonic infrastructure that mapped onto a spatioadministrative hierarchy with Beijing at the center, broadcasting sounds intimately connected to Communist ideology, economic collectivization, and industrialization. The political, then, was sensed spatially and affectively by means of this built infrastructure designed to encompass the nation sonically.

I now fast forward several decades and turn to a second sonic infrastructure that is representative of the marked shift in China's political and economic rationalities beginning in the 1980s.

Dakou Die

Dakou die, known in English as "cutout discs," are surplus media discarded by (mostly) North American and European record companies and retailers—CDs, cassettes, and DVDs, often marked by a small incision in the spine of the case or the outer edge of the disc itself. Ubiquitous throughout China in street stalls, at electronics markets, and on the shelves of music fans in the 1990s and 2000s, dakou die and their role in the emergence and evolution of China's domestic music scene and market have been extensively discussed in the journalistic and academic presses in China and abroad (De Kloet 2010; Li 2020).

Many popularly circulating terms gesture toward the wider importance of dakou die in forging generational and subcultural identities as well as the medium's connection to broader cultural transformations. These include: *dakou qingnian* (dakou youth), *dakou yidai* (dakou generation), and *dakou wenhua* (dakou culture). Music critic, experimental musician, and poet Yan Jun's verse about dakou die connects dakou die's sources in the waste discarded by other nations to their generative role in Chinese youth culture in the 1990s: "We are the 'Dakou Generation.' We are chewing the rubbish, swallowing the fragments of the world, growing vigorously" (Yan, n.d.).

Dakou die circulation brings attention to one way that China's full-speed and sometimes chaotic entrance into neoliberal globalization beginning in the 1980s was audible in unusual and unexpected ways. Following Yan's insight, it is important to acknowledge that the circulation of dakou die to and within China was embedded in a broader infrastructure—the global waste trade—which connected SEZs in southern China to Europe and North America via the sale and transportation of e-waste including physical media. Attending to the connections between dakou die and this broader infrastructure also brings attention to the overlooked ecological, material, and economic contexts of dakou die as a media system (Maxwell and Miller 2012).

David Harvey (2007, 120) calls the coincidence of the turn to neoliberal policies in the US and Britain and Deng Xiaoping's initiation of economic reforms in the aftermath of the Cultural Revolution "a conjectural accident of world-historical significance." Just as global capitalism was restructuring, China emerged in the 1980s as a powerhouse of industrial production with an enormous reserve of labor. During the same period, a global trade in waste was rapidly expanding. E-waste, plastics, and other potential recyclables—those that either require significant labor in order to realize value or carry significant toxic risk in the extraction process—were circulated as negative commodities from the Global North to the Global South (Frey 2012; Laha 2015). Shantou, a port city in eastern Guangdong Province and one of the five original SEZs, became a major hub in the global waste infrastructure. With Shantou's port as a destination for the world's trash, communities around Shantou became major trash sorting facilities, and the markets of Shantou became a destination for buyers who resold dakou die, among other things, throughout China.

By the 1990s dakou die were arguably the most important medium through which foreign popular music entered China. Picked up by salvagers in the trash markets in Shantou and resold through middlemen who brought them to secondhand markets in cities throughout China, dakou die inspired a generation of listeners and musicians by supplementing and inspiring an emerging domestic popular music industry, bypassing broadcast media that was privatizing but still controlled by the state, and circumventing strict laws regarding the import or domestic reissue of foreign books, films, and music. Dakou die articulated a developing youth culture and concomitant new modes of being an individual and linked the PRC to global economic and cultural flows through newly established SEZs in southern China. Thus, a sonic byproduct of neoliberal globalization in China could be heard through this peculiar sonic infrastructure embedded in the global waste trade.

As sonic infrastructure, dakou die manifest China's reentry into global cultural flows in the late twentieth century and directly link this reconnection to a process of neoliberal globalization in which China plays a central role. Dakou die are thus deeply tied to the Reform and Opening Up policy of Deng Xiaoping and are an example of the unintended cultural consequences of economic reform as well as the eroding state control of what was heard, where, when, and by whom. Official culture was circumvented by new media flows enabled by small-scale entrepreneurialism, and neoliberal desiring subjects (Rofel 2007) were formed through new listening practices. At the same time, a spatial hierarchy with Beijing at the center subtly shifted toward a reintegration with European and North American urban centers mediated through SEZs that functioned as portals to faraway places, elevating the role of these cities—and southern China more broadly—in national life.

Just as the sensory effects of wired radio in part functioned through the visibility of the speaker itself, the cutouts in the sides of dakou die are scars that bring attention to the unusual voyage that a polycarbonate plastic container of sound has made. Thus, like in the case of the wired radio loudspeakers, dakou die highlight one of the key insights of the anthropology of infrastructure—that the poetic dimensions of infrastructures are sensed alongside the goods they transmit; that is, sonic infrastructures act as signifiers in and of themselves, signifiers in which the "palpability of the sign" (Jakobson 1960) is a dominant and determining function. This echoes to some degree Marshal McLuhan's (1964) famous axiom, "the medium is the message." Put more simply, the ways that sounds circulate are as important as the sounds themselves, and listening involves not just hearing but also sensing the infrastructures that transmit mediated sounds and in turn sensing the political and economic rationalities that undergird these particular sonic infrastructures.

Having discussed wired radio in the Mao era and dakou die in the reform era in order to further develop the infrastructural approach to circulations of sound that I am proposing in this chapter, I now turn to a more extended discussion of Xingwaixing Records, applying such an approach to the contemporary sonic infrastructures most important to the bands at the center of this book.

Xingwaixing Records and China's Transforming Music Industry

"CLOSE LISTENING WITH A POINT OF VIEW"

In the late 1990s and early 2000s, what started as a relatively obscure and niche-market record company based in Guangzhou met with outsized success and eclipsed its competitors to become a pioneer of a transforming global music industry as well as one of China's largest distributors of CDs. Out of the dust of a crumbling music industry challenged both by piracy and by new digital music distribution services, Guangdong Xingwaixing Wenhua Chuanbo Youxian Gongsi (henceforth Xingwaixing, English name Starsing Records) grew through innovative business practices that taken together represent a structural shift in the Chinese music industry. As sonic infrastructures, Xingwaixing's ventures reflect and contribute to spatial reconfigurations tied to China's evolving economic and political rationalities and have given rise to listening practices that constitute new notions of self and subjectivity in contemporary China.

Xingwaixing was founded by Zhou Xiaochuan in 1997 and started out by recording, producing, publishing, and promoting CDs of traditional Chinese instrumental music. Finding the market somewhat limited, Zhou began to seek out cooperative partnerships with major record companies. At first, Zhou targeted, in his words, "comparatively unpopular music, really anything but mainstream pop music" (personal communication, December 12, 2014),[2] which included western classical music as well as jazz, rock, world music, and new age. In part Zhou sought out music with copyright values that were significantly depreciated, especially for Chinese distribution rights. What set Xingwaixing's CD publishing business apart, however, was an emphasis on introducing the music in its context. Speaking of that time in the company's history, Zhou emphasizes the efforts the company took to make accurate translations of lyrics ("no matter whether it was French or English or Gaelic or an African dialect") as well as writing well-researched introductions to the artists and the music in Chinese for the liner notes. This contrasted with the widely available dakou die, pirated CDs, and MP3 downloads available at the time, which offered listeners schizophonic (Schafer 1977) listening experiences that separated sound from source and context.[3]

Zhou's philosophy is encapsulated in Xingwaixing's corporate slogan, *You guandian de lingting*, which can be translated as "Close listening with a point of view." *Lingting* is a compound verb that describes close, respectful listening and is often used in reference to live performances or recordings of art music or important speeches. As articulated in this slogan, it implies an informed experience of close listening that inspires both affective connection to the music and reflection on the music's meaning and significance in a global context. The "point of view" is described in corporate literature as "a way of thinking arrived at through meticulous reflection." Thus, Xingwaixing has positioned itself as not only a publisher of recorded music but as a tastemaker, a curator of quality music. As Zhou himself relates, "From the start, we have recommended good music according to our own aesthetic standards. So, a lot of people have learned about music through our recommendations and through buying our CDs, and over the long term, they develop confidence in our brand."

The expansion of Xingwaixing beginning in the late 1990s was closely tied to broader economic development, privatization of industry, and media liberalization that started in the 1980s in which southern China broadly (and the Pearl River Delta region specifically) played a major role. Discussing this period in China, Zhang and Ong (2008, 2) suggest that new economic policies of the reform era shifted much more than the economic rationality of China and that privatization may be understood as an "ensemble of techniques that free up not only entrepreneurialism but also powers of the self." Under China's particular fusion of neoliberalism and socialism, privatization tied together new forms of economic participation with new forms of selfhood and desire (Rofel 2007), giving rise to new kinds of subjectivities. In this context, Xingwaixing's "close listening with a point of view" may be understood as a privatized listening practice that is representative of new notions of selfhood, consumerism, and desire in postsocialist China.

This listening practice was enabled, furthermore, by new business practices and infrastructures pioneered by Xingwaixing. In order to maximize profit, Zhou sought to consolidate and better monetize the business by controlling more aspects of the supply chain. Thus, CDs, jewel cases, and printed liner notes were manufactured in factories in the Pearl River Delta that were closely controlled by Xingwaixing. In addition to distributing through major established media resellers, Xingwaixing also began to sell through its own online portal as well as through a network of physical storefronts throughout China. Taken together, this corporatized music industry with many cogs represents a privatized sonic infrastructure tied to the economic rise of the Pearl River Delta region. There is a pointed connection to transnational culture that is not piecemeal and chaotic like that of the dakou era but that is regulated by nonstate actors—educated cosmopolitans whose "point of view" (*guandian*) appeals to an emerging middle-class consumer who performs his own economic rise through "close listening" (*lingting*). As Yu (2009, 9) and other scholars of media and communications in China argue, "the ideational change from 'masses' (qunzhong) to 'audience' (guanzhong) [was] a defining moment in Chinese media culture." The slogan *You guandian de lingting* encapsulates this change; consumers who purchase CDs published by Xingwaixing perform "close listening with a point of view" and listen from a privatized "point of view," which is a radical departure from the "point of view" cultivated in relation to earlier sonic infrastructures.

SONIC AND SPATIAL TRANSFORMATIONS IN CONTEMPORARY CHINA

In addition to new forms of listening promoted by Xingwaixing, as discussed in the previous section, the physical linkages and musical circulations promoted reveal and reinforce spatial reorganizations that have underpinned China's broader transformations in recent decades. In China, a four-tiered scalar hierarchy of province, district, county, and township under one central capital has a historical legacy of nearly two thousand years, and it persists as a defining spatioadministrative construct (Oakes and Schein 2006, 13; Wang 2005, 9). During the Mao era, this was the most important such construct, and it was mirrored by the physical infrastructure of the wired radio system discussed earlier. Several intertwined developments have partially disrupted or complicated this spatial and scalar system beginning in the early reform era and accelerating in recent years.

First, on an administrative level, the establishment of SEZs (beginning with Shenzhen, Zhuhai, Shantou, Xiamen, and Hainan, all in southern China, in the early 1980s) drastically disrupted this system by introducing alternative economic and political units that jumped scales and were intended to forge new linkages between China and the world through designated conduits, as highlighted in the previous discussion of dakou die. Second, China's rapid urbanization has elevated cities other than Beijing into important economic, political, and cultural centers. Third, "transboundary formations" (Cartier 2001) such as the Pearl River Delta (Zhujiang Sanjiaozhou) and Greater Bay Area (Yuegang'ao Dawanqu) articulate new spatial formations that reorient scalar constructs, integrate the Special Administrative Regions (and former colonies of foreign powers) of Hong Kong and Macau, and connect to Chinese-speaking communities outside the boundaries of the PRC state. Finally and most importantly, all of the above spatial transformations have instigated and been furthered by new mobilities and modes of translocal belonging (Oakes and Schein 2006) that have arisen alongside economic reforms. These new mobilities and modes of belonging are deeply tied to China's *huji zhidu* (household register system), commonly referred to as the *hukou* system (Chan 2009), as discussed in greater detail in the introduction.

Against these backdrops, it is first worth noting that Xingwaixing Records is based in Guangzhou. Guangzhou is China's third largest city, and it has played a central role in the economic transformation of China in recent decades. Being located in Guangzhou is significant particularly in the context of what several scholars of the media have observed as "a reconfigured place hierarchy in the nation [that] has ushered in a new national mediascape featuring the Pearl River Delta as a region distinctively associated with real potentials to rival the centre in terms of political, social and cultural impact" (Sun and Chio 2012, 4; Zhao 2008). From the establishment of the original SEZs in the 1980s through Deng Xiaoping's Southern Tour in 1992 that cemented associations of the region with economic reforms, southern China was often characterized as relatively culturally liberal and more globally engaged than other regions of China. This provides an important context for the ways in which Xingwaixing forged links with the rest of the world through institutionalized circulations of recorded sound.

From its base in Guangzhou and beginning in the 1990s, Xingwaixing's primary business consisted of licensing and rereleasing albums from the rest of the world, thereby reintegrating larger numbers of Chinese listeners into global sonic flows from which the PRC had been largely isolated during the 1950s through the 1980s. As Xingwaixing expanded, Zhou sought out contractual relationships with major international record companies as exclusive agent or partner. As the exclusive mainland China agent of Universal and partner to Sony and Warner, Xingwaixing is deeply tied to the global recording industry. In addition, Xingwaixing is the exclusive mainland China agent to several major Asian independent labels that represent Chinese-language stars, including Taiwan's Rock Records and Tapes (Gunshi Changpian) and Hong Kong's Gold Typhoon (Jinpai Dafeng). In these ways, Xingwaixing has been an important actor in linking Chinese listeners to musical sounds from around the world and reconnecting the PRC to global and regional East Asian circulations of music.

LIUZHEN YINYUE AND YYQ

New business practices pursued by Xingwaixing in recent years have creatively engaged new opportunities enabled by evolving technologies, changing demographics, and shifting cultural politics. According to Zhou, in 2014 CDs accounted for about 70 percent of Xingwaixing's business. The remaining 30 percent was an expanding portfolio of new business activities, many of which connect music makers and listeners in China in new ways and in so doing trace and reinforce translocal connections between places within and beyond China. The spatialities of these new sonic infrastructures markedly contrast with not only the spatioadministrative hierarchy mimicked by wired radio and the ad hoc global space echoed by dakou die but also with the global and regional integration exhibited by the more traditional music industry model pursued by Xingwaixing in the 1990s and early 2000s.

Mabang and Wanju Chuanzhang have been central to these new initiatives. As discussed in previous chapters, it is significant that both of these bands are based in Guangzhou, but for each, an alternative regional identity is central to their musical concept, and elements of that regional identity—the dialect being sung, the lyrical themes and content, and elements of musical style—are self-consciously reformulated and recombined with cosmopolitan and globally oriented musical practices. In the case of each of the bands, the music itself articulates new modes of spatial belonging that are mirrored by the sonic infrastructures through which the music reaches listeners, modes that may broadly be termed *translocal*, implying a capacity to belong to multiple places and a mode of existence in between places. Such translocal spatial imaginaries and modes of belonging are harnessed and promoted through related sonic infrastructures that Xingwaixing has assembled, including a sublabel devoted to independent bands, Liuzhen Yinyue, and a social-networking site, YYQ.com.

Liuzhen Yinyue is a sublabel under Xingwaixing that describes itself in corporate literature as "dedicated to the support and promotion of independent and original music" (*duli yinyue* and *yuanchuang yinyue*). These two terms deserve unpacking. The first term, *duli yinyue* (independent music), may be understood within the context of a transnationally circulating "indie" ideology. As Keith Negus (1992, 16) put it, "the 'indie'—imbued with connotations of a radical, alternative and more sincere way of producing music . . . operate[s] as a romantic ideology informing . . . buying habits, [and connecting] the value of the music [with] the record label releasing it."[4] Paying attention to economic logics behind a counterculture ethos that is increasingly both mainstream and global, it is worth mentioning that the winner of the 2016 season of the popular music reality television series Zhongguo Hao Gequ was Hanggai, the Mongolian folk fusion band and longtime darling of China's independent music scene whose albums, incidentally, have been rereleased on the Liuzhen label.

The second term, *yuanchuang yinyue* (original music), emphasizes forms of creativity as they relate to (somewhat idealized) *duli* modes of production, positioning "original" music in opposition to mainstream Mandarin-language pop music. The names of the sublabel, Liuzhen Yinyue in Chinese and Zen Music in English, highlight this strategy. The Chinese name, Liuzhen Yinyue, may be translated as Keeping Real Music and expands into the sublabel's slogan, which foregrounds authenticity and innovation: "*Liu*xia zhege shidai *zhen*shi de shengyin" (Preserving the real sounds of this era). Zen Music, the unrelated English name, on the other hand, points to the global ambitions of the label, deploying a commonly romanticized aspect of East Asian culture.

While the sublabel was originally conceived along Xingwaixing's original business model of licensing, rereleasing, and marketing previously released albums to new audiences but with a focus on independent music from throughout China, the sublabel altered its practice in 2014 and has since functioned as an important conduit for independent musicians particularly in southern China. As a new, small, and experimental part of a much larger corporation, Liuzhen Yinyue seeks to integrate traditional music-industry business models with new strategies to reach a listening public that is both fragmented and networked; globally conscious, yet devoted to local and regional identities. Focusing on artist management and live commercial performances more than on the distribution of recordings, Liuzhen signed four bands from around southern China (including Mabang and Wanju Chuanzhang) and celebrated its formal launch in June 2014 in Guangzhou. Each band signed a five-year contract with Liuzhen, which receives a portion of all performance fees that the band receives in exchange for managing the band and giving it access to the significant resources at its disposal for recording, branding, and promotion. During its first years in existence, it was closely intertwined with a second venture by Xingwaixing, YYQ.com (*Yinyue Quan*, literally Music Circle).

In recent years online platforms and smartphone apps have become major avenues through which independent bands promote themselves and fans discover new music. While general social media platforms Weibo, Weixin, and Douban remain dominant in China, Xingwaixing's startup, YYQ.com, sought to become a major player by offering a social-networking site devoted entirely to music and, more importantly, an integrated platform through which bands could promote themselves, distribute their music, gain performance opportunities, reach out to fans, and even custom order and sell band merchandise to fans.[5] Zhou describes YYQ.com in terms of a larger business strategy to sell not CDs or even MP3s but "a service that permeates every aspect of customers' lives" (Ye 2011).[6]

YYQ frequently sponsors performances showcasing diverse up-and-coming bands at venues in Guangzhou and other cities and employs a full-time photographer and music reporter to document performances for feature stories on their website while encouraging sharing of these stories through other social media. YYQ's efforts point to and attempt to harness the power of rapidly developing and ever-evolving networks of niche-market music scenes devoted to specific genres ranging from folk and reggae to hip-hop and metal. Zhou describes this as a reaction to the "many market subdivisions . . . that have arisen with the whole internet world. Music fans can hear all the music from all over the world. Fans can develop an appetite for all sorts of different things. However, to engage in actual musical interaction is in fact quite difficult." YYQ aims to facilitate this "actual musical interaction" and to monetize it. YYQ's on-the-ground connections to local venues in multiple cities thus foster local and translocal music scenes that self-consciously demarcate themselves from mainstream Mandarin-language pop.

In summer 2014 I traveled with Wanju Chuanzhang and Mabang as they performed in six cities in Guangdong and Fujian Provinces on the first leg of a cross-country tour that was intended to function as a national rollout of the Liuzhen Yinyue brand. Sponsored by Xingwaixing, YYQ.com, and Liuzhen Yinyue, "Yueye shiba cheng" (*Yueye* is a pun that elides the words "cross-country" and "music"; *shiba cheng* means simply "eighteen cities") planned to bring six bands to established local music venues in eighteen cities for three dates each. Each night featured two of Liuzhen Yinyue's bands along with one local band from the host city.

The most well-attended shows of the first leg of the tour were in Xiamen and Quanzhou. Both Wanju Chuanzhang and Yizhi (also known by their English name, Afinger), a hip-hop group from Shantou also signed to Liuzhen, sing in Min subdialects of Chinese and have developed followings throughout Min-speaking areas in northern Guangdong and Fujian Provinces. In this way, Liuzhen Yinyue's business strategy draws on the already deeply translocal music scenes and fan networks that have grown alongside China's independent music scene in recent decades. It also accesses communities of listeners aligned by various local dialects, a topic I explore at length in chapter 4. At the same time, the tour attempts to cross-market unfamiliar bands to new audiences and to harness the reach of mainstream media such as radio and television in order to bring music that has often been celebrated precisely for its niche-market appeal and local identity to a larger audience, resembling efforts elsewhere in the world (Garland 2014).

As sonic infrastructures, YYQ.com and Liuzhen Yinyue build on and further enable actual and vicarious mobilities that connect smaller cities and rural areas to major urban centers. The translocal connections they forge are bidirectional. Liuzhen Yinyue has largely signed artists who hail from outside major metropolitan areas, but its corporate offices, recording studio, and most of the musicians themselves are based in Guangzhou, and it reaches listeners through live shows it organizes in smaller cities as well as through social media and online streaming services accessed anywhere through smartphones. These translocal linkages mirror the modes of spatial belonging that many people in southern China have experienced in their mobile lives and trace the economic connections that have enabled the region to maintain a leading role in China's development. At the same time, these infrastructures enable connections to listeners in other regions of China and in the broader world while promoting the status of southern China as an important center for cultural innovation, thus strengthening a consolidated southern Chinese regional identity. As audiences and performers connect in new ways and major corporations adapt to a changing listening public, a new kind of sonic infrastructure emerges consisting of corporations, websites, independent music venues, radio stations, smartphones, and informal fan networks. Through privatized practices of "close listening with a point of view" promoted by Xingwaixing, this sonic infrastructure enables the new spatial configurations central to China's broader transformations to be heard and felt through circulations of the music of bands like Wanju Chuanzhang and Mabang.

Sound, City, Soil: Sonic Infrastructures and Soundscapes

Shengxiang, chengshi, nitu. In June of 2013, Taigu Hui, a luxury mall in Guangzhou's Tianhe District, featured an exhibition of collaborative works by folk musician Zhu Fangqiong and sculptor Zhou Song under this title, translated by the organizers as "Sound, City, Soil." Staged in Taigu Hui's Glass Box, a large, airy space perched atop the mall with commanding views of the sky and the city, the exhibit featured thirteen ceramic works by the artists. Each work encased a sounding high-fidelity speaker within a flowing and uniquely resonant ceramic shape with finishes ranging from the raw red color of earth to the flawlessly smooth white of traditional porcelain.

A reporter covering the exhibition for the Guangzhou daily newspaper *Xinxi Shibao* wrote, "Art is not mysterious, it is not distant—it is a part of life. The vitality and appeal of art allows city dwellers, surrounded by the noises of the city, to find a way to solitarily reflect. It makes you ponder, in this forest of earth, every chunk of earth has its own unique sound—each, transmitting different messages, telling different stories, waiting for you to listen" (Xu 2013).

Forged from the clay of the earth, each speaker produced by Zhu and Zhou has a unique resonance—the electrical signals that vibrate the speakers encased in ceramic become sounds that are in turn altered by the particular shape and constitution of the earth through which they resonate. Observing the beautiful form of the speaker, as the *Guangzhou Daily* reporter noted, a listener is reminded that all sounds are perceived multisensorily, and furthermore, in particular spatially situated ways.

Sound, City, Soil—this sculpture exhibition provokes reflection on several questions that this chapter has explored. How are sounds, cities, and space coconstituted in contemporary China? How does sound—particularly when heard through technologies as varied as public loudspeakers, discarded CDs, and headphones attached to smartphones—create senses of space and place through its mobility? How do the material and spatial qualities of the media through which sounds circulate inflect the ways the sounds themselves are sensed? Finally, what is the relationship between these sonically and materially constituted senses of space and place and economic, political, and cultural formations?

In Zhu and Zhou's sculptural works, sounds emitted from speakers are transformed by their embeddedness in pieces of earth shaped by the sculptors' hands. For many attendees who saw, heard, and felt these sculptures, this exhibition brought attention to the ways that sounds may be multisensorily perceived through and within the materials and spaces that carry them, a concept that resonates with the theoretical project of this chapter and with discussions in sound studies more broadly.

The turn to a sounded anthropology (Samuels et al. 2010; Porcello et al. 2010) has been enormously generative of critical concepts and approaches for engaging with sound (Novak and Sakakeeny 2015). Examining the relationships between sound, space, and self, the approach grounded in sonic infrastructures that I have outlined in this chapter draws inspiration from, but also aims to nuance, the soundscape concept (Samuels et al. 2010; Schafer 1977), which is widely invoked but has also been critiqued for its universalizing tendencies and for the vague ways in which it is sometimes popularly deployed (Kelman 2010; Sterne 2014).

Like the soundscape construct, sonic infrastructures "simultaneously [index] a set of sonic-spatial practices, the metadiscourses that describe them, and the cultural and sensory conditions that make it possible to—even passively—experience sonic space in certain terms" (Sterne 2014, 183). Like a soundscape, a sonic infrastructure is a "publicly circulating entity that is a produced effect of social practices, politics, and ideologies while also being implicated in the shaping of those practices, politics, and ideologies" (Samuels et al. 2010, 330). However, by invoking infrastructure, I mean to draw attention to the complexities of the technical and cultural systems that make up soundscapes in contemporary societies and to attend to the ways these soundscapes and media systems may also intertwine with broader movements, practices, discourses, and objects. I mean to bring attention to the materialities and spatialities of the broad array of structures through which sounds are mobile and to the historical layering of systems that constitute an infrastructural whole. Questioning the spatial understanding of "landscape" implied in many uses of the term *soundscape*, I also mean to engage with space not as a predetermined category but as a process and to complicate the "-scape" of the soundscape with a critical ear to spatial processes as inherently economic, political, and cultural.

These interventions are provoked by on-the-ground realities in contemporary China, where configurations of space, notions of self, and structures of media systems have transformed in rapid and sometimes chaotic ways that bring attention to the broader intertwinedness and occasional disjunctures of these transformations. In China (and elsewhere), sonic infrastructures both reveal and shape the political and economic systems in which they are embedded. They contribute to new ways of configuring space; of understanding the nested relationships between the local, the national, and the global; and of molding subjectivities under shifting and complex political rationalities. Like Zhu and Zhou's clay speakers, they do all this not only by transmitting sounds but by being sensed—heard, seen, and felt—themselves.

EPILOGUE

Music, China, and the Political

In the decade leading up to the establishment of the PRC in 1949, musical workers trained at the Lu Xun Academy of Art traveled throughout rural China transcribing local folk songs and reworking them so that, infused with new political content, the sounds and words could return to the voices and minds from which they came and inspire revolutionary consciousness.[1] These arts workers might have walked some of the same roads that imperial musicians traveled in the Han Dynasty (206 BCE—220 CE), sent by the emperor throughout the vast landmass he ruled to collect folk songs. Hearing these songs, the emperor hoped to better understand and govern these diverse regions. Remolding them into ritual music, he hoped to bring about social harmony through musical performance.[2]

In 2008 I traveled through rural Yunnan Province with the band San Duojiao, collaborating with musicians in several villages and small towns where band members (or their parents) had grown up. Band members, now based in Guangzhou, referenced these histories as they discussed our three-week-long trip as *caifeng*—"collecting airs," a term that carries residues of China's three-thousand-year history of bringing sounds and lyrics from the margins to the center as part of broader territorial and political projects.[3] Mabang and Wanju Chuanzhang also invoke the term *caifeng* to describe musical fieldwork in their lead singers' home regions.

Whether carried out by the state two thousand years ago or by independent musicians in China's major cities today, recontextualizations of local musical, lyrical, and narrative materials recast and reformulate ideas of territories, centers, and margins and negotiate evolving notions of the self, space, publics, and state as well as all of their interrelationships.

While this book has largely focused on contemporary China, it proceeds from the assumption that configurations and experiences of modernity and of globalization are hardly singular and uniform (Appadurai 1996; Chakrabarty 2000; Rofel 1999) and that it is crucial for any theorization of contemporary culture to draw on the distinctive histories of knowledge in the place or places it attempts to describe. Thus, any understanding of contemporary popular music in China—even and especially one that draws on notions of cosmopolitanism, circulation, and hybridity—should also pay attention to situated musical histories in China that extensively reference space, place, and governmentality. Casual references by contemporary musicians to two-thousand-year-old folk-song collecting practices and a Guangzhou music venue, Yuefu, named after a Han Dynasty governmental agency charged with managing music, demonstrate the extent to which China's long musical history intersects with contemporary musical practices.

From the two-millennium-old *Guofeng* (Airs of the States) section of the *Shijing* (Book of Odes), which categorized folk verse according to region of origin,[4] to the massive *Anthology of Chinese Folksong* divided into chapters by place and *minzu*[5] to the concept of *secaiqu* (color areas) in Chinese musicology as a way to describe regional variation in Han folk song (Miao and Qiao 1987), there is a strong tradition in China of viewing place, person, and musical sound as fundamentally linked. China's long history of song collection, regional performance gathered under an imperial or national umbrella, and philosophical and political discourse that explicitly theorize the relationships between music, person, place, and governance must be considered as a context for contemporary thinking about these issues.

In proposing *tianxia* as a way of thinking "musical cosmopolitanism with Chinese characteristics," this book has explored the various ways a cohort of musicians in Guangzhou sonically and aurally conceptualize connections between China's third largest city, their hometowns in lesser-developed areas of China, and faraway places outside of China. Historically, tianxia was a way of conceiving the world where the center—an imperial capital—emanated outward, incorporating difference through cultural and political processes of absorption. As a structure of feeling inflecting contemporary modes of musical circulation and forms of musical creativity, tianxia frames new ways of producing knowledge about the world through music, of merging transnationally circulating forms of popular music with regional Chinese traditions, and of asserting creative authority in an increasingly connected musical world.

Tianxia also speaks to the significance of the current political moment. China is reasserting its role in the world through various means including Xi Jinping's Belt and Road Initiative and is extending its sphere of influence through economic and cultural activities throughout the world. At the same time, the Chinese state is tightening its grip on power, and the public sphere is increasingly regulated and intertwined with state policies. Since Xi Jinping's assumption of the office of president in 2013 (and the abolition of presidential term limits in 2018), three decades of incremental liberalization of cultural domains since Reform and Opening Up have given way to a period of increased state interventions in citizens' lives. The delicate balance of neoliberalism and authoritarianism in China's postsocialist modernity is being recalibrated.

When I have presented the work that has culminated in this book at academic conferences where I am one of the few scholars working on China, I often receive some sort of question about whether the musicians I work with suffer from political repercussions under an authoritarian Chinese regime because of their musical activities. While the "social" in China is still a space severely intertwined with state policies, the music at the center of this book—and, with limited exceptions, rock, independent, and popular music in China more broadly—is not overtly or explicitly political and does not fit into neat binaries of hegemony and resistance as outsiders expect and desire.[6] One of the goals of this book is to nuance tendencies in Anglophone music scholarship about China—especially, but not only, about rock and popular music—that privilege certain questions and approaches and may obscure more subtle political issues surrounding evolving notions of the world, the individual, the state, and space.

To understand this preoccupation, it is worth briefly considering the intellectual history of considering the state as a central analytical figure in and context for musical production in China. While there is certainly a very real and *longue durée* engagement in China with the relationship between state and music, as already discussed, it is also important to emphasize European and American scholars' early fascination with the political significance of Chinese music and to understand the legacy of this approach. Dutch diplomat, mystery novelist, and scholar Robert Hans van Gulik's *The Lore of the Chinese Lute: An Essay in Ch'in Ideology* (1940) looked to the extensive record of writings on the *guqin* in relationship to Confucian philosophies. Embodying the foundation of an approach to and understanding of the political dimensions of music in China that would be pursued in American ethnomusicology, he wrote,

> The significance of music appears to be twofold, depending on whether it is viewed in its universal, cosmological and superhuman aspect, or, on the other hand, *in its specialized, political*, human aspect. In its universal aspect music is the harmony inherent in all nature, embracing heaven and earth. In its

> specialized aspect it is applied to man, both as an individual and *as a member of the political unity, the State.* (Van Gulik 1940, 24, emphasis added)

After Van Gulik, foundational scholars of Chinese music working in American universities focused on the *guqin* with attention to its relationship to political ideologies (Lieberman 1977), on the relationship of ancient music to ethics and politics (Thrasher 1980), and on the political mobilization of song in the PRC (Kagan 1963; Yung 1984). Much recent scholarship has also furthered and nuanced understandings of the connections between music and statecraft in China (Brindley 2012; Mittler 1997; Guy 2005). Tuohy (2001) offers a broader theoretical framework for understanding the political use of song in twentieth-century China and identifies a pattern of "sonic nationalism" that stretches back to Confucian ritual music and that penetrates most levels of music making in contemporary China. All sounds are connected, she argues:

> They form a piece, a monumental piece composed through the discourse and practices of twentieth-century musical nationalism that link them to each other within the organizational form of the Chinese nation. The vocabulary and contexts of the nation, in turn, reconfigure musical discourse and practice; new terms such as *minzu* . . . label pieces in music books, and performances occur within designated national spaces. Two-thousand-year-old song anthologies become models for collating the nation's current diversity, concerts commemorate earlier social-political movements, and national media daily broadcast a musical synchronicity that sonically encompasses the country. (Tuohy 2001, 107)

While vestiges of explicit musical nationalism are ubiquitous in contemporary China, it is important to recognize that they form only one part of a complex soundscape that also includes local folk musics, regional operatic forms, singing competition television series, independent and popular music, and many other forms of music making.

That said, similar perspectives have also structured much of the Anglophone scholarly work on popular music in contemporary China. Three broad tendencies in this work are worth noting: first, a geographic focus on Beijing and northern China; second, a focus on rock music; and third, an emphasis on hegemony/resistance models and approaches from cultural studies in understanding music's relationship to state power.[7] These tendencies may lead to skewed perspectives on the broader worlds of popular music heard in China, the majority of which is not produced in Beijing, not rock and roll, and not remotely subversive.

Given the historical legacy of music's role in Chinese statecraft, it is perhaps no wonder that political approaches to music are significant "gatekeeping concepts" regulating Anglophone research on Chinese music. Appadurai defines gatekeeping concepts as ideas "that seem to limit anthropological theorizing about the place in question, and that define the quintessential and dominant questions of interest in the region" (1986, 357). As caste is to India and reciprocity is to Polynesia, the authoritarian state is to Chinese music—"a few simple theoretical handles become metonyms and surrogates for the civilization or society as a whole" (357). This reproduces a cold war attitude toward China that is being reignited with the contemporary rebalancing of world power toward Asia. Furthermore, echoing anthropologist Lila Abu-Lughod (1990, 41), it romanticizes resistance and is "ultimately more interested in finding resistors and explaining resistance than with examining power."

Certainly this historical legacy is important and even permeates the contemporary soundscape of China. A reproduction of the fifth-century bells of Marquis Yi of Zeng[8] were used in a specially commissioned orchestral work by Tan Dun that was performed at the Hong Kong handover ceremony in 1997, and the opening ceremony of the 2008 Olympics featured a performance by 2008 synchronized drummers that drew on conventions of Confucian ritual music. But the state is certainly not the only analytical figure in and context for musical production in China. I am not arguing that scholars should ignore questions of power in studies of Chinese music; music is an ideal lens on the changing state-society relationships in postsocialist China. However, to cite the historical legacy of state control of musical production and then argue that rock music challenges state authority and is part of an emerging liberal public sphere oversimplifies a complex dynamic. Rather than diametrically oppose state-sponsored music with independent music, it is more productive to look to the alignments and cleavages between them as a diagnostic of power (Abu-Lughod 1990) and attempt to unravel some of the ways in which multiple boundaries—between urban and rural, local and global, Han and minority, private and public, socialist and capitalist, authoritarian and neoliberal—are intertwined and mutually constituting.

*

To this end, and having considered a multitude of contexts and meanings of the music of Wanju Chuanzhang and Mabang, from the languages in which it is sung to the sonic infrastructures through which it circulates, it is worth dwelling in these final pages on the most basic way that the bands have chosen to identify themselves: their names. As discussed in chapter 2, Mabang derives its name from the horse caravans that traveled along the Ancient Tea Horse Road (*Chama Gudao*, also known in English as the Southern Silk Road), transporting tea and other goods along mountainous routes in China's southwest. The name alludes to a Chinese cosmopolitan formation that connects contemporary mobilities to Chinese cosmopolitanisms that stretch back two thousand years while evoking China's southwest, borderlands, movement, masculinity, and depictions of ancient China. The name of the second band, Wanju Chuanzhang (Toy Captain), playfully references the maritime routes that converge on Nan'ao Island, an island off China's southeastern coast. The name alludes to the theme—and, as Li Yihan reminds us in chapter 3, the feeling—of the sea that runs through Wanju Chuanzhang's music, weaving together lyrics about seaside living with a musical style the band describes as *haiyang minyao* (ocean folk). The name also evokes histories of migration between Minnan-speaking regions of China (in Guangdong and Fujian) and broader Southeast Asia, another major theme in the stories told through Wanju Chuanzhang's lyrics.

These band names, in addition to evoking modes of transport, mobility, migration, and movement, also resonate with the remarkably mobile lives all of the band members have lived. Just as Deng Xiaoping's Reform and Opening Up was beginning to have widespread impact, drummer Dao Jianghua left a stable future in an ethnic song and dance troupe in Yunnan Province to busk on the streets of the island of Hainan, one of the first Special Economic Zones (SEZs). He went on to become a successful musician in Shenzhen (another SEZ), and eventually a central figure in Guangzhou's music business. Mabang's lead singer Ye Honggang left his home in a steel-mining town in Guangxi to pursue music—and occasional short-term welding work—in Shenzhen before moving to Guangzhou and becoming active in its *minyao quan* (folk circle). Dao and Ye's mobilities—as well as the mobilities of all the musicians discussed in chapters 5 and 6—have been shaped by political and economic reforms in China—most significantly by reforms of the hukou household registration system but also by broader economic development that has attracted large numbers of people to China's cities, particularly those in the Pearl River Delta region.

For each of these musicians, actual corporeal mobility has been intertwined with vicarious musical mobility shaped by the shifting media landscape of China, a landscape whose ongoing transformation has given rise to particular ways of listening to diverse musics from China and abroad. For Dao Jianghua, listening to smuggled cassette tapes of George Michael and Madonna in the 1980s stirred a thirst for learning about ways of making music different from those his training in a state-sponsored ethnic song and dance troupe had exposed him to. Later, he learned about reggae and dub through friends in Guangzhou, which led him to listen widely and alter the way he approached drumming. The Hong Kong rock band Beyond deeply influenced several band members early in their lives; as Cantonese speakers, they sang along with the clever lyrics and loved Beyond's musical style, which was markedly different from ideological *tongsu gequ* produced by the PRC state.

In the 1990s, a thriving circulation of *dakou* (cutout) media, tied to neoliberal globalization through the global waste trade, brought all of these musicians in contact with schizophonic sounds from around the world through a chaotic form of musical circulation I discuss in chapter 7. Bob Dylan, the Eagles, and the Beatles were among the musicians that particularly influenced Li Yihan and Ye Honggang as songwriters. In the 2000s the ways these musicians listened to music shifted dramatically once again. Record labels like Xingwaixing began to rerelease popular music from around the world; passing through official channels, these releases were part of well-curated and well-documented collections that offered contextualized introductions and liner notes. Even more importantly, the internet—at first sites like Xiami and Douban and Xingwaixing's own YYQ, and now dominant services Wangyi Yun Yinyue (NetEase Cloud Music) and QQ Music—began to offer vast troves of music and information about it for interested listeners. These included the obscure American West Coast emo favored by Gao Fei, the Japanese genre of visual kei that inspired Li Yihan to form his own band, and the French electro-dub adored by Dao Jianghua.

These cosmopolitan listening practices in turn have shaped the ways these musicians think about and make music. Aforementioned actual and vicarious mobilities intertwine, and global popular musics serve as palettes that these musicians selectively draw from as they create music reflective of their own lives and own mobilities. For Wanju Chuanzhang, this means reformulating diverse music from coastal regions—music understood broadly as *lading yinyue* (Latin music) and encompassing salsa, flamenco, reggae, and other styles—into *haiyang minyao* (ocean folk), as I discuss in chapter 3. For Mabang, it means blending elements of rock and reggae with *caidiao* opera and "original ecology" (*yuanshengtai*) folk musics, as I discuss in chapter 2. An important element of expressing the local for both bands is the use of local languages (*fangyan*) instead of standard Mandarin, a subtle and complex form of aesthetic resistance to national hegemony that I discuss in chapter 4.

These new forms of musical cosmopolitanism are particularly significant against a historical backdrop wherein music, person, and place were understood as deeply linked. From the 160 "Airs of the States" preserved in the

Shijing to explicit Confucian thinking about music in the *Yueji* (Classic of music) that understands music as expressive of the inner nature of people and the political stability of regions, traditional thinking about music and place in China posits a dynamic relation wherein music reflects—but can also shape—emplaced ways of being in the world. This is perpetuated in official discourse throughout the twentieth century, from discussions of musical endemicity (*difangxing*) in Maoist cultural policy, to a massive cartographic anthology of music produced beginning in the 1980s, to televisual performances of the nation such as the 2019 National Day Evening Gala that performatively enact orthodox ways of understanding interconnected political, spatial, and human hierarchies (Kielman 2020).

The most important insight of this long history of thinking about music, place, and person in China is the idea that music not only *expresses* but can also *reformulate* all of these notions. This perspective is poetically captured by a seventh-century commentator on the *Yueji*, Kong Yingda, who wrote, "Music comes from people, yet returns to affect people. This is like rain coming from the mountain yet returning to rain upon the mountain, like fire coming from wood yet returning to burn wood" (in Cook 1995, 13). Contemporary musical cosmopolitanisms in China must be understood as knowledge-making processes where notions of self, state, publics, and space as well as local, regional, national, and global imaginaries are constantly recreated in a dynamic process of resounding.

This process of emergence (Williams 1977), in turn, is intimately connected to a contemporary context of neoliberal transformation of economic, political, and cultural realms in China. In contemporary China under "neoliberalism with Chinese characteristics" (Harvey 2007), "socialism from afar" (Zhang and Ong 2008), or "flexible postsocialism" (Zhang 2012), new subjectivities and ways of being a person and a citizen have emerged alongside the rise of a transformed consumer culture and a privatized media industry. Shifting understandings of music and its meanings and new forms of musical cosmopolitanism not only coincide with China's broader transformations; rather, music both reflects and shapes these transformations. Music produces worlds.

Acknowledgments

My deepest gratitude goes to the musicians and others at the center of this book. Meeting Dao Jianghua in 2006 opened up a world of music and people passionate about it in southern China; our long friendship has shaped not only this book but also the path of my life since those first years in Guangzhou. Ye Honggang's musical and intellectual curiosity, creativity, and openness have led me to think about music and life in new ways. Li Yihan's generosity and devotion to the music are an inspiration to me as a musician, scholar, and person. David Wong is behind the scenes in most of the performances, rehearsals, recording sessions, and other activities described in this book, and I thank him for his friendship, unending logistical help, and for many long conversations about music that helped me formulate the ideas in this book. Zhou Xiaochuan's support for Liuzhen Yinyue made this work possible, and I thank him for allowing me to interview him. I thank Fan Feng, A Fei, Yu Dian, Gao Fei, Zhou Yi, Yu Zhenhai, Liao Peng, Elizabeth, Xiao Budian, and Xiao Sun for all of the experiences and conversations we have shared as our musical lives have overlapped.

My colleagues at the Chinese University of Hong Kong (CUHK) have formed a supportive and invigorating community while I have written this book. I thank Chan Kai Young, Victor Chan, Cheong Wai Ling, Amanda Hsieh, Lee Tong Soon, Wendy Lee, Jeff Levenberg, Poon Kiu Tung, Nathan Seinen, Brian Thompson, Tseng Sun Man, and Victor Vicente. Special thanks are reserved for Fred Lau; from conversations while I was a graduate student and serving on my dissertation committee to now acting as my department chair, he has been a generous mentor whose knowledge and experience has helped to shape this project in many ways. I thank my students at CUHK, especially all of my graduate students—Jonathan Chan, Winnie Chan, Chang Le, Daniel Chu, Fang Bo, Fu Biwen, Hu Qifang, Jiang Haoran, Mi Pengxuan, Zhou Yi, and Zhang Wenzhao—for stimulating conversations about music in China and for their help with various tasks related to the preparation of this book.

Work toward this book started during my studies at Columbia University. I could not wish for a more generous and insightful adviser and mentor than Ana Maria Ochoa Gautier; the breadth of her knowledge and the ways she shares it are an inspiration, and this project has benefited from them deeply. I thank Chris Washburne for his steadfast support and mentorship stretching back to my undergraduate days and for pushing me to make the connections between fieldwork, musicianship, and cultural theory that are the foundation of this book. Kevin Fellezs opened up new ways of thinking about both popular music and the potentials of scholarly endeavors. Aaron Fox, Ellen Gray, and Alessandra Ciucci all deeply shaped my understanding of the interdisciplinary possibilities of an anthropology of music. Timothy Oakes's insights were extremely helpful in expanding my work in new directions. Finally, I thank all of my fellow graduate students in ethnomusicology at Columbia for creating such a friendly, vibrant, and intellectually stimulating community.

I am extremely grateful to executive editor Elizabeth Branch Dyson, senior editorial associate Mollie McFee, and production editor Elizabeth Ellingboe at the University of Chicago Press for helping me shape and focus this project and for bringing this book to fruition. Many thanks to the two anonymous reviewers who offered helpful and productive comments on the initial manuscript and to Steve LaRue, whose careful copyediting of the book makes it eminently more readable.

This book was made possible by generous institutional support at many stages. Publication with the University of Chicago Press was supported in part by a publication subvention grant from the Faculty of Arts of the Chinese University of Hong Kong. The work described in this book was substantially supported by a grant from the Research Grants Council of the Hong Kong Special Administrative Region, China (Project No. CUHK 24606718). The Weatherhead East Asian Institute at Columbia University was very generous in their support of this project at several stages; I benefited from a semester of unencumbered writing support from WEAI's Julie How Fellowship as well as two summers of preliminary fieldwork in Guangzhou supported by the Institute's PhD Training Grant. Finally, the year of fieldwork in 2014 on which this book is largely based was made possible by a Fulbright-Hayes Doctoral Dissertation Abroad grant.

I thank my parents, George and Karen Kielman, for nurturing a curiosity about the world and a love of music that has led me down this path. I thank my wife Genny Griffiths for helping refine and think through many of the ideas and writing in this book. Most of all, I thank her, Halina, and Frances for sharing this journey together.

Notes

Chapter One

1. All English translations of Chinese materials in this book are by the author unless otherwise noted.

2. The scroll was a gift from the calligrapher to the owners upon the opening of the venue's predecessor in 2007. The phrase was also adopted as the slogan of a second location of the venue located in Shenzhen.

3. The term *musical cosmopolitanism* is invoked by ethnomusicologists to refer to a range of practices. My own focus is not a coherent movement that blends indigenous sounds with popular musics in order to create a nationalist popular music, such as in the Zimbabwean context discussed by Turino (2000). Nor is it akin to what Motti Regev terms *aesthetic cosmopolitanism* (Regev 2013), where conventions from North American and European popular music practices structure the interrelated musical and cultural worlds of everything in their paths while at the same time functioning as resources for the articulation of cultural uniqueness. I am more inspired by works such as Ryan Skinner's (2015), which sketches a locally situated, historically constituted cosmopolitan formation invoking Achille Mbembe's notion of "Afropolitanism" in order to interpret urban Malians' intertwined musical and ethical orientations toward the world.

4. As a foundational political concept, Zhao contrasts *tianxia* with the Greek idea of *polis*, comparing the "world perspective" of *tianxia* to the citizenship-focused notion of *polis*. This distinction is also significant in understanding *tianxia* in relation to the English *cosmopolitanism*.

5. These critiques are largely on two grounds. The first is that tianxia outlines a utopian world order and political institution without offering any details of how it might be realized. The second is that inherent in tianxia is what international relations scholar William Callahan (2008, 749) calls "a conversion of difference" and the replacement of one imperialism with another, presumably Chinese-led and built on premodern East Asia.

6. Zhao (2005, 3) situates his formulation of tianxia as part of broader efforts to "rethink China": "The historical significance of 'rethinking China' lies in recovering China's own ability to think, reconstructing its world views, values and methodologies, and thinking about China's future, Chinese concepts about the future and China's role and responsibilities in the world."

7. Announced by President Xi Jinping in 2013, the Belt and Road Initiative consists of infrastructure projects, trade agreements, and political alliances connecting China to a number of nations in Southeast Asia, South Asia, Central Asia, and Africa.

8. As Wang (2017, 2) observes, "Sustained by affective ties rather than coercion, tianxia distinguishes the inside from the outside less by geography and ethnicity than by cultural competence. Boundaries are fluid and relational: whoever attains cultural norms can be an insider, and the outsider can move in on merit."

9. Ye pronounces this phrase with a hard *k* sound ("Zou kee-lie") instead of the *ch* of standard Mandarin, marking his speech as a southwest variant of Mandarin. I discuss this, and the broader linguistic practices central to this music, further in chapter 4.

10. As the unequal mobilities experienced by the musicians I work with, the persistence of the hukou system, and a broader "geography of inequality" (Sun and Chio 2012) all remind us, however, mobilities—both actual and vicarious—are themselves contingent and unequal. This situation forces this book also to follow Steingo (2015) in pushing back against a tendency of ethnomusicologists to propose an ever-increasing and unfettered mobility of people and sounds.

11. In an Oxford handbook devoted to "mobile music studies," Gopinath and Stanyek (2014) also cite Urry's work and propose "mobile music" as a "cultural practice" (1) that emerged in the late nineteenth century with electrification and developed in tandem with new technologies from the portable gramophone to the smartphone. They outline an area of inquiry—"mobile music studies"—that focuses on mobile devices, technologies, practices of listening, and markets. While they do consider the "the movement of human populations," the authors' stated focus is musical "mobilization, wherein listening technologies are made mobile in various ways and to varying degrees" (28). Contrasted with Gopinath and Stanyek, my use of "mobility" as an analytic casts a wider net by focusing on connections between the mobilities of people and the mobilities of musics.

12. With *emergent*, I invoke the sense in which Raymond Williams (1977, 123) uses the term: contrasted with "residual" and "dominant" culture, "emergent" culture is where "new meanings and values, new practices, new relationships and kinds of relationships are continually being created."

13. I use the word *vicarious* in its everyday sense to mean "experienced imaginatively through another person or agency" (*Oxford English Dictionary Online*). Drawing attention to the intertwining of experience and imagination, I also mean to invoke Appadurai's (1990) discussion of imagination as social practice and follow him in bringing together three senses of the word: first, the idea of images, especially as mechanically reproduced (Benjamin [1936] 1986); second, the concept of the imagined community (Anderson 1983); and third, the French idea of imaginary (*imaginaire*) as a "constructed landscape of collective aspirations" (Appadurai 1990, 6).

14. My division of actual and vicarious mobilities simplifies Urry's categorization of five distinct kinds of mobility: *corporeal* travel of people; physical movement of *objects*; *imaginative* travel; *virtual* travel; and *communicative* travel (Urry 2007, 47). It also is informed by Appadurai's (1990) notion of five "-scapes"—ethnoscapes, technoscapes, financescapes, mediascapes, and ideoscapes—describing five dimensions of global cultural flows.

15. It is through this "emergence," furthermore, that the musical, economic, and political connect through the spatial. In this case the cultural economy and the broader economy exist in dynamic relation; as Cunningham et al. (2008) point out, in some cases, creative industries are an "*innovation system* of the economy" (5, emphasis in the original), wherein "the economic value of the creative industries . . . does not stem from their relative contribution to economic value, but from their contribution to the coordination of new ideas or technologies and thus to the process of economic and cultural change" (5).

16. Wang (2005) discusses an administrative scale system of provinces and counties (*junxian*) stretching back to the Han Dynasty (206 BCE–220 CE) and argues that contemporary

spatialities draw directly on this *junxian* system and furthermore perpetuate a center-periphery relationship where all localities are defined in a hierarchical relationship to the capital. Wang also invokes classical Chinese ideas of place and governance, including the concept of *yindi zhiyi* (each according to its geoculture), a system whereby local officials were allowed to localize central decrees, as well as *dili zhi*, which also described the "geoculture" of each place, "thus linking the notion of administration to both the natural and cultural geography of a place" (12). Through this historically informed perspective, Wang situates the relevance of contemporary regionalisms and the ways place-based identities are subsumed under a state-defined and ethnically based "Chinese-ness."

17. Dirlik (2008) reiterates that the tendency to map societies and consolidate identities in terms of nations, civilizations, or cultures is a feature of (western) modernity that erases alternative ways of conceiving of space and that this tendency has shaped understandings of "China" domestically and abroad. Looking at Chinese diversity in terms of ethnicity, regionalism, and transnational contact zones, Dirlik argues that "cultural constitution has been a product not of the diffusion of social and cultural practices from some center but of dialectical encounters in many contact zones" (3). Connecting his argument to the broader critique of the "culture concept," Dirlik advocates moving away from approaches that homogenously and isomorphically map people and ways of life onto spaces and instead looking to hybridity and contact zones as agents in the production of "culture(s)." Dirlik's work provokes scholars to examine the particular cultural and geographic histories of China as they are both connected to *and distinct from* parallel histories that have led to dominant European Enlightenment thinking and, in turn, to investigate how these histories inflect the discursive production of concepts of culture, concepts of space, and concepts of the local in China.

18. I am building on currents in anthropology that advocate moving away from studying "cultures in places" toward ethnographically informed approaches that seek to understand social and economic processes that connect people and places (Gupta and Ferguson 1997) as well as anthropology's increasing attention to movements and migrations (Clifford 1997; Friedman 2015; Ong 1999; Sun 2002). As Gupta and Ferguson (1997) write, "cultural territorializations (like ethnic and national ones) must be understood as complex and contingent results of ongoing historical and political processes. It is these processes, rather than pregiven cultural-territorial entities, that require anthropological study" (5). Gupta and Ferguson go on to stress that, though many studies have interrogated the local and its connection to some larger scale (region, nation, globe), these studies often overlook that the local itself—as both a space and a scale—is "discursively and historically constructed" (6).

19. Oakes and Schein (2006) stress four characteristics of *translocal* as they deploy the term. First, *translocal* refers to more than physical mobility; rather, it connects "the interdependence of the subjective dimension of translocality—vicarious mobilities and translocal imaginaries—with . . . physical movements" (3). Second, they point out that translocal flows inevitably bring about new forms of economic and social inequality. Third, they argue that these new flows invigorate rather than erase local place-based identities. Fourth, they are careful to historicize current "translocality" within the context of a long history of translocal flows and attempt to trace the ramifications of the changing role of the state in defining conceptions of space, place, and scale.

20. Since the 1990s several ethnographic studies have nuanced an understanding of the ways music and sound may participate in constructions of the local in globally connected societies. Manuel (1993) demonstrates how mobile media technologies in India decentralize networks of

music distribution and result in a fractured, democratized, and dispersed musical landscape where local variation is much more substantial. Rather than extinguish local forms of creativity, he finds that (democratic participant) mass mediation reinvigorates a sense of the local. By studying Zouk as a "local" musical phenomenon in both its original location and in the global networks through which it circulates, Guilbault (1993) explores how music contributes to forging local identities and communities through broader circulations. In postapartheid South Africa, Meintjes (2003) elucidates how the recording studio is a site where conceptions of local and global are negotiated through timbre. Diehl (2002) demonstrates how discourses of authenticity, tradition, and musical reinvention link Tibetan refugees to both an imagined and idealized homeland and to new lives in their adopted country. Samuels (2004) suggests that the indexical gesture that links particular expressive forms to identities (of place or otherwise) are "polyphonic and ambiguous" (169) and finds that mass-mediated commercial music may develop deep connections to place-based identities. Luvaas (2009) explores the worlds of Indonesian indie pop musicians who pointedly avoid mixing indigenous or local cultural forms with transnationally circulating pop sounds and instead "use transnational aesthetics to challenge existing constructions of locality, supplanting the 'local' of the national and colonial past with a chosen, empowering positionality grounded in a dialectical relationship with the global" (249). These and other scholars (Erlmann 1999; Lipsitz 1994; Slobin 1993; Stokes 2004; Taylor 1997; Turino 2000) offer inspiration for the present discussion.

21. For example, Luvaas (2009), Regev (2013), and Shin (2009).

22. The text is in Chinese and English; I include here the English text as the official translation.

23. *Lingnan* is used in everyday contexts to refer to Cantonese culture; thus, Guangzhou is also being cast here as the center of a regional and linguistically defined Chinese culture stretching over Guangdong and Guangxi Provinces as well as the Special Administrative Regions of Hong Kong and Macau.

24. Cartier (2001) offers a more in-depth discussion of these economic transformations as well as of the effects of their implementation particularly in southern China.

25. *Hong* is often translated as "factories," though the buildings were not themselves factories and the term itself refers to the business entity rather than the building or location.

26. Guangzhou's connections—through Shamian Island—to Hong Kong and Macau—as well as to faraway places like Calcutta and Mauritius, also swept up in colonial machinations—are beautifully explored in Amitav Ghosh's historical novel *Sea of Poppies* (2008) and the Ibis Trilogy of which it is a part.

27. In a 1993 article that was in part reacting to the saturation in popular music studies of theoretical approaches and methodologies borrowed from cultural studies, Sara Cohen (1993, 127) wrote, "an ethnographic approach to the study of popular music, used alongside other methods . . . would emphasize that popular music is . . . human activity involving social relationships, identities, and collective practices." More recently, David Pruett (2011) has advocated for fieldwork-based studies among the producers of mainstream popular music as "culture bearers" in the traditional ethnomusicological sense.

28. "The use of hallucinatory drugs, love-ins, public nudity, light shows, the Indian sitar, beards and dirty bodies, communal sex orgies—the extreme fringes of the hippie world that were indicative of losing touch with reality. . . . Who would have ever thought that the amplified guitar—through the manipulations of clever management—would ever serve as the vehicle for such a social nightmare!" (Hood 1971, 17). Despite Hood's intense distaste toward the musical

and social worlds of rock music, it is worth noting that he is suggesting that it is worthy of academic study and that ethnomusicology is the appropriate discipline from which to study it.

Chapter Two

1. See also Fabbri (1982), Holt (2007), Brackett (2016), and Born and Haworth (2017).

2. DeLanda (2006) develops the concept of "relations of exteriority" in order to emphasize the autonomy of component parts of assemblages, which may be transplanted into different assemblages wherein they function differently; thus the whole can never be reduced to the sum of the properties of its component parts.

3. Holt (2007, 24) observes, "The concept of *practice* opens up a different understanding of genre conventions because it shifts focus away from objectified ontologies (sign, category, recording, etc.) and toward agency and process. . . . Studying musical practice allows us to see how genre elements are in play and how the dialectic between repetition and change is negotiated at particular moments."

4. I refer to lead singer Ye Honggang and drummer Dao Jianghua by their full given names and other band members by their artist names (*yiming*) used widely in public discourse about the bands and in informal social settings. In chapters 5 and 6, I also refer to Ye Honggang and Dao Jianghua by their nicknames (A Gang and Xiao Dao), as they are relevant to their public musical identities that I am discussing there.

5. This process is outlined in greater detail in chapter 5.

6. Mifen Yuedui began to record a new album three times in as many years, but each time a major obstacle kept them from bringing the project to completion. In 2012 they came closest to finishing a complete album; they spent a week at Hong Kong bassist, recording engineer, and promoter Peter Scherr's home studio, the same man who produced Wanju Chuanzhang's 2012 album that I discuss in chapter 3. However, Scherr faced a major health crisis at the end of that year and stopped working on the album. He relocated to the US, and the project files that contained the recording in progress were never retrieved.

7. I discuss Liuzhen Yinyue, this process, and the business models surrounding it, much more extensively in chapter 7.

8. This and subsequent quotes from Ye Honggang in this chapter are from an interview with the author on December 10, 2014.

9. Occasionally and more specifically, their music was referred to as *chengshi minyao* (urban folk) or *xiandai minyao* (modern folk).

10. The appropriation of nonwestern musics by western musicians and the power imbalances inherent in both musical collaborations and digital sampling of so-called world music was a major topic discussed by ethnomusicologists in the 1990s. See Erlmann (1996), Feld (1996a), Meintjes (1990), and Zemp (1996).

11. Examples of bands that fit in this last category who have performed at aforementioned "world music" festivals in China include Zhaoze (Swamp), a Guangzhou-based postrock band centered around a traditional seven-stringed zither *guqin* thickly layered with effects; Beijing-based Shanren Yuedui (Mountain Person Band), which draws on folk, rock, and minority musics of Yunnan Province; Beijing-based Hanggai, which layers Mongolian instrumentation and throat singing over heavy rock; and Toyota-based Turtle Band, a "13 piece punk orchestra that fuses traditional Japanese carnival beats with other musical elements including distorted guitar, Indian music, and Korean traditional music, all held together with a punk rock background" (http://www.turtleisland.jp).

12. This bio is used widely online and in promotional materials, including Mabang's press kit.

13. Located in Guangzhou and established in 1932, Xinghai Conservatory is an esteemed institution in China despite having less international name recognition than Central Conservatory in Beijing and Shanghai Conservatory.

Chapter Three

1. The use of local dialects by both Wanju Chuanzhang and Mabang is the subject of the next chapter, so I treat it only very briefly here.

2. Translated from the Chinese text posted on Douban, other online media, and included in Wanju Chuanzhang's official press kit used through 2014.

3. It is worth noting that this mode of drawing on genres from far away resembles that of tianxia as political system, emphasizing absorption of difference over conversion.

4. I include a translation of the Chinese album title here, though the official English name of the album is *South Island, Marine Flavor Was a Nice Feeling.*

5. Scherr operated a company, Chuangyi Yinyue Zai Zhongguo (Creative Music in China), that organized tours of several North American jazz and other groups in mainland China and also produced independent records for several bands in southern China.

6. In preparing for both the 2015 release of Mabang's debut album and the 2016 release of Wanju Chuanzhang's sophomore album on the Liuzhen Yinyue label, I worked closely with the lead singers of each band to create English translations of all lyrics to be included in the liner notes. English translations in Wanju Chuanzhang's 2012 album liner notes were done by a friend of the band from Singapore; I largely adhere to his translation of the lyrics of "Beach Party" with minimal changes for clarity. As I discuss in chapter 4, the inclusion of lyrics in standard Chinese in the liner notes was particularly important to both bands because a majority of listeners has limited to no comprehension of the lyrics when simply listening. For both bands, Chinese lyrics are included as a textual accompaniment to the songs in beautifully produced liner notes; it is hoped that listeners will read the lyrics and enjoy them as much as they will listen to and enjoy the music. English lyrics are included as well for a hoped-for international audience, and it is hoped by both lyricists that non-Chinese speakers might read and enjoy their lyrics as well.

7. Approximately two-thirds of China's "floating population" are male.

8. The dominance of Douban and Xiami in the mid-2010s as services through which people accessed music have since been overtaken by Wangyi Yun Yinyue (NetEase Cloud Music) and QQ Music in a rapidly changing online media landscape. I discuss Xingwaixing's own entrance into this business in chapter 7.

9. Another particularly insightful example of such scholarship is Condry's (2006) analysis of the culturally situated meanings of hip-hop in Japan.

10. Novak (2008, 16) notes, furthermore, that "listening is not the final link of a chain of musical transmission, but the very crucible of musical innovation" and that "practices of listening reinterpret and recontextualize musical genre in ways that complicate our notions of local music."

Chapter Four

1. The particular dialect that Li Yihan sings in is Yun'aohua (Yun'ao dialect) and is named after Yun'ao Township, where Li grew up. In casual speech, including by Li, Yun'ao dialect is often referred to as simply "Nan'ao Dao fangyan" (Nan'ao Island dialect) or "Nan'aohua" (Nan'ao

language). Often, it is simply glossed as Chaozhouhua or Chaoshanhua, which it is a variety of; this slippage also points to the overlapping scales by which fangyan are variously categorized. Yun'ao dialect's relationship to the more widely spoken southern Min dialects Chaozhouhua and Hokkien is discussed later in this chapter. For ease of readability and to avoid confusion, I refer to the dialect throughout this chapter as simply Nan'ao dialect.

2. The terms *Chaozhouhua* and *Chaoshanhua* are used interchangeably and represent standard Mandarin pronunciations of the dialect name, rendered in Hanyu Pinyin. *Chaoshan* is a term used to describe the broader region and is a contraction of the names of the two major cities that anchor the region, Chaozhou and Shantou. *Teochew* and *Chiuchow* are also common romanizations of *Chaozhou* (derived from Chaozhouhua and Cantonese pronunciations respectively) and are more widely used in English to refer to the language, culture group, and region. I use *Chaozhouhua* throughout this chapter following my practice elsewhere of using Hanyu Pinyin.

3. Like many artists, lead singer Li Yihan has written down stock responses for standard questions he receives frequently from media interviewers; it is this distilled text I include here, though he sometimes expands on this verbally.

4. The term *Hokkien* is commonly used in English to refer to this widely spoken southern Min dialect; the term is a nonstandard romanization of the pronunciation in the dialect of its province of origin, Fujian. As spoken in Taiwan, it is referred to as "Holo" or "Taiyu" (Taiwanese). It is also spoken extensively in Southeast Asia and in overseas Chinese communities elsewhere.

5. Apart from the explicit mention of place names, the reading of the bubble quotations on the poster as local dialects is conveyed by the use of particular vocabularies unique to the dialects. For a discussion of the ways in which local dialects are conveyed in written Chinese, see Gunn (2006).

6. Because of the variety of sounds that may be associated with one Chinese character depending on what dialect it is read in, the linguistic standardization at the center of Chinese nation building during the twentieth century was at least as focused on the sounds of language as on their standardized inscription. While a new vernacular literature promoted a written language that was based on standard Mandarin as it was actually spoken (as opposed to Classical Chinese), mass media, including music, also played a large role in standardizing the *sound* of standard Mandarin.

7. Liu (2013) discusses this law and its implications more extensively, and my analysis draws on her insightful interpretations.

8. Gunn draws on Derrida in order to discuss the relationship of the written Chinese language to the diversity of dialects it may represent and relates this discussion to Hobsbawm's understanding of linguistic standardization's role in national integration. Against this backdrop and informed by the linguistic undercurrents in Gramsci's discussions of hegemony, Bourdieu's concept of language as symbolic power, and theories of performativity (Austin 1962), Gunn (2006, 7) views language use as a "social act" and observes that "uses of local language may be read as postcolonial resistance to the performative of China by showing another agency, or it may be read as creating an identity to be aligned with flows of capital" (14).

9. While Gunn and Liu come from comparative literature backgrounds and focus primarily on literature, television, and the internet, Liu's (2014) work also touches on music, discussing hip-hop and internet circulations of DIY songs in local dialects.

10. Influenced by Jakobson and following Feld, several ethnomusicologists, including Fox (2004) and Samuels (2004), have explored how vocalizations in sung speech index region, class, and social group and, furthermore, how "the heightened presence of the singing voice produces a site where speech and song intertwine to produce timbral socialities" (Feld et al. 2005, 341).

11. The most common system is referred to as Chaozhou Pinyin Fang'an and is popularly referred to as peng'im, the Chaozhouhua pronunciation of pinyin.

Chapter Five

1. In addition to many years of close work with the people whose *yinyue shenghuo* are recorded in these chapters, each biography is drawn in part from a formal interview completed toward the end of my sustained year of fieldwork in 2014. I began the interviews by explaining some of the goals of these chapters and guided the discussions with questions that elicited reflections on growing up in their hometowns, on their musical developments from a young age, and on the developments of their careers as musicians. Each interview lasted between one and three hours and was conducted in Mandarin. In what follows, I intersperse translations of musicians' own words with my own narration. Where the specific Chinese words used may contain nuance not readily apparent in the English, I include the original Chinese in parentheses. I discuss my relationships and collaborations with each individual while foregrounding the narrative of their musical lives as they tell it.

2. Throughout this book, I refer to most musicians by their artists' names (*yiming*) as opposed to by their given names. In the biographies that follow, in cases where the artists' names hold special significance in relation to given names, I explain the connection. In these two chapters, I use artists' names in all cases, as these names are connected to and expressive of the musical lives described in the chapters. In the rest of this book, I refer to Dao Jianghua (Xiao Dao), Li Yihan (Xiao Li), and Ye Honggang (A Gang) by their given names.

3. For the sake of smooth reading, I do not cite each quotation I include in these biographies. Interviews, all conducted by the author in Mandarin and unpublished until now, took place in Guangzhou between December 1 and December 20, 2014.

4. Gangtai music refers to pop music originating in Hong Kong and Taiwan. The word *gangtai* elides the Mandarin names of Hong Kong (Xianggang) and Taiwan.

5. Further discussion of *tongsu gequ* may be found in Jones (1992).

6. *Dakou die*, literally "cutout discs," are surplus cassettes and later CDs that traveled to China from North America and Europe via the global waste trade. I discuss the phenomenon in more detail in chapter 7.

7. "Nothing to My Name," Cui Jian's famous song that became an anthem of the Tiananmen protests.

8. A hukou is a family registration that functions as a sort of residence permit tying one to one's place of birth, as I discuss at greater length in the introduction.

9. The venue was called *Putong Yibai* (Regular 100).

10. The English phrase "Live House" is used by Chinese speakers to refer to music venues; the word, and the concept, is derived from the Japanese *raibu hausu*, which is a Japanese *wasei-eigo*, a word that is an English loan word that has come to have a specific different or nuanced meaning in its Japanese usage.

11. Huang (2014) offers an overview of the varied and nuanced meanings of this term, particularly in relation to music. In everyday use, the term carries many of the same connotations as *hipster* in English, though I choose not to translate it as such.

12. It was also well known by an English name, C:Union, and was meant to visually resemble musical notation while phonically alluding to the original Chinese.

13. See Rees (2016) for an in-depth discussion of the term.

14. The zhongkao, "middle test," is the standardized test administered at the end of middle school (*chuzhong*). It determines one's track in high school (*gaozhong*). The importance of this test and the pressure surrounding it is underscored by the many mentions of this test and the even more important *gaokao* high school graduation equivalent in all of these biographies.

15. This bar was named after Dou Wei's seminal rock band formed in 1987.

16. Genjudi is a well-known music venue in Shenzhen that hosted some of China's most well-known rock, folk, and independent musicians in the 1990s. It is the same bar that I describe in the previous biography; I worked with several other Guangzhou-based musicians to take an ownership stake in this bar and manage it starting in 2008. The bar is now once again under new ownership, but it is still a prominent venue.

17. *Kuaican* is an inexpensive fast-food takeout meal meant for one person consisting of one or more vegetable or meat dishes on rice.

18. Panyu is a southern district of Guangzhou, semisuburban and forty-five minutes from downtown by subway.

19. He specifies the character with the chengyu *hainabaichuan*, "all rivers flow into the sea."

20. The percussion that Fan Feng plays has changed over time. In 2004 he was playing bongos, but by 2007 he had begun to play a djembe.

Chapter Six

1. The western coast of Taiwan lies less than two hundred miles directly east of Nan'ao.

2. Sina Weibo, the most popular microblogging service in China.

3. His father's elder brother's son (his cousin), to whom he refers as big brother (*gege*).

4. Zhou Yi goes by his given name.

5. Xie Tingfeng, a Hong Kong singer popular at the time.

6. This is a private (*minban*; *sili*) college, which is rare in China. It is not funded or accredited by the central government.

Chapter Seven

1. Emphasizing infrastructure as a key actor in these processes builds on work by ethnomusicologists that invokes the concept of infrastructure directly or indirectly in order to explore issues of musical circulation (Novak 2013), recording industries and physical media (Manuel 1993), and technology and hardware (Steingo 2015).

2. Unless otherwise noted, subsequent quotations from Zhou Xiaochuan all draw from the same interview with the author in Zhou's office in Guangzhou on December 12, 2014.

3. Such dislocated sounds are typical of what Novak (2011, 606) discusses in terms of "an emergent open source culture of global media."

4. Discussing indie circulations between North and South America, Garland (2014, 4) explores the term in depth as "both a musical genre and a mode of organizing musical production and circulation in a still-emerging music industry landscape."

5. YYQ was rolled into a new and related venture by Xingwaixing in 2019, Cuckoo Music, as major streaming services QQ Music and Wangyi Yun Yinyue (NetEase Cloud Music) became dominant in overlapping market segments.

6. Rather than be sidelined by the internet, Zhou sees the move to digital services as essential to the survival of the industry: "Since I've been working in the music industry, I feel that the

internet has consistently exploited music. But I think that, more and more, the music industry ought to be able to effectively make use of the internet as a tool."

Epilogue

1. For an in-depth discussion of this process, see Holm (1991).

2. Von Falkenhausen (1993) offers an archaeological and historical examination of the role of *bianzhong* suspended bells in early China with broader observations about the musical and political contexts of ritual music. Cook (1995) offers a detailed analysis of the Confucian text, the *Yueji* (Record of Music). Fu (2008) discusses village music within the local political and social structures of the Zhou Dynasty. These and many other scholars offer insight into the relationship of music to governance in ancient China.

3. The etymology of the word *caifeng* is related to the use of *feng* in the *Shijing* (Du and Di 2005), and the twentieth-century practice of *caifeng* is explicitly connected to the folk song collection practices that produced the *Shijing*. The *Shijing* is a collection of three hundred and five poems that are said to date from the eleventh through sixth centuries BCE. There is significant and most likely unresolvable debate about the origins of the *Shijing* (Wong and Lee 1989; Mittag 1993). Scholars believe that an emperor in the Zhou Dynasty (1046–256 BCE) sent music officials throughout Chinese territory (present-day Eastern-central China) to collect the lyrics of folk songs so that he might better understand the diverse people he ruled. Confucius (551–479 BCE) is said to have later edited what was originally a collection of over three thousand songs down to three hundred and five. It is hard to overstate the extent of the collection's impact on Chinese culture. By the Han Dynasty (206 BCE–220 CE), the collection was considered one of the five classics that formed the backbone of consolidated Confucian thought.

4. The first 160 poems of the *Shijing* are classified as *guofeng*, often translated as "Airs of the States." They are organized under the headings of fifteen names of semiautonomous states (*guo*) during the Zhou Dynasty (1046–256 BCE) and Warring States Period (475–221 BCE). The poems are understood to be the lyrics of folk songs collected in these states. Han Dynasty scholars took *feng* to mean a system of teaching, while neo-Confucian scholars in the Song Dynasty interpreted *feng* to mean a musical form or style. *Feng* in modern Chinese means air or wind; as part of the compound word *fengsu* it may mean custom; as part of *fengge* it may mean style. The precise meaning of *feng* in *guofeng* is heavily debated, but these echoes in modern Chinese all represent popular interpretations of the term. Unifying all these interpretations of *guofeng* is a categorization by place and a belief that the songs are somehow linked to or expressive of the places from which they came.

5. In the aftermath of the Cultural Revolution (1966–1976), Chinese scholars, musicians, officials, and government institutions embarked on a massive folk song collecting project. The project was connected to a broad rejuvenation of the arts and academia that formed an intellectual counterpart to Deng Xiaoping's economic reform policies. Initiated in 1979 and jointly sponsored by the Ministry of Culture and the Chinese Musician's Association, the *Zhongguo Minjian Yinyue Jicheng* consists of over three hundred volumes of musical transcriptions, lyrics, and explanatory notes. Published piecemeal beginning in the early eighties, new volumes continue to be added to the collection. The anthology attempts to record the entirety of Chinese folk musical activities in all thirty provinces and autonomous regions. The anthology is not only devoted to folk song (*min'ge*); parallel collections also exist for narrative singing (*Zhongguo Quyi Yinyue Jicheng*), local operatic traditions (*Zhongguo Xiqu Yinyue Jicheng*), and instrumental

music (*Zhongguo Minjian Qiyuequ Jicheng*). The largest section of the anthology is the *Zhongguo Minjian Gequ Jicheng* (Anthology of folk songs of the Chinese peoples). Jones (2003) gives a broad introduction to the collection as a whole and offers some insight into the processes behind collecting and organizing the anthology.

6. The intellectual histories of popular music studies and cultural studies, as well as the North American and European contexts on which many of their theoretical assumptions were based, also instigate such an expectation.

7. Taken together, the three most influential English-language monographs on Chinese popular music (Jones 1992; Baranovitch 2003; De Kloet 2010) offer insight into evolutions in both China's popular and independent music scenes and scholarly approaches to them. They document the flowering and development of China's music scenes from state-sponsored ideological music and a small urban rock scene in the 1980s to a complex mosaic of corporate, state-sponsored, and independent musics in the early 2000s. Theoretically, they reveal a move away from strict models of hegemony/resistance toward an understanding of popular music as an arena for the forging of new kinds of subjectivities. At the same time, they all to varying degrees retain a political perspective that understands popular music as existing in opposition to state power.

8. Discovered in 1977 and dating from the fifth century BC, this set of bronze bells buried with the Marquis Yi of Zeng offered new insights about ancient Chinese musical practice, in particular as it related to governance, as discussed at length by Von Falkenhausen (1993). It is significant also, however, that the bells are regularly invoked in academic and popular discourse about connections between sound and state in a broad historical perspective.

Works Cited

Abu-Lughod, Lila. 1990. "The Romance of Resistance: Tracing Transformations of Power through Bedouin Women." *American Ethnologist* 17 (1): 41–55.

———. 1997. "The Interpretation of Culture(s) after Television." *Representations*, no. 59 (July): 109–34.

Althusser, Louis. 1971. *Lenin and Philosophy and Other Essays*. New York: Monthly Review Press.

Anderson, Benedict. 1983. *Imagined Communities: Reflections on the Origin and Spread of Nationalism*. London: Verso.

Appadurai, Arjun. 1986. "Theory in Anthropology: Center and Periphery." *Comparative Studies in Society and History* 28 (2): 356–61.

———. 1990. "Disjuncture and Difference in the Global Cultural Economy." *Public Culture* 2 (2): 1–24.

———. 1996. *Modernity at Large: Cultural Dimensions of Globalization*. Minneapolis: University of Minnesota Press.

Austin, J. L. 1962. *How to Do Things with Words*. Cambridge, MA: Harvard University Press.

Bakhtin, Mikhail Mikhailovich. (1937) 2004. *The Dialogic Imagination: Four Essays*. Austin: University of Texas Press.

Baranovitch, Nimrod. 2003. *China's New Voices: Popular Music, Ethnicity, Gender, and Politics, 1978–1997*. Berkeley: University of California Press.

Bates, Eliot. 2016. *Digital Tradition: Arrangement and Labor in Istanbul's Recording Studio Culture*. Oxford: Oxford University Press.

Bauman, Richard. 1984. *Verbal Art as Performance*. Prospect Heights, IL: Waveland Press.

Becker, Howard. 1982. *Art Worlds*. Berkeley: University of California Press.

Benjamin, Walter. (1936) 1986. "The Work of Art in the Age of Mechanical Reproduction." In *Illuminations*, edited by Hannah Arendt, 214–18. New York: Schocken Books.

Bolter, J. David, and Richard A. Grusin. 1999. *Remediation: Understanding New Media*. Cambridge, MA: MIT Press.

Born, Georgina, and Christopher Haworth. 2017. "From Microsound to Vaporwave: Internet-Mediated Musics, Online Methods, and Genre." *Music and Letters* 98 (4): 601–47.

Bourdieu, Pierre. 1991. *Language and Symbolic Power*. Edited by John B. Thompson. Cambridge, MA: Harvard University Press.

Brackett, David. 2016. *Categorizing Sound: Genre and Twentieth-Century Popular Music*. Oakland: University of California Press.

Briggs, Charles L., and Richard Bauman. 1992. "Genre, Intertextuality, and Social Power." *Journal of Linguistic Anthropology* 2 (2): 131–72.

Brindley, Erica Fox. 2012. *Music, Cosmology, and the Politics of Harmony in Early China*. Albany: State University of New York Press.

Bryant, Lei Ouyang. 2007. "Flowers on the Battlefield Are More Fragrant." *Asian Music* 38 (1): 88–122.

Buckley, Chris. 2018. "China Blocks a Memorial Service to Sichuan Earthquake Victims." *New York Times*, May 12, 2018.

Callahan, William A. 2008. "Chinese Visions of World Order: Post-Hegemonic or a New Hegemony?" *International Studies Review* 10 (4): 749–61.

Campbell, Jon. 2011. *Red Rock: The Long, Strange March of Chinese Rock & Roll*. Hong Kong: Earnshaw Books.

Cartier, Carolyn. 2001. *Globalizing South China*. Oxford: Blackwell.

Casey, Edward S. 1996. "How to Get from Space to Place in a Fairly Short Stretch of Time: Phenomenological Prolegomena." In *Senses of Place*, edited by Steven Feld and Keith H. Basso. Santa Fe, NM: School of American Research Press.

Chakrabarty, Dipesh. 2000. *Provincializing Europe: Postcolonial Thought and Historical Difference*. Princeton, NJ: Princeton University Press.

Chan, Kam Wing. 2009. "The Chinese Hukou System at 50." *Eurasian Geography and Economics* 50 (2): 197–221.

Chang, Won Ho. 1989. *Mass Media in China: The History and the Future*. Ames: Iowa State University Press.

Chang, Xin 常新. 2014. "Youxian guangbo" 有线广播 [Wired broadcasting]. *Suzhou Zazhi* 苏州杂志, no. 1, 15.

Chen, Chuanbo, and C. Cindy Fan. 2016. "China's Hukou Puzzle: Why Don't Rural Migrants Want Urban Hukou?" *China Review* 16 (3): 9–39.

Clifford, James. 1997. *Routes: Travel and Translation in the Late Twentieth Century*. Cambridge, MA: Harvard University Press.

Cohen, Sara. 1993. "Ethnography and Popular Music Studies." *Popular Music* 12 (2): 123–38.

Collier, Stephen J. 2011. *Post-Soviet Social: Neoliberalism, Social Modernity, Biopolitics*. Princeton, NJ: Princeton University Press.

Condry, Ian. 2006. *Hip-Hop Japan: Rap and the Paths of Cultural Globalization*. Durham, NC: Duke University Press.

Cook, Scott. 1995. "'Yue Ji' 樂記—Record of Music: Introduction, Translation, Notes, and Commentary." *Asian Music* 26 (2): 1–96.

Corbin, Alain. 1998. *Village Bells: Sound and Meaning in the Nineteenth-Century French Countryside*. New York: Columbia University Press.

Cunningham, Stuart, John Banks, and Jason Potts. 2008. "Cultural Economy: The Shape of the Field." In *The Cultural Economy*, edited by H. K. Anheier and Y. R. Isar, 15–26. London: SAGE.

De Kloet, Jeroen. 2005. "Sonic Sturdiness: The Globalization of 'Chinese' Rock and Pop." *Critical Studies in Media Communication* 22 (4): 321–38.

———. 2010. *China with a Cut: Globalisation, Urban Youth and Popular Music*. Amsterdam: Amsterdam University Press.

DeLanda, Manuel. 2006. *A New Philosophy of Society: Assemblage Theory and Social Complexity*. London: Continuum.

Deleuze, Gilles, and Félix Guattari. 1977. *Anti-Oedipus: Capitalism and Schizophrenia*. New York: Viking Press.

———. 1987. *A Thousand Plateaus: Capitalism and Schizophrenia*. Translated by Brian Massumi. Minneapolis: University of Minnesota Press.

DeNora, Tia. 2000. *Music in Everyday Life*. New York: Cambridge University Press.

Diehl, Keila. 2002. *Echoes from Dharamsala: Music in the Life of a Tibetan Refugee Community*. Berkeley: University of California Press.

Dirlik, Arif. 2008. "Timespace, Social Space, and the Question of Chinese Culture." *Boundary 2* 35 (1): 1–22.

Du, Yaxiong 杜亚雄, and Di Xiaoyan 邸晓嫣. 2005. "'Caifeng' haishi 'tianye gongzuo'?" "采风"还是"田野工作"? [Caifeng or fieldwork?]. *Wuhan Yinyue Xueyuan Xuebao* 武汉音乐学院学报, no. 1, 20–23.

Duara, Prasenjit. 1995. *Rescuing History from the Nation: Questioning Narratives of Modern China*. Chicago: University of Chicago Press.

———. 2000. "Local Worlds: The Poetics and Politics of the Native Place in Modern China." *South Atlantic Quarterly* 99 (1): 13–45.

———. 2009. *The Global and Regional in China's Nation-Formation*. London: T & F Books.

Erlmann, Veit. 1996. "The Aesthetics of the Global Imagination: Reflections on World Music in the 1990s." *Public Culture* 8 (3): 467–87.

———. 1999. *Music, Modernity, and the Global Imagination: South Africa and the West*. New York: Oxford University Press.

———, ed. 2004. *Hearing Cultures: Essays on Sound, Listening and Modernity*. New York: Berg.

Fabbri, Franco. 1982. "A Theory of Musical Genres: Two Applications." *Popular Music Perspectives* 1:52–81.

Faudree, Paja. 2012. "Music, Language, and Texts: Sound and Semiotic Ethnography." *Annual Review of Anthropology* 41 (1): 519–36.

Feld, Steven. 1994. "From Schizophonia to Schismogenesis: On the Discourses and Commodification Practices of 'World Music' and 'World Beat.'" In *Music Grooves: Essays and Dialogues*, edited by Charles Keil and Steven Feld, 257–98. Chicago: University of Chicago Press.

———. 1996a. "Pygmy POP. A Genealogy of Schizophonic Mimesis." *Yearbook for Traditional Music* 28 (January): 1–35.

———. 1996b. "Waterfalls of Songs: An Acoustemology of Place Resounding in Bosavi, Papua New Guinea." In *Senses of Place*, edited by Steven Feld and Keith H Basso. Santa Fe, NM: School of American Research Press.

———. 2000. "A Sweet Lullaby for World Music." *Public Culture* 12 (1): 145–71.

———. 2012. *Jazz Cosmopolitanism in Accra: Five Musical Years in Ghana*. Durham, NC: Duke University Press.

———. 2015. "Acoustemology." In *Keywords in Sound*, edited by David Novak and Matt Sakakeeny, 12–21. Durham, NC: Duke University Press.

Feld, Steven, Aaron A. Fox, Thomas Porcello, and David Samuels. 2005. "Vocal Anthropology: From the Music of Language to the Language of Song." In *A Companion to Linguistic Anthropology*, edited by Alessandro Duranti, 321–45. New York: Blackwell.

Fox, Aaron A. 2004. *Real Country: Music and Language in Working-Class Culture*. Durham, NC: Duke University Press.

Frey, R. Scott. 2012. “The E-Waste Stream in the World-System.” *Journal of Globalization Studies* 3 (1): 79–94.

Friedman, Sara. 2015. *Exceptional States: Chinese Immigrants and Taiwanese Sovereignty*. Oakland: University of California Press.

Frith, Simon. 1989. “Why Do Songs Have Words?” *Contemporary Music Review* 5 (1): 77–96.

———. 1996. *Performing Rites: On the Value of Popular Music*. New York: Oxford University Press.

Fu, Daobin. 2008. “Village People, Village Music and the Theoretical Significance of the Concept That Poetry Can Harmonize People.” *Frontiers of Literary Studies in China* 2 (3): 321–48.

Garland, Shannon. 2014. “Music, Affect, Labor, and Value: Late Capitalism and the (Mis)Productions of Indie Music in Chile and Brazil.” PhD diss., Columbia University.

“Geji lingdao jiguan yingdang youxiao de liyong wuxiandian guangbo” 各级领导机关应当有效地利用无线电广播 [All levels of leadership ought to effectively make use of radio broadcasting]. 1950. *Renmin Ribao* 人民日报, June 6.

Ghosh, Amitav. 2009. *Sea of Poppies*. New York: Picador.

Giddens, Anthony. 1991. *Modernity and Self-Identity: Self and Society in the Late Modern Age*. Stanford, CA: Stanford University Press.

Ginsburg, Faye D., Lila Abu-Lughod, and Brian Larkin, eds. 2002. *Media Worlds: Anthropology on New Terrain*. Berkeley: University of California Press.

Gopinath, Sumanth, and Jason Stanyek, eds. 2014. *The Oxford Handbook of Mobile Music Studies*. New York: Oxford University Press.

Graham, Stephen, and Simon Marvin. 2001. *Splintering Urbanism: Networked Infrastructures, Technological Mobilities and the Urban Condition*. New York: Routledge.

Gramsci, Antonio. 2000. *The Gramsci Reader: Selected Writings, 1916–1935*. Edited by David Forgacs. New York: New York University Press.

Greenblatt, Stephen. 2010. *Cultural Mobility: A Manifesto*. New York: Cambridge University Press.

Guilbault, Jocelyne. 1993. *Zouk: World Music in the West Indies*. Chicago: University of Chicago Press.

Guilbault, Jocelyne, and Roy Cape. 2014. *Roy Cape: A Life on the Calypso and Soca Bandstand*. Durham, NC: Duke University Press.

Gunn, Edward M. 2006. *Rendering the Regional: Local Language in Contemporary Chinese Media*. Honolulu: University of Hawai‘i Press.

Gupta, Akhil, and James Ferguson, eds. 1997. *Anthropological Locations: Boundaries and Grounds of a Field Science*. Berkeley: University of California Press.

Guy, Nancy. 2005. *Peking Opera and Politics in Taiwan*. Urbana: University of Illinois Press.

Harvey, David. 2007. *A Brief History of Neoliberalism*. New York: Oxford University Press.

Hirschkind, Charles. 2006. *The Ethical Soundscape: Cassette Sermons and Islamic Counterpublics*. New York: Columbia University Press.

Hobsbawm, E. J. 1990. *Nations and Nationalism since 1780: Programme, Myth, Reality*. New York: Cambridge University Press.

Holm, David. 1991. *Art and Ideology in Revolutionary China*. New York: Oxford University Press.

Holt, Fabian. 2007. *Genre in Popular Music*. Chicago: University of Chicago Press.

Hood, Mantle. 1960. “The Challenge of ‘Bi-Musicality.’ ” *Ethnomusicology* 4 (2): 55–59.

———. 1971. *The Ethnomusicologist*. New York: McGraw-Hill.

Huang, Shan. 2014. "Independence at Large: Contemporary China's Alternative Music Scenes and the Cultural Practices of Post-Socialist Urban Youth." MA thesis, University of South Carolina.

Hung, Chang-Tai. 1996. "The Politics of Songs: Myths and Symbols in the Chinese Communist War Music, 1937–1949." *Modern Asian Studies* 30 (4): 901–29.

Ives, Peter. 2004. *Language and Hegemony in Gramsci*. London: Pluto Press.

Jakobson, Roman. 1960. "Closing Statement: Linguistics and Poetics." In *Style in Language*, edited by Thomas A. Sebeok, 350–77. Cambridge, MA: MIT Press.

Jan, George P. 1967. "Radio Propaganda in Chinese Villages." *Asian Survey* 7 (5): 305–15.

Jones, Andrew F. 1992. *Like a Knife: Ideology and Genre in Contemporary Chinese Popular Music*. Ithaca, NY: East Asia Program, Cornell University.

———. 2001. *Yellow Music: Media Culture and Colonial Modernity in the Chinese Jazz Age*. Durham, NC: Duke University Press.

Jones, Stephen. 2003. "Reading between the Lines: Reflections on the Massive 'Anthology of Folk Music of the Chinese Peoples.'" *Ethnomusicology* 47 (3): 287–337.

Kagan, Alan L. 1963. "Music and the Hundred Flowers Movement." *Musical Quarterly* 49 (4): 417–30.

Kelman, Ari V. 2010. "Rethinking the Soundscape: A Critical Genealogy of a Key Term in Sound Studies." *Senses & Society* 5 (2): 212–34.

Kielman, Adam. 2020. "Sites and Sounds of National Memory: Performing the Nation in China's Decennial National Day Celebrations." *International Communication of Chinese Culture* 7 (2): 147–68.

Kurpaska, Maria. 2010. *Chinese Language(s): A Look through the Prism of the Great Dictionary of Modern Chinese Dialects*. New York: De Gruyter Mouton.

Laha, Somjita. 2015. "(In)formality in E-Waste Movement and Management in the Global Economy." PhD diss., University of Manchester.

Larkin, Brian. 2008. *Signal and Noise: Media, Infrastructure, and Urban Culture in Nigeria*. Durham, NC: Duke University Press.

———. 2013. "The Politics and Poetics of Infrastructure." *Annual Review of Anthropology* 42 (1): 327–43.

Lefebvre, Henri. 1991. *The Production of Space*. Oxford: Blackwell.

Li, Cheng 李盛. 2012. "Youxian guangbo yu xiangcun dongyuan (1952–1983)" 有线广播与乡村动员 (1952–1983) [Wired radio and rural mobilization (1952–1983)]. MA thesis, Lanzhou University.

———. 2014. "Jianguo chu xiangcun youxian guangbo xingqi de yuanyin tan xi" 建国初乡村有线广播兴起的原因探析 [An analysis of the reasons for the rise of village wired radio in the early decades of the PRC]. *Xinwen yanjiu dao kan* 新闻研究导刊, no. 7, 123.

Li, Huiling 李慧玲. 2007. "Nongcun youxian guangbo de lishi he xianzhuang" 农村有线广播的历史和现状 [The history and current situation of rural wired broadcasting]. *Qingnian Jizhe* 青年记者, no. 9, 55–56.

Li, Zhongwei. 2020. "Listening to the Scrap: Contested Materialities of Music in 1990s China." In *Popular Music, Technology, and the Changing Media Ecosystem*, edited by Tamas Tofalvy and Emília Barn, 149–64. Cham, Switzerland: Palgrave Macmillan.

Li, Zhun 李准. 1956. "Nongmin xin'ai de pengyou—youxian guangbo" 农民心爱的朋友——有线广播 [The peasants' beloved friend: Wired broadcasting]. *Renmin Ribao*, March 15, 1956.

Lieberman, Fredric. 1977. "The Chinese Long Zither Ch'in: A Study Based on the Mei-An Ch'in-P'u." PhD diss., University of California, Los Angeles.

Lipsitz, George. 1994. *Dangerous Crossroads: Popular Music, Postmodernism, and the Poetics of Place*. London: Verso.

Liu, Alan P. L. 1971. *Communications and National Integration in Communist China*. Berkeley: University of California Press.

Liu, Jin. 2013. *Signifying the Local: Media Productions Rendered in Local Languages in Mainland China in the New Millennium*. Boston: Brill.

——. 2014. "Alternative Voice and Local Youth Identity in Chinese Local-Language Rap Music." *Positions: Asia Critique* 22 (1): 263–92.

Luvaas, Brent. 2009. "Dislocating Sounds: The Deterritorialization of Indonesian Indie Pop." *Cultural Anthropology* 24 (2): 246–79.

Ma, Jianxiong, and Cunzhao Ma. 2016. "The Mule Caravans as Cross-Border Networks: Local Bands and Their Stretch on the Frontier between Yunnan and Burma." In *Myanmar's Mountain and Maritime Borderscapes: Local Practices, Boundary-Making and Figured Worlds*, edited by Su-Ann Oh, 237–57. Singapore: ISEAS—Yusof Ishak Institute.

Mak, Angela Ka Ying. 2007. "Advertising Whiteness: An Assessment of Skin Color Preferences among Urban Chinese." *Visual Communication Quarterly* 14 (3): 144–57.

Manuel, Peter. 1993. *Cassette Culture: Popular Music and Technology in North India*. Chicago: University of Chicago Press.

Marcus, George E. 1995. "Ethnography in/of the World System: The Emergence of Multi-Sited Ethnography." *Annual Review of Anthropology* 24 (January): 95–117.

Mathews, Gordon. 2017. *The World in Guangzhou: Africans and Other Foreigners in South China's Global Marketplace*. Chicago: University of Chicago Press.

Maxwell, Richard, and Toby Miller. 2012. *Greening the Media*. New York: Oxford University Press.

McLuhan, Marshall. 1964. *Understanding Media: The Extensions of Man*. New York: McGraw-Hill.

Meintjes, Louise. 1990. "Paul Simon's Graceland, South Africa, and the Mediation of Musical Meaning." *Ethnomusicology* 34 (1): 37–73.

——. 2003. *Sound of Africa! Making Music Zulu in a South African Studio*. Durham, NC: Duke University Press.

——. 2012. "The Recording Studio as Fetish." In *The Sound Studies Reader*, edited by Jonathan Sterne, 255–82. New York: Routledge.

Miao, Jing 苗晶, and Qiao Jianzhong 喬建中. 1987. *Lun Hanzu min'ge jinsi secaiqu di huafen 論漢族民歌近似色彩區的劃分* [An approximate division of Han folk songs into local color areas]. Beijing: Wenhua Yishu Chubanshe.

Middleton, Richard. 1990. *Studying Popular Music*. Philadelphia: Open University Press.

——, ed. 2000. *Reading Pop: Approaches to Textual Analysis in Popular Music*. New York: Oxford University Press.

Mittag, Achim. 1993. "Change in Shijing Exegesis: Some Notes on the Rediscovery of the Musical Aspect of the 'Odes' in the Song Period." *T'oung Pao*, 2nd. ser., 79 (4/5): 197–224.

Mittler, Barbara. 1997. *Dangerous Tunes: The Politics of Chinese Music in Hong Kong, Taiwan, and the People's Republic of China since 1949*. Wiesbaden: Harrassowitz.

Negus, Keith. 1992. *Producing Pop: Culture and Conflict in the Popular Music Industry*. London: Edward Arnold.

——. 1999. *Music Genres and Corporate Cultures*. New York: Routledge.

Novak, David. 2008. "2.5 × 6 Metres of Space: Japanese Music Coffeehouses and Experimental Practices of Listening." *Popular Music* 27 (1): 15–34.

——. 2010. "Cosmopolitanism, Remediation, and the Ghost World of Bollywood." *Cultural Anthropology* 25 (1): 40–72.

——. 2011. "The Sublime Frequencies of New Old Media." *Public Culture* 23 (3 [65]): 603–34.

——. 2013. *Japanoise: Music at the Edge of Circulation*. Durham, NC: Duke University Press.

Novak, David, and Matt Sakakeeny, eds. 2015. *Keywords in Sound*. Durham, NC: Duke University Press.

Oakes, Tim, and Louisa Schein, eds. 2006. *Translocal China: Linkages, Identities, and the Reimagining of Space*. London: Routledge.

Ochoa, Ana María, and Carolina Botero. 2009. "Notes on Practices of Musical Exchange in Colombia." *Popular Communication* 7 (3): 158–68.

Ochoa Gautier, Ana María. 2014. *Aurality: Listening and Knowledge in Nineteenth-Century Colombia*. Durham, NC: Duke University Press.

Ong, Aihwa. 1999. *Flexible Citizenship: The Cultural Logics of Transnationality*. Durham, NC: Duke University Press.

Ortner, Sherry B. 2005. "Subjectivity and Cultural Critique." *Anthropological Theory* 5 (1): 31–52.

——. 2006. *Anthropology and Social Theory: Culture, Power, and the Acting Subject*. Durham, NC: Duke University Press.

Porcello, Thomas. 2004. "Speaking of Sound Language and the Professionalization of Sound-Recording Engineers." *Social Studies of Science* 34 (5): 733–58.

Porcello, Thomas, Louise Meintjes, Ana Maria Ochoa, and David W. Samuels. 2010. "The Reorganization of the Sensory World." *Annual Review of Anthropology* 39 (January): 51–66.

Pruett, David B. 2011. "When the Tribe Goes Triple Platinum: A Case Study Toward an Ethnomusicology of Mainstream Popular Music in the U.S." *Ethnomusicology* 55 (1): 1–30.

Rees, Helen, ed. 2009. *Lives in Chinese Music*. Urbana: University of Illinois Press.

——. 2016. "Environmental Crisis, Culture Loss, and a New Musical Aesthetic: China's 'Original Ecology Folksongs' in Theory and Practice." *Ethnomusicology* 60 (1): 53–88.

Regev, Motti. 2013. *Pop-Rock Music: Aesthetic Cosmopolitanism in Late Modernity*. Cambridge: Polity Press.

Rice, Timothy. 2003. "Time, Place, and Metaphor in Musical Experience and Ethnography." *Ethnomusicology* 47 (2): 151.

Roberts, Dexter, and Jasmine Zhao. 2016. "This Is How China Preps for the Big Test." *Bloomberg Businessweek*, June 2, 2016.

Rofel, Lisa. 1999. *Other Modernities: Gendered Yearnings in China after Socialism*. Berkeley: University of California Press.

——. 2007. *Desiring China: Experiments in Neoliberalism, Sexuality, and Public Culture*. Durham, NC: Duke University Press.

——. 2017. "China's Tianxia Worldings: Socialist and Postsocialist Cosmopolitanisms." In *Chinese Visions of World Order: Tianxia, Culture, and World Politics*, 212–36. Durham, NC: Duke University Press.

Ruskin, Jesse D., and Timothy Rice. 2012. "The Individual in Musical Ethnography." *Ethnomusicology* 56 (2): 299–327.

Samuels, David W., Louise Meintjes, Ana Maria Ochoa, and Thomas Porcello. 2010. "Soundscapes: Toward a Sounded Anthropology." *Annual Review of Anthropology* 39 (January): 329–45.

Samuels, David William. 2004. *Putting a Song on Top of It: Expression and Identity on the San Carlos Apache Reservation*. Tucson: University of Arizona Press.

Schafer, R. Murray. 1977. *The Tuning of the World*. New York: Knopf.

Schnitzler, Antina von. 2008. "Citizenship Prepaid: Water, Calculability, and Techno-Politics in South Africa." *Journal of Southern African Studies* 34 (4): 899–917.

Shin, Hyunjoon. 2009. "Have You Ever Seen the Rain? And Who'll Stop the Rain? The Globalizing Project of Korean Pop (K-Pop)." *Inter-Asia Cultural Studies* 10 (4): 507–23.

Sigley, Gary. 2013. "The Ancient Tea Horse Road and the Politics of Cultural Heritage in Southwest China: Regional Identity in the Context of a Rising China." In *Cultural Heritage Politics in China*, edited by Tami Blumenfield and Helaine Silverman, 235–46. New York: Springer.

Skinner, Ryan Thomas. 2015. *Bamako Sounds: The Afropolitan Ethics of Malian Music*. Minneapolis: University of Minnesota Press.

Slobin, Mark. 1993. *Subcultural Sounds: Micromusics of the West*. Hanover, NH: Wesleyan University Press.

Soja, Edward W. 1989. *Postmodern Geographies: The Reassertion of Space in Critical Social Theory*. Haymarket Series. New York: Verso.

Steingo, Gavin. 2015. "Sound and Circulation: Immobility and Obduracy in South African Electronic Music." *Ethnomusicology Forum* 24 (1): 102–23.

———. 2016. *Kwaito's Promise: Music and the Aesthetics of Freedom in South Africa*. Chicago: University of Chicago Press.

Sterling, Marvin D. 2010. *Babylon East: Performing, Dancehall, Roots Reggae, and Rastafari in Japan*. Durham, NC: Duke University Press.

Sterne, Jonathan. 2014. "Soundscape, Landscape, Escape." In *Soundscapes of the Urban Past: Staged Sound as Mediated Cultural Heritage*, edited by Karin Bijsterveld. Berlin: Transcript.

Stokes, Martin, ed. 1994. *Ethnicity, Identity, and Music: The Musical Construction of Place*. Oxford: Berg.

———. 2004. "Music and the Global Order." *Annual Review of Anthropology* 33 (January): 47–72.

———. 2008. "On Musical Cosmopolitanism." *Macalester International* 21, art. 8.

Sun, Wanning. 2002. *Leaving China: Media, Migration, and Transnational Imagination*. Lanham, MD: Rowman & Littlefield.

Sun, Wanning, and Jenny Chio, eds. 2012. *Mapping Media in China: Region, Province, Locality*. New York: Routledge.

Szego, C. K. 2003. "Singing Hawaiian and the Aesthetics of (In)Comprehensibility." In *Global Pop, Local Language*, edited by Harris M. Berger and Michael Thomas Carroll, 291–328. Jackson: University Press of Mississippi.

Taylor, Timothy Dean. 1997. *Global Pop: World Music, World Markets*. New York: Routledge.

Thompson, E. P. 1967. "Time, Work-Discipline, and Industrial Capitalism." *Past & Present*, no. 38 (December): 56–97.

Thompson, Paul, and Brett Lashua. 2014. "Getting It on Record: Issues and Strategies for Ethnographic Practice in Recording Studios." *Journal of Contemporary Ethnography* 43 (6): 746–69.

Thrasher, Alan. 1980. "Foundations of Chinese Music: A Study of Ethics and Aesthetics." PhD diss., Wesleyan University.

Tuohy, Sue. 2001. "The Sonic Dimensions of Nationalism in Modern China: Musical Representation and Transformation." *Ethnomusicology* 45 (1): 107–31.

———. 2003. "The Choices and Challenges of Local Distinction: Regional Attachments and Dialect in Chinese Music." In *Global Pop, Local Language*, by H. M. Berger and M. T. Carroll. Jackson: University Press of Mississippi.

Turino, Thomas. 2000. *Nationalists, Cosmopolitans, and Popular Music in Zimbabwe*. Chicago: University of Chicago Press.

Urry, John. 2007. *Mobilities*. Malden, MA: Polity Press.

Van Gulik, Robert Hans. *The Lore of the Chinese Lute: An Essay in Ch'in Ideology*. Tokyo: Sophia University, 1940.

Von Falkenhausen, Lothar. 1993. *Suspended Music: Chime-Bells in the Culture of Bronze Age China*. Berkeley: University of California Press.

Wallerstein, Immanuel Maurice. 1974. *The Modern World-System*. Studies in Social Discontinuity. New York: Academic Press.

Wang, Ban, ed. 2017. *Chinese Visions of World Order: Tianxia, Culture, and World Politics*. Durham, NC: Duke University Press.

Wang, Jing, ed. 2005. *Locating China: Space, Place, and Popular Culture*. New York: Routledge.

Washburne, Christopher. 2008. *Sounding Salsa: Performing Latin Music in New York City*. Philadelphia: Temple University Press.

Waterman, Christopher Alan. 1990. *Jùjú: A Social History and Ethnography of an African Popular Music*. Chicago: University of Chicago Press.

Werbner, Pnina. 2006. "Vernacular Cosmopolitanism." *Theory, Culture & Society* 23 (2/3): 496–98.

Wong, Siu-Kit, and Kar-Shui Lee. 1989. "Poems of Depravity: A Twelfth Century Dispute on the Moral Character of the 'Book of Songs.'" *T'oung Pao*, 2nd ser., 75 (4/5): 209–25.

Williams, Raymond. 1977. *Marxism and Literature*. Oxford: Oxford University Press.

Xu, Yir 徐毅儿. 2013. "Niba hui changge: 'Kua jie' rang yishu geng qinmin" 泥巴会唱歌: "跨界" 让艺术更亲民 [Mud can sing: "Boundary-crossing" makes art more accessible to the people]. *Xinxi Shibao* 信息时报, June 27.

Yan, Jun. N.d. "How to Repair Dakou Cassettes." http://www.yanjun.org/archives/1146.

Yan, Margaret Mian. 2006. *Introduction to Chinese Dialectology*. Munich: LINCOM Europa.

Yang, Mayfair Mei-hui. 2002. "Mass Media and Transnational Subjectivity in Shanghai: Notes on (Re)Cosmopolitanism in a Chinese Metropolis." In *Media Worlds: Anthropology on New Terrain*, edited by Faye D. Ginsburg, Lila Abu-Lughod, and Brian Larkin, 189–210. Berkeley: University of California Press.

Yano, Christine Reiko. 2002. *Tears of Longing: Nostalgia and the Nation in Japanese Popular Song*. 206. Cambridge, MA: Harvard University Asia Center.

Ye, Qingyi 叶清漪. 2011. "Zhou Xiaochuan: Rang yinyue xiaofei geng bianjie, rang yinyue wuchubuzai" 周小川: 让音乐消费更便捷, 让音乐无处不在 [Making music consumption easier, making music ubiquitous]. *Nandu Yule Zhoukan* 南都娱乐周刊, April 8.

Yu, Haiqing. 2009. *Media and Cultural Transformation in China*. New York: Routledge.

Yu, Sabrina Qiong. 2012. *Jet Li: Chinese Masculinity and Transnational Film Stardom*. Edinburgh: Edinburgh University Press.

Yu, Yu-Hsiu. 1963. "Radio in the Villages." *China Reconstructs*, April 1963.

Yung, Bell. 1984. "Model Opera as Model: From Shajiabang to Sagabong." In *Popular Chinese Literature and Performing Arts in the People's Republic of China, 1949–1979*, edited by Bonnie McDougall, 144–64. Berkeley: University of California Press.

Zak, Albin. 2001. *The Poetics of Rock: Cutting Tracks, Making Records*. Berkeley: University of California Press.

Zemp, Hugo. 1996. "The/An Ethnomusicologist and the Record Business." *Yearbook for Traditional Music* 28 (January): 36–56.

Zhang, Li. 2001. *Strangers in the City: Reconfigurations of Space, Power, and Social Networks within China's Floating Population*. Stanford, CA: Stanford University Press.

———. 2012. "Afterword: Flexible Postsocialist Assemblages from the Margin." *Positions* 20 (2): 659–67.

Zhang, Li, and Aihwa Ong, eds. 2008. *Privatizing China: Socialism from Afar*. Ithaca, NY: Cornell University Press.

Zhao, Tingyang 赵汀阳. 2005. *Tianxia tixi: Shijie zhidu zhexue daolun* 天下体系: 世界制度哲学导论 [The Tianxia system: An introduction to the philosophy of a world institution]. Nanjing: Jiangsu Education Press.

———. 2009. "A Political World Philosophy in Terms of All-under-Heaven (Tian-Xia)." *Diogenes* 56 (1): 5–18.

Zhao, Yuezhi. 2008. *Communication in China: Political Economy, Power, and Conflict*. Lanham, MD: Rowman & Littlefield.

Zhongguo de youxian guangbo 中国的有线广播 [Cable broadcasting in China]. 1988. Beijing: Beijing Guangbo Xueyuan Chubanshe.

Index

Page numbers in italics refer to figures.